EPICURI

CW01641867

In this book, Tim O'Keefe reconstructs the theory of freedom of the ancient Greek philosopher Epicurus (341-271/0 BCE). Epicurus' theory has attracted much interest, but our attempts to understand it have been hampered by reading it anachronistically as the discovery of the modern problem of free will and determinism. O'Keefe argues that the sort of freedom which Epicurus wanted to preserve is significantly different from the 'free will' which philosophers debate today, and that in its emphasis on rational action it has much closer affinities with Aristotle's thought than with current preoccupations. His original and provocative book will be of interest to a wide range of readers in Hellenistic philosophy.

TIM O'KEEFE is Assistant Professor of Philosophy at Georgia State University. Since 2001 he has been the Ancient Philosophy Area Editor for the *Internet Encyclopedia of Philosophy.*

EPICURUS ON FREEDOM

TIM O'KEEFE

CAMBRIDGE
UNIVERSITY PRESS

CAMBRIDGE UNIVERSITY PRESS
Cambridge, New York, Melbourne, Madrid, Cape Town, Singapore, São Paulo, Delhi

Cambridge University Press
The Edinburgh Building, Cambridge CB2 8RU, UK

Published in the United States of America by Cambridge University Press, New York

www.cambridge.org
Information on this title: www.cambridge.org/9780521114912

First published 2005
This digitally printed version 2009

A catalogue record for this publication is available from the British Library

ISBN 978-0-521-84696-7 hardback
ISBN 978-0-521-11491-2 paperback

For Anne and Quinn

Contents

Acknowledgments

In the long process of working out my thoughts about the topic of Epicurus on freedom, I've received help from many people. I'm happy to acknowledge some of them here.

David O'Connor's seminar on ancient ethics gave me an engaging and sympathetic introduction to Epicureanism. Although my disagreements with David Sedley will be obvious in what follows, reading his pioneering work first sparked my interest in the role of the swerve in preserving our freedom.

Many of the arguments here were originally developed during work on my dissertation at the University of Texas at Austin. It was a wonderful place to study, largely because the faculty and students of the joint program in Ancient Philosophy formed a supportive and enriching community. In particular, I'd like to thank Steve White and Jim Hankinson for their continuing help and friendship. Steve White provided answers, often leavened with dreadful puns, to many questions of mine. Jim Hankinson gave feedback on much of the ms. Also, his work has provided for me a model of how to engage in the study of ancient philosophy.

Sylvia Berryman and Hal Thorsrud each looked over drafts of the whole book; their prompt and generous comments were immensely helpful. I hope that one day soon I can return the favor. The detailed input of the anonymous reviewers from Cambridge University Press, and of David Sedley, was also quite useful.

This book is dedicated to Anne Farrell and Quinn O'Keefe. Anne has been invaluable as a sounding board and in-house editor and reviewer. More importantly, her love has helped sustain me and bring me happiness. Quinn's entry into the world during the late stages of revision to this book did not directly assist me in my writing—if anything, the opposite is true—but he was a source of joy and of comic relief. Also, he helped convince me that the Stoic version of the Cradle Argument is closer to the mark than the Epicurean one.

Note: Although no part of this book simply reprints previously published articles *verbatim*, in some sections there is considerable overlap of content. I dealt with the swerve's role as an origin of collisions (chapter 5) in O'Keefe (1996). The ontological status of sensible qualities for Democritus and Epicurus (section 4.1.2) is treated at greater length in O'Keefe (1997), and Epicurean reductionism and *On Nature* 25, the subjects of much of chapter 4, are discussed in O'Keefe (2002). Some of the consideration of the 'traditional' interpretation in chapter 2 appeared previously in O'Keefe (2003a).

Abbreviations

Adv. Colot.	Plutarch, *Against Colotes*
Arr.	Arrighetti, *Epicuro, Opere*
DA	Aristotle, *de Anima*
de Int.	Aristotle, *de Interpretatione*
De lib. arb.	Augustine, *De libero arbitrio*
DF	Cicero, *De finibus*
DK	Diels and Kranz, *Die Fragmente der Vorsokratiker*
DL	Diogenes Laertius, *Lives of the Philosophers*
DRN	Lucretius, *De rerum natura*
Ep. Hdt.	Epicurus, *Letter to Herodotus*
Ep. Pyth.	Epicurus, *Letter to Pythocles*
Ep. Men.	Epicurus, *Letter to Menoeceus*
KD	Epicurus, *Principal Doctrines*
L&S	Long and Sedley, *The Hellenistic Philosophers*
M.	Sextus Empiricus, *Against the professors*
MA	Aristotle, *de Motu Animalium*
Meta.	Aristotle, *Metaphysics*
PH	Sextus Empiricus, *Outlines of Pyrrhonism*
Pol.	Aristotle, *Politics*
NE	Aristotle, *Nicomachean Ethics*
Tim.	Plato, *Timaeus*
SV	Epicurus, *Vatican Sayings*

Introduction

One of the most startling and distinctive aspects of Epicurean philosophy is the atomic motion known as the 'swerve.' The Epicureans are materialists, holding that the only things that exist *per se* are bodies and 'void,' which is just empty space.[1] Bodies are simply conglomerations of atoms, which are uncuttable, extended bits of 'full' space flying through the void as a result of their weight, past motions, and collisions with other atoms. But the Epicurean poet Lucretius writes that if all atomic motion were the deterministic result of past motions and weight, we would not have the 'free volition' (*libera voluntas*) which allows each of us to move ourselves as we wish. Since we evidently do have the power to move ourselves as we wish, there must be a third, indeterministic cause of atomic motion, in addition to weight and past motions – a 'swerving' of the atoms to the side at uncertain times and places, which saves us from fate.

In part, this book is an attempt to discern the role the swerve plays in preserving human freedom. However, the swerve cannot be studied in isolation; it must be understood in the context of Epicurus' ethics, philosophy of mind, and metaphysics in general. So the subject of this book is Epicurus' overall theory of human freedom. I will argue that the swerve plays only a peripheral role in Epicurus' overall theory, and that an overemphasis on the role of the swerve has significantly distorted our understanding of Epicurus' ethics, philosophy of mind, action-theory, and metaphysics, as scholars read swerves into parts of Epicurus' philosophy where they are not mentioned at all.

Epicurus' theory of freedom deserves attention not only because of its place within Hellenistic philosophy, but because of the way it has shaped how we conceive of the issue of free will today. Epicurus plays a key role in the birth of the traditional 'problem of free will and determinism'

1 See Sedley (1988b) for an extended discussion of the notion of void in atomism. He argues that there is an important shift from the early atomists, who regard void as a negative substance that occupies space (and could move around), to the Epicureans, who regard it as simply empty space.

– that is, the seeming incompatibility of causal determinism and the sort of 'ability to do otherwise' that is necessary for moral responsibility. Because Epicurus believes that freedom and determinism are incompatible, and because he denies that determinism is true in order to preserve our freedom, Epicurus has been hailed as the first person to discover the free will problem, and the first to offer a libertarian solution to it.[2] But I think that this is mistaken. There is a great variety of 'freedom and determinism' problems, and Epicurus is responding to concerns quite distinct from the ones that motivate the traditional problem of free will and determinism. Epicurus *is* pivotal in the story of how our problem of free will and determinism arose, but not because he himself formulated this problem. Instead, his own position was appropriated and significantly reshaped in debates by subsequent philosophers, and through a process that owes a great deal to historical quirk and happenstance, Epicurus helped to form a libertarian conception of the freedom of the will that he himself would have repudiated.

Because of textual difficulties, understanding Epicurus' position on freedom and the role the swerve plays in it is not easy. Almost all of Epicurus' own writings are lost, and none of those that we do have mention the swerve. Because of this, in order to reconstruct Epicurus' position we must rely on reports by later sources, some of them hostile or undiscerning. We also need to try to see how Epicurus might be responding to problems he saw in the positions of earlier philosophers. Because of these obstacles, a multiplicity of competing and incompatible explanations of how the swerve is supposed to save us from fate have been proposed. Before turning to the main argument of the book, in the remainder of this introductory section I provide a little background for those unfamiliar with the texts and issues. First I present key figures and texts that will play a part in the subsequent story, then I lay out the main thread of the book's argument, chapter by chapter.

0.1 FIGURES AND TEXTS[3]

Sources on Epicurus. Our picture of Epicurus' thought is gleaned from the works of many figures, but three will be particularly important to my discussion.

2 For example, see Huby (1967); Long and Sedley (1987) vol. 1 p. 107; Asmis (1990) 275.

3 For more information on the sources on Epicurus and Hellenistic philosophy generally, see Mansfeld (1999). For more information on the dates of the figures below (excluding Aristotle and Democritus), see Dorandi (1999).

Epicurus himself (341–271/0 BCE). Epicurus was a voluminous writer, but almost all of his writings are lost. However, some useful material is still left. *Diogenes Laertius* (*c.* 230 CE) wrote a ten-book *Lives of the Philosophers*, filled with digests of philosophers' opinions and amusing tales of their lives and deaths, many of them spurious, along with samples of Diogenes' own wretched poetry. Fortunately, his treatment of Epicureanism (in book 10) contains three letters Epicurus wrote which summarize his philosophy. The *Letter to Herodotus* (*Ep. Hdt.*) is a digest of Epicurus' metaphysics, broadly conceived, which includes discussions of the causes of atomic motion (which surprisingly does not mention the swerve) and of the nature of the mind. The *Letter to Pythocles* (*Ep. Pyth.*) gives explanations of meteorological phenomena. The *Letter to Menoeceus* (*Ep. Men.*) is a summary of Epicurus' ethics and an exhortation to the Epicurean way of life. In *Ep. Men.* 133–134 Epicurus says that one should reject the "fate of the natural philosophers," because not all things occur of necessity – instead, some depend on us. Again, Epicurus does not mention the swerve here, and the exact point he is making is not entirely clear. Diogenes also preserves the *Principal Doctrines* (*KD*), a series of maxims that deal primarily with ethical matters. The *Principal Doctrines* and all three letters are invaluable starting-places for understanding Epicurus' philosophy, but because they are merely summaries and maxims, they still leave many questions unanswered.

Another source that has figured quite prominently in recent discussions is the extant portions of *On Nature book 25*. *On Nature* is Epicurus' *magnum opus*. The passages we have contain a self-refutation argument against those who hold that all things occur "of necessity," and a description of human psychological development, including the relationship between psychological states and the atoms that constitute the mind. Unfortunately, the text is in terrible shape. It was contained in a library in an Epicurean villa in the village of Herculaneum, which was buried in the eruption of Mount Vesuvius in 79 CE that also destroyed Pompeii. The carbonized scrolls were unearthed in the eighteenth century, and work continues today in unrolling, deciphering, translating, and interpreting their contents. In addition to being riddled with lacunae, the text also bristles with unexplained technical terminology, making interpretation of it even more difficult.[4]

4 An excellent introduction to the history of the Herculaneum papyri is Sedley (1998) 94–98, and Sedley (1998) 98–133 discusses the length, style, and contents of *On Nature.*

Lucretius (*c.* 94–55 BCE). Lucretius was a committed Epicurean and a remarkable poet; besides this, we know next to nothing about him. Lucretius is celebrated for his single work, *De rerum natura (On the nature of things)*, a six-book exposition of the parts of Epicurean philosophy that in ancient times would have been known as 'physics,' quite broadly construed.[5] *DRN* includes discussions of the existence of atoms and void, Epicurus' philosophy of mind and theory of perception, the nature of the gods, the development of society, diseases, and much else.

Several sections of *DRN* are particularly important for my purposes. The first is *DRN* 2 216–293. It occurs in the middle of a discussion of atomic motion and contains two arguments for why there must be an atomic swerve – to explain why there are atomic collisions and to preserve our freedom. Second is *DRN* 4 877–906, where Lucretius briefly describes what is going on at the atomic level in Epicurean action theory. Also important is *DRN* 3 94–416, which gives an account of Epicurean philosophy of mind; particularly significant are lines 258–322, which concern how people can control their own natural temperaments through the use of reason. Surprisingly, Lucretius does not mention the swerve anywhere besides *DRN* 2 216–293.

Lucretius was a poet, not an original philosopher. It is possible that at points he might have misunderstood what is going on in Epicurean philosophy,[6] but generally the presumption should be he is reliable, as a committed and intelligent Epicurean who was very likely drawing directly on Epicurus' own writings.[7]

Cicero (106–43 BCE) was a Roman statesman and amateur philosopher, who was killed at the orders of Antony. He was an adherent of the skeptical Academy. During an enforced hiatus from Roman politics in 45 to 43 BCE, he decided to serve his countrymen by writing expositions in

5 See, for instance, *DL* 10 29–30, who reports that Epicureans divide philosophy into three parts: canonic (basically, epistemology), ethics, and physics, and that physics covers the entire study of nature.

6 A possible (though quite controversial) example of this is Lucretius' representation of Epicurean theology. Long and Sedley (1987) vol. I 144–149 argue that Epicurus views the gods *merely* as idealized thought-constructs of what supremely blessed humans would be, but that Epicurus' coyness on the issue (in order to avoid censure) misled Lucretius and some other later Epicureans into thinking that the gods literally exist eternally as solid bodies living in the *intermundia*, the empty space between the *cosmoi*. I accept Long and Sedley's thesis, but many do not.

7 See Sedley (1998), particularly chapters 3 through 5, for a quite detailed treatment of the way Lucretius draws on Epicurus. Even if one does not fully accept Sedley's thesis that Lucretius' "sole philosophical source and inspiration from early in book I until late in book VI is Epicurus' great physical treatise, *On nature*" (Sedley (1998) 93), he nonetheless demonstrates that Lucretius was intimately familiar with and dependent upon Epicurus' own writings.

Latin of the major philosophical systems of the day. These included works on ethics, epistemology, the gods, *etc.* Two works are particularly important for this study. To a lesser extent, I will be drawing on *De finibus* (*On ends*), the first two books of which contain an extended exposition of Epicurean ethics, followed by Cicero's scathing criticisms. But much more important is *De fato* (*On fate*), only portions of which survive. This treatise concerns the question of whether causal determinism is compatible with justified praise and blame. However, it also deals with arguments that try to draw fatalist conclusions from logical considerations concerning the fixity of the truth-value of statements about the future. In addition to talking about how Epicurus uses the swerve to combat such arguments, Cicero also lays out the positions of the Stoic Chrysippus and one of the heads of the skeptical Academy, Carneades, concerning these questions (see below for more on these figures).

Cicero must be used with more care than Epicurus or Lucretius, but he is still an important source. Cicero, like Lucretius, is not an original philosopher – he is more of a philosophical enthusiast, who may sometimes misunderstand the position he is talking about. Also, he admits that for many of his books he only paraphrased works written by Stoics and Epicureans, in which they laid out their views. Still, Cicero studied philosophy extensively. He was also very hostile toward Epicureanism. This sometimes causes him to be uncharitable when interpreting Epicurus' views. Nonetheless, although he does not always succeed, Cicero tries to be fair in presenting the views of various philosophers before criticizing them. The purpose of his philosophical treatises – which is also consistent with his philosophical position – is to lay out, side by side, the arguments of various philosophers so as to allow the reader to make his own decision as to their merits. Many of his treatises (such as the *De finibus*) are in dialogue form, with spokesmen of various schools offering extended expositions of their positions.

Key predecessors of Epicurus. Epicurus said he was entirely self-taught, but this claim is usually not taken seriously. Philosophers often view Epicurus' arguments on determinism and freedom as responding to two of his predecessors, Democritus and Aristotle, although there is little agreement on what exactly Epicurus is responding to, or in what way.

Democritus (*c.* 460–370 BCE). Along with Leucippus, Democritus was one of the originators of atomism. Epicurus largely appropriated his metaphysics from him. However, he objected to two aspects of Democritus' thought. Democritus said that, in reality, only atoms and the void exist, while properties like whiteness and sweetness exist only "by convention." From this, Democritus derived pessimistic conclusions about our ability to gain knowledge about the world from our senses. Epicurus wished to resist this skepticism, which he thought untenable, and he insisted on the reality of sensible qualities. Secondly, Epicurus attributed to Democritus the view that all things occur 'of necessity,' which Epicurus thought amounts to denying that anything depends on us as agents. Such fatalism was as unacceptable to Epicurus as Democritus' skepticism.[8]

Aristotle (383–322 BCE). The most extensive treatment of issues of personal responsibility we have prior to the Hellenistic period is that of Aristotle in *Nicomachean Ethics* 3 1. Aristotle died about fifteen years before Epicurus arrived in Athens. His discussion is interesting and influential. However, it seems initially to bypass entirely issues of determinism and freedom of the will. Aristotle's presumption is that agents are responsible for their actions, and he focuses on the types of excusing factors – varieties of force and ignorance – that render action involuntary and hence unfit candidates for praise and blame. At first, such an analysis would seem more at home in compatibilist than in libertarian theories of freedom. But in any case, Aristotle seems not even to raise the issue of free will and determinism. Aristotle's 'four causes' – even his so-called 'efficient cause' – do not map easily onto the modern notion of an efficient cause.[9] The thesis of universal causal determinism, as it is usually used in modern debates over free will and determinism, would be difficult to formulate in Aristotelian terms.

Despite this, several parts of Aristotle's discussion have sometimes been thought to point toward the current debate and also to have influenced Epicurus. One is his assertion in *NE* 3 1 that voluntary actions are ones that have their 'origin in the agent himself.' A second is in *NE* 3 5 where Aristotle says that, when actions are up to us, we have the power either to act or not to act. A third is Aristotle's discussion, in *NE* 3 5, of arguments that try to show that we are not responsible for our actions because the characters from which these actions spring are formed by factors which are ultimately beyond our control.

8 For a good selection of the reports on Democritus that attest to these features of his thought, see Kirk, Raven, and Schofield (1983) 402–433.

9 See e.g., *Physics* 2 3 194b23–35 for a quick summary of Aristotle's four causes, and Hocutt (1974) and Vlastos (1969/1973) section 1 for how Aristotle's notion of *aitia* differs from the modern notion of cause. Further discussion of this claim about Aristotle's 'four causes' can be found in section 3.1.

Another important text is *de Interpretatione 9*. *De Interpretatione* is primarily a text in semantics. In *de Int.* 9, Aristotle considers whether the Principle of Bivalence – the principle that every statement either is true or is false – holds universally. Aristotle considers a fatalist argument based on the Principle of Bivalence. According to this argument, if all statements have been true or false all along, this would include statements about what will occur in the future, and this would make it impossible for us to affect the future. Aristotle rejects this fatalist conclusion, and (on most but not all interpretations of *de Int.* 9) as a result thinks that the Principle of Bivalence does not hold true of all statements. Statements about particular, contingent events in the future (such as "there will be a sea battle tomorrow") are, at least for now, neither true nor false.[10] A similar argument for the necessity of the future that was taken to have fatalist implications, the 'Master Argument,' is both put forward and endorsed by Diodorus Cronus (died *c.* 284 BCE); this formulation of the argument was much debated by philosophers in the Hellenistic period, and is no less a subject of modern controversy.

Key Successors of Epicurus. Epicurus is the main subject of this book, but part of the story I wish to tell concerns how Epicurus' account had an impact on subsequent controversy, and how later thinkers remolded his account for their own purposes. Two figures play a crucial role:

Chrysippus (*c.* 280–207 BCE). Chrysippus was third head of the Stoa, which was founded by Zeno of Citium around 300 BCE. The Stoics were sharply opposed to the Epicureans on many topics. For instance, they emphasized that virtue is the only thing that is intrinsically good, whereas Epicureans held that virtue is only instrumentally valuable. More important for this book are the Stoic views on God and fate. According to the Stoics, God and the *cosmos* are identical. The world is organized in accordance with God's benevolent plan, which ensures that things will turn out the way they do. Epicurus vehemently disagreed with all this. However, the earlier heads of the Stoa, Zeno and Cleanthes, had not clearly worked out exactly how fate operated, as far as we know. Chrysippus was the first person to link up fate and causal determinism explicitly. He identified fate with the unwinding of a sequence of causes, affirming that *every single* event that occurs is both causally determined and fated. Chrysippus also gave an analysis of how causal determinism is compatible both with effective agency and with justified praise and blame.

10 This orthodox interpretation of *de Int.* 9 has been challenged; see section 6.2.1 for further discussion.

Carneades (214–129/8 BCE). Carneades was one of the most influential leaders of the skeptical Academy. Arcesilaus (316/5–241/0 BCE) moved Plato's Academy in a skeptical direction *c.* 265, shortly after Epicurus' death. Arcesilaus turned away from system building and instead concentrated on attacking the doctrines of others, particularly the Stoics. In doing so, he could claim to be following the example of Socrates, as depicted in many of Plato's dialogues. Carneades continued Arcesilaus' practice and developed an array of arguments against others' positions, particularly the epistemology of the Stoics as laid out by Chrysippus. However, he went beyond Arcesilaus in his procedure. Not content with rebutting others' arguments, Carneades also developed positive arguments of his own in favor of various views – not because he endorsed them himself, but in order to counterbalance the arguments of others for opposing views. Carneades employed this tactic in the case of determinism and freedom. In order to battle Chrysippus, Carneades modified Epicurus' position. He reaffirmed that freedom is incompatible with causal determinism but argued that it is compatible with the Principle of Bivalence's holding true universally. He also argued that free agency can be defended without recourse to any fundamental physical indeterminacy like the swerve.

0.2 MAP OF WHAT WILL COME

I begin chapter 1 with a survey of different types of possible "free will and determinism" problems. I then summarize some of the main interpretations of Epicurus and categorize them based upon what problem they take Epicurus to be addressing with the swerve. After that, I look at the way in which Epicurus (and Epicureans) describe the sort of freedom they are concerned to defend, as well as what they *should* care about, given their ethics and metaphysics. I argue that most interpreters have mistakenly assimilated Epicurus' concerns to those of modern libertarians. It is both much more plausible and more charitable to ascribe to Epicurus a concern to defend rational agency rather than libertarian free will.

In chapter 2, I look at Lucretius' poem *De rerum natura.* I argue that Lucretius' description of the swerve in *DRN* 2 251–293 does not give us good reason to think that there is a swerve involved in the production of every free action. In fact, he gives us little information about how the swerve is supposed to help preserve our freedom, other than that it somehow prevents what will occur from being predetermined. However, his description of the *libera voluntas* that the swerve helps safeguard makes it clear that *libera voluntas* is *not* a libertarian freedom of the will. Instead,

Lucretius cares about our ability to move ourselves as we wish, in order to get what we desire.

In chapter 3, I consider supposed Aristotelian antecedents in the *Nicomachean Ethics* to Epicurus' position. I agree with others who have thought that both Aristotle and Epicurus wish the agent to be the 'origin' of both his actions and his own character. However, for neither Aristotle nor Epicurus does this have any anti-determinist implications.

Chapter 4 is primarily an examination of Epicurus' philosophy of mind. I argue that Epicurus has an identity theory of mind: the mind is identified with a group of atoms in the chest, and mental events and states are identified with atomic events and states. I give an extended analysis of the extant portions of Epicurus' *On Nature* 25. In these passages, Epicurus is concerned to rebut the fatalist implications of Democritean eliminative materialism, not the deterministic implications of his reductionist materialism. (I also argue, *inter alia*, that Epicurus' response to the skeptical implication of Democritus' metaphysics, in which Epicurus defends the reality of properties like whiteness and sourness, is consistent with his having a reductionist metaphysics.)

The overarching negative conclusion of chapters 2, 3 and 4 is that none of these texts allow us to discern the role of the swerve, and that the various attempts to use them for this purpose fail. The main positive doctrine that emerges from considering these texts is that Epicurus wishes to preserve our ability to use our reason to control our action and shape our character, a view that is (in itself) compatible both with causal determinism and with an identity theory of the mind.

In chapters 5 and 6, I turn to my own view of the swerve. Chapter 5 concerns the role the swerve plays in explaining atomic collisions. In chapter 6, I describe how the swerve is supposed to help preserve human freedom. Epicurus' reasons for positing the swerve are inadequate; he makes a number of mistakes that are subsequently uncovered by Chrysippus and Carneades. Nonetheless, I argue that my interpretation is preferable to the others both on textual grounds and on grounds of charity. In the Epilogue, I take up the question of how the traditional 'problem of free will' arose, if Epicurus was not concerned with it, and I look at the way in which Epicurus inadvertently contributed to its birth. I argue that Carneades should be credited (or blamed) for first formulating a libertarian position on the 'traditional' problem of free will and determinism, and that via Cicero's *De fato*, it was transmitted to the western philosophical tradition in St. Augustine's *On Free Choice of the Will*.

CHAPTER I

What sort of an incompatibilist is Epicurus?

If our sources can be trusted, Epicurus asserts an incompatibility between *libera voluntas* (sometimes translated as 'free will') and determinism, and he denies that determinism is true, positing a mechanism, the swerve, by which it is rendered false, saying that the swerve is needed in order for us to be free. Because of this, Epicurus has been hailed as the first person to discover the free will problem. But this is too hasty. Much of the recent discussion of Epicurus has been muddled by assimilating his position and his concerns to those of modern libertarians. Before we answer the question of *how* the swerve is supposed to secure our freedom, at least two other questions need to be addressed: What *type* of freedom is the swerve supposed to secure? And why should we *care* about having freedom in this sense – that is, why does it matter? Only if Epicurus is concerned to secure the same type of freedom as are modern libertarians, and for the same sort of ethical concerns, are we justified in calling Epicurus a 'libertarian.'[1] Before considering in detail the passages in which

1 So, for instance, I find Jeffrey Purinton's discussion highly unsatisfactory. Purinton writes that Epicurus is a 'libertarian' because he asserts '(1) that, although some things happen 'by necessity' and others happen 'by chance' some things are genuinely 'due to us,' (2) that praise and blame properly attach to 'what is due to us,' and therefore (3) that we are not 'enslaved to the fate of the physicists,' not subject, that is, to physical determinism.' (Purinton (1999) 254). Each step (1)–(3) is questionable as a support for attributing libertarianism to Epicurus, since one could accept that Epicurus advances each of them (as I do) and yet still reject the identification of Epicurus' with the libertarian position. This is because what Epicurus means by phrases like some things being "up to us" and some things being "by necessity" is still at issue, it is not obvious that Epicurus' *primary* concern is with praise and blame, and one cannot simply straightforwardly identify the "fate of the physicists" with physical determinism. Because of this, when Purinton says, "Now set aside all textual evidence and simply ask what a would-be libertarian atomist is *obliged* to say" (p. 258), and then goes on to criticize various other interpretations of Epicurus because they do not sufficiently respect either his libertarianism or his atomism, many of his criticisms are question-begging. That is because much of his argument presupposes his definitions of libertarianism and atomism, and other parties to the debate would simply deny that Epicurus is a libertarian or an atomist, as Purinton uses the terms.

Epicurus' theory of freedom and the role of the swerve are discussed, in this chapter I will lay some conceptual groundwork that I hope will clarify the following discussion. First, I will set forth (rather schematically) some varieties of 'problems of free will,' and I will situate interpretations of Epicurus, including my own, in terms of these varieties. Then I will consider the terminology that Epicurus and those who report on Epicurus' position use when discussing our freedom, to see what sort of freedom he is concerned to defend. Finally, I will look into what sort of freedom Epicurus *ought* to be concerned to defend, given his ethics and psychology.

1.1 *The problems of free wills and determinisms*

We can represent different types of "free will and determinism" problems by thinking of them as involving combinations of three factors. The first is a type of determinism. The second is something that is threatened by that determinism. And finally, since determinism is supposed to present a *problem* for us (at least potentially), there is something ethically significant that has as a necessary condition what determinism threatens. The three factors would plug into the following sort of schema:

Type of determinism *X* threatens (at least potentially) *Y*, and *Y* is a necessary condition for *Z*.

X. Three types of determinism are often discussed.[2]

The most common type of determinism featured in contemporary debates is *causal* determinism – roughly, the thesis that the "laws of nature" along with past states of the universe determine exactly one unique future.[3] In ancient discussions, this thesis would not have been put in terms of "laws of nature." Nonetheless, it is recognizable when Lucretius describes how, without the swerve, new motion would always arise from old motion in an invariable order stretching back to infinity (*DRN* 2 251 ff), and again when the Stoics portray fate as an everlasting, inviolable, and interconnected sequence of causes which determines everything that occurs, past, present and future.[4]

The second type is *logical* determinism – roughly, the thesis that every proposition either is true or is false, including propositions about what

2 The terminology of 'logical' and 'epistemic' determinism is from Long and Sedley (1987) vol. I 466.

3 For a detailed contemporary specification of causal determinism along these lines, see van Inwagen (1983) section 3.3 58–65.

4 See the sources in L&S section 55 for many reports of this sort of view, especially 55J, K, L, and O.

will occur in the future.[5] The classic source for this thesis is Aristotle's discussion in *de Int.* 9, along with the 'Master Argument' of Diodorus Cronus.[6]

The final type of determinism is *epistemic* determinism, more commonly known as foreknowledge – the doctrine that some agent knows everything that will occur. In ancient sources, this was usually discussed merely as a way of illustrating logical determinism, not as a separate type of determinism, and some contemporary thinkers maintain that there is not any problem of 'foreknowledge' separable from the issue of logical determinism. However, when an essentially omniscient God is introduced as the foreknower, some think that this presents special determinist problems of its own above the problems posed by logical determinism.[7]

Y. Likewise, we can distinguish, in a rough and ready way, three different things that determinism might be thought to threaten.

The first is the *ability to do otherwise than one does.* I am now typing, but I believe I have the ability to refrain from doing so. As Aristotle puts it, "For where it is in our power to act, it is also in our power not to act, and *vice versa*" (*NE* 3 5 1113b 7–9).[8] Bobzien calls this 'two-sided' freedom of the will, or freedom between doing some action and not doing it.[9]

5 See Bernstein (2002) for a good overview of this thesis. Bernstein, however, would dislike the term 'logical determinism,' since he thinks that fatalist arguments that proceed from considerations of future truth do not draw merely on logical principles—or at least, those that do so are uninteresting and grossly fallacious. Bernstein believes that more philosophically interesting fatalist arguments depend on semantic and temporal considerations, so he would probably prefer a term like 'semantic-temporal determinism.' In my formulation of the thesis, I do not mean to exclude views according to which the primary truth-bearers are something other than propositions.

6 I discuss the 'Master Argument' and the *de. Int.* 9 arguments in much more detail in chapter 6. A good summary of the Master Argument can be found in Barnes, Bobzien and Mignucci (1999) 88–92. Gaskin (1995) is an excellent, if rather dense and technical, treatment of both Aristotle's 'Sea Battle' argument and Diodorus' 'Master Argument.' See Sedley (1977) for more on Diodorus and the 'Dialectical/Megarian' School of which he was a part.

7 See Aristotle *de Int.* 9 18b33–19a7 for an example of using prior predictions merely as a way of illustrating logical determinism, and Zagzebski (2002) 61–62 and Bernstein (2002) 75–80 for discussions of whether God's foreknowledge poses special determinist problems above logical determinism, along with references to much of the recent literature on this question.

8 Unless otherwise noted, translations of Aristotle are from Barnes (1984), sometimes with minor modifications.

9 Bobzien (2000) 288. By using the quotation from Aristotle to illustrate the idea that we have the ability to do otherwise than we do, I do not mean to imply that his own understanding of this ability is libertarian rather than compatibilist.

The second can be designated *ultimate origination* or *ultimate control.* After Frankfurt's famous counterexamples,[10] many people came to think that it is not an ability to do otherwise at the moment of decision that is key to freedom, but that one's actions can ultimately be traced back to the agent himself. Perhaps my current beliefs and states of character determine what I am now doing, and make it so I cannot do otherwise. (In fact, it may be thought that this is what the virtuous person is like.) This need not preclude my action being free, as long as "the springs of action are truly an agent's own."[11] Determinism is thought to threaten this by making the agent's character itself traceable back to factors of heredity and environment outside of the agent and over which the agent has no control. Ancient precedents to this concern have been found in Aristotle's doctrine that the *archê* (origin or principle) of voluntary action must be internal to the agent (*NE* 3 1) and his concern to defend the agent's responsibility for his own character so that he will be responsible for the actions that flow from that character (*NE* 3 5). (However, see chapter 3 for my argument that Aristotle's concerns are *not* really that similar to worries about 'ultimate origination.')

Finally, determinism might be thought to undermine *the openness or contingency of the future.* This is often conceived of in terms of an asymmetry between the future, which is 'open' to us, versus the fixity of the past, which we can do nothing to change.

Z. Lastly, there are at least two different ways in which the loss of the ability to do otherwise, ultimate control, or the openness of the future may affect us.

First, it may destroy the possibility of *moral responsibility.* People behave in all sorts of unfortunate ways, but they would not be *culpable* for acting in those ways if determinism were true.

Second, determinism may be thought to undermine *effective/rational deliberation or action.* If what is going to occur has already been determined, what's the point in deliberating about which action to perform?

10 Frankfurt (1969); see Part v of Kane (2002) for an overview and discussion of the voluminous literature Frankfurt has sparked. As Fischer puts it, Frankfurt examples "contain a fail-safe mechanism that does not actually play any role in the relevant agent's deliberations, choices, and behavior, but whose presence ensures that the agent deliberates, chooses, and behaves just as he actually does" (Fischer (2002) 281), *e.g.*, a neuroscientist monitoring the agent's brain for signs that he will not do some action *a*, and who will press a button to ensure that the agent will do *a* if the sign appears, but who (as it turns out) never has to press the button, as the agent simply goes ahead and does *a.* The agent is responsible for this action (if anyone is responsible for any action), but the neuroscientist ensures that the agent did not have the ability to do otherwise than he did.

11 Haji (2002) 212.

Now that I have laid out the three different factors, let's consider some ways in which they can be combined to form different free will and determinism problems. We will then be in a position to look at some of the main schools of interpretation of Epicurus' theory in terms of what *type* of free will problem they take Epicurus to be addressing and how the swerve is supposed to help solve it. (I will also describe how they draw on the various texts and predecessors of Epicurus described above (section 0.2) as evidence.)

The 'traditional' problem of free will and determinism concerns the charge that causal determinism threatens our ability to do otherwise than we do, and that this sort of ability is necessary in order to be morally responsible for one's actions.[12] Compatibilists either try to produce an analysis of "could have done otherwise" that is compatible with determinism,[13] or they simply deny the so-called 'Principle of Alternative Possibilities' (PAP). (PAP states that a person is morally responsible for what she has done only if she could have done otherwise.)[14]

According to *Cyril Bailey, Elizabeth Asmis, Jeffrey Purinton*, and *Don Fowler* (from now on Bailey *et al.*), who advocate what I will dub *the 'traditional' interpretation*, Epicurus is addressing something like this 'traditional' problem of the incompatibility of casual determinism and moral responsibility, via PAP.[15] Epicurus appropriates most of his atomistic metaphysics from Democritus. Like Democritus, he identifies the mind with a conglomerate of atoms. However, he recognizes that Democritus' atomism has unacceptable deterministic consequences. If all atomic motions are causally necessitated, then our decisions, being identified with atomic motions in our minds, would likewise be causally necessary. And if this were true, we would not have the ability to do otherwise than is necessary for moral responsibility.

To avoid this problem, Epicurus denies that all atomic motions are causally determined by introducing the swerve, an indeterministic atomic motion. Our volitions, which produce our actions, are identical to (or at least constituted by) swerves that occur in our minds. Thus, for any action

12 See van Inwagen (1983) chapter 3 for an influential version of such an argument, and Kapitan (2002) for an overview of the recent debate on such arguments.

13 See Berofsky (2002) for an overview of recent compatibilist analyses of "could have done otherwise."

14 Frankfurt-style cases are one major reason for abandoning PAP (see n. 10). For a very different reason for rejecting PAP (which I am quite sympathetic to), see Dennett (1984) chapter 6.

15 Bailey (1928) 838–842 and (1947) 318–323, 433–437, Asmis (1970) and (1990); Purinton (1999); and Fowler (2002) commentary on *DRN* 2 251–293 and appendix. Fowler has not usually been grouped with Bailey *et al.* See O'Keefe (2003*a*) 463 for my reasons for putting him in this group.

we take, we could have acted differently – if the volition/swerve producing that action had not occurred, or had occurred at a different time.

The main textual support for this interpretation is Lucretius' discussion in *DRN* 2 251–293 of the role the swerve plays in preserving our freedom, which (proponents claim) makes it clear that an atomic swerve is directly involved in the production of every free action. Recent advocates of this position also claim that Epicurus is appropriating Aristotle's concern, as expressed in *NE* 3 1 and 3 5, that voluntary actions must have their origin in the agent himself and it must be in the agent's power either to perform or not to perform them.

Members of another family of interpretation, *the 'anti-reductionist' interpretation*, agree with the 'traditional' interpretation that Epicurus is dealing with the 'traditional' problem of free will and determinism, and that Epicurus finds this problem vexing because of his Democritean inheritance.[16] However, they think that Epicurus' main concern is to combat the unacceptable consequences of Democritus' *reductionist* atomism – his contention that, in truth, *only* atoms and void exist. Epicurus denies that the mind and its powers can be exhaustively explained in terms of the motions of atoms, because doing so would lead to rejecting the reality of emergent psychological properties like volitions. (This supposedly parallels Epicurus' response to Democritus' skepticism: Democritus denies the reality of emergent qualities like colors, which leads him to doubt that the senses can be a source of knowledge, whereas Epicurus affirms their reality.) The remains of *On Nature* 25 that discuss psychological development provide the main textual support for anti-reductionist interpretations.

This anti-reductionism is related to Epicurus' denial of determinism in various ways by different advocates of anti-reductionism. The most influential is David Sedley's thesis that for Epicurus the self is an emergent phenomenon that acquires a power of volition that transcends the laws that bind atomic motion and can even 'reach down' and cause changes at the atomic level. (As Sedley puts it, the self is *radically* emergent. For this reason, I label Sedley's view *the 'radical emergence' interpretation.*) However, the self would not be able to exercise this power if physical laws were sufficient on their own to determine all atomic motions. As a minimal indeterminacy at the atomic level, the swerve allows the self 'elbow room'

16 Proponents of anti-reductionist interpretations include David Sedley (Sedley (1983) and (1988*a*); Long and Sedley (1987) section 20); Julia Annas (Annas (1992) chapter 7 and (1993)); and Philip Mitsis (Mitsis (1988) chapter 4).

where it can exercise its power to act one way or the other *within* the laws of physics, but in a way that is not *determined* by the laws of physics.[17]

Another 'problem of free will,' in addition to the traditional one, is that causal determinism threatens our ability to have 'ultimate control' over our actions, which is necessary for moral responsibility. Many libertarians recently have given up PAP but still think that, in order for a person to be morally responsible for his actions, they cannot be traced back to causes beyond the agent's control.[18]

David Furley and Suzanne Bobzien, both proponents of *the 'internal cause' interpretation*, propose that Epicurus has a similar worry.[19] According to them, Epicurus is not concerned to show that the agent 'could have done otherwise' at the moment of choice, or that she has some sort of 'two-sided power,' either to perform an action or not to perform it, as a necessary condition for moral responsibility. And so, Epicurus is not concerned to put a swerve directly in the production of every free action. Instead, both say, the role of the swerve is to save us from 'internal necessity,' as Lucretius puts it in *DRN* 2 289–293, that is, the way our *characters* would be necessitated if determinism were true. If the formation of one's character were able to be traced entirely to external factors of environment and heredity beyond one's control, the actions that flow from one's character would also be traceable entirely to factors external to the agent, and thus they would not really be free.

The swerve saves us from this necessity by breaking the chains of cause and effect that otherwise would allow the agent's present character and desires to be traced to causes external to him; in turn, this lets his actions have an 'internal origin.'

Two pieces of Epicurean literature are cited in favor of this interpretation. One is Lucretius' claim that swerves save us from 'internal

17 Sedley (1983) 41. Trevor Saunders (1984) accepts Sedley's view of the radically emergent self, but his view of the role of swerve is quite different and does not fit easily into the matrix of positions I am sketching out here. I discuss Saunders' view in n. 8 of chapter 2.

18 For an influential recent view along these lines, see Kane (1996), particularly chapters 5 and 6. Eleonore Stump attributes a libertarian view of this sort to Augustine, and her discussion is a brief and clear introduction to issues concerning PAP vs. 'ultimate origination.' See Stump (2001). Pereboom calls people who advocate versions of incompatibilism that focus on alternate possibilities 'leeway incompatibilists' and those who focus on an incompatibilist condition on the causal history of an action 'causal history incompatibilists.' Pereboom himself falls into the latter category and denies that we have free will. Pereboom (2001) 1–37 provides a good introduction to some of these issues. He also gives a sustained argument that Frankfurt-style scenarios render PAP false (and hence 'leeway incompatibilism' false) but do not falsify the basic intuition that free actions must not be produced by deterministic processes that trace back to causal factors beyond an agent's control.

19 Furley (1967) study II, "Aristotle and Epicurus on Voluntary Action," and Bobzien (2000).

necessity;' the other is Epicurus' discussion of character development in *On Nature* 25. Proponents of this interpretation claim that the way Aristotle responds in *NE* 3 5 to exculpatory arguments from psychological determinism provides both precedent and inspiration for Epicurus' view.

My own thesis is that Epicurus' *main* concern is not with justified praise and blame, but with preserving the rationality and efficacy of deliberating about one's future actions, although he thinks that determinism is incompatible with both. The reason for this is that a necessary condition on effective deliberation is the openness and contingency of the future, and determinism makes the future necessary. Furthermore, even though Epicurus posits the swerve in order to render causal determinism false, the sort of deterministic argument that Epicurus is concerned to rebut is the *fatalist* argument given in *de Int.* 9 and by the Megarians, which moves from considerations of future *truth*, to the fixity of the future, to the pointlessness of deliberation. Epicurus thinks that, if the Principle of Bivalence (the principle that every statement either is true or is false) held universally, this would make the future fixed in a way such as to render us helpless. (And so we can call my view *the 'bivalence' interpretation.*) Epicurus thinks that both logical and causal determinism are incompatible with the contingency of the future, and the swerve renders both false, since logical and causal determinism are mutually entailing. The swerve plays no direct role in the production of action or the formation of character.

The main textual support for attributing this role for the swerve to Epicurus is Cicero's *De fato*. There is precedent for the sort of position Epicurus adopts in Aristotle's rejection of the Principle of Bivalence for similar reasons in *de Int.* 9. If I am right about this, to assimilate Epicurus' concerns to those of modern libertarians is highly misleading.

The different types of interpretations can be summarized as shown in Table 1.1

In order to establish the 'bivalence interpretation,' I need to go through the texts that bear on the Epicurean position regarding human freedom. But before doing so, let me first establish its initial plausibility by showing that none of the terminology Epicureans use when discussing human freedom preclude it, and that the *sort* of 'free will and determinism' problem that I take Epicurus to be concerned with is one he *should* be concerned with, given his ethics and psychology, whereas – even apart from considerations of how successfully the swerve addresses these problems – the other sorts of free will and determinism problems should not even trouble Epicurus at all.

Table 1.1.

Name of interpretation	*X* Type of determinism	*Y* what determinism threatens	*Z* what *Y* is necessary for	How the swerve solves this problem
Traditional interpretation	Causal	The ability to do otherwise than one does	Moral responsibility	Volitions are identical with indeterministic swerves.
Radical emergence interpretation	Causal	The ability to do otherwise than one does	Moral responsibility	Swerves allow the self to exercise its power in the gaps they leave.
Internal cause interpretation	Causal	Ultimate origination of one's character and actions	Moral responsibility	Swerves prevent one's character from being entirely causally determined by external factors.
Bivalence interpretation	Both logical and causal	The openness and contingency of the future	Primarily effective deliberation and action; secondarily justified praise and blame	Swerves ensure that what will occur in the future has not been always fixed.

1.2 Terminology and contexts

Epicurus is concerned to defend human freedom, but none of the terminology he uses (or that others use who report on the Epicurean position) show that he is worried about preserving the ability of an agent to do otherwise than he does, much less that he conceived of this two-way ability in libertarian terms. *Libera voluntas* is often translated 'free will,' but depending on the context, it can mean something like 'unfettered impulse.'[20] After all, Cicero is willing to describe even the compatibilist Chrysippus, who certainly did not have a two-sided libertarian conception of freedom of will, as wanting to free (*libero)* our minds from necessity of motion and to accommodate the views of those who think that the movements of our minds are voluntary (*voluntarius*).[21] (For this reason, I will usually translate *voluntas* as 'volition,' since it is not potentially misleading in the way 'will' is, and while I think that the Epicurean theory of *libera voluntas* actually ends up being something like a theory of 'unfettered impulse,' using that as a translation would be highly tendentious.)[22]

Likewise, Epicurus says that how we act and develop "depends on us" (παρ' ἡμᾶς) and that our actions arise through us ourselves or from us ourselves (δι' ἡμῶν αὐτῶν or ἐξ ἡμῶν αὐτῶν). That our actions are παρ' ἡμᾶς is compatible with them simply being caused by us (*e.g.*, that I caused myself to walk, so that my walking "depended on me"), and need not imply that, however we act, it is "up to us" whether to act one way rather than another (*e.g.*, that it was up to me *whether or not* to walk). In fact, Bobzien argues at length, and I think convincingly, that to say our actions are παρ' ἡμᾶς is more naturally read as indicating that we are causally responsible for our actions (what she calls a 'one-sided causative' παρ' ἡμᾶς) and has no implications about free choice.[23] To say that actions are δι' ἡμῶν αὐτῶν or ἐξ ἡμῶν αὐτῶν also has no implications of free choice. In fact, Chrysippus defends the thesis that certain things originate "from us" (ἐξ ἡμῶν),[24] and when the Stoics are concerned to

20 See Annas (1992) 177 n. 3 and Bobzien (2000) 310–1 for more detailed discussion of the term *libera voluntas*.

21 *De fato* xvii 39. That Cicero thinks that Chrysippus' compatibilist project is unsuccessful does not damage the main point, that a concern to uphold *libera voluntas* (or something described using cognate terms) does not immediately imply a libertarian concern for two-sided freedom of choice, any more than Daniel Dennett's asserting that we have 'free will' in some sense shows that he is a libertarian, or that he thinks an ability to do otherwise is essential for human freedom.

22 See Annas (1992) 176–177 for an argument that Lucretius uses *voluntas* in order to translate *hormê* from Epicurus and that *hormê* would best be translated as 'impulse.'

23 Bobzien (2000) 293–298. Especially convincing is her point that Epicurus says in *On Nature* 25, in a parallel construction, that our actions both "depend on" [παρά] us and also "depend on" [παρά] our beliefs. She says that it makes sense to say that our actions are *a result of* our beliefs, but not that our beliefs make a decision *whether or not* to perform an action. Annas also notes that Epicurus uses παρά ("depends on us") instead of ἐπί with the dative ("up to us") when talking about our responsibility for our actions (Annas (1993) 55–56 and n. 12), and she thinks this usage indicates that Epicurus wants simply to defend the "intuitive" idea that we are agents, and that he "seems not to want to defend a very strong and possibly unintuitive version of the idea " (Annas (1992) 129).

24 Eusebius, *Evangelical Preparation* 6.8.25–9 (L&S 62F).

describe precisely what type of agency we do have and are at pains to *deny* the thesis that freedom is a matter of having free choice between opposite actions, they say repeatedly that what is up to us is what happens *through* us (δι' ἡμῶν).[25]

The passages which report the Epicurean views on determinism and freedom indicate that Epicurus *is* concerned about defending something like the view that we have moral responsibility. The much later Epicurean Diogenes of Oinoanda claims that all censure and admonition would be abolished if fate controlled what we did, and Cicero, in reporting the worry that motivates the various parties to the fate and free volition debate, says that if fate were operative, there would be no justice in either praise or blame. Epicurus, likewise, when arguing that some things 'depend on us,' says praise and blame properly attach to such things, and in his anti-fatalist argument in *On Nature* 25, he asserts that our practices of rebuking, opposing and reforming each other presuppose that the cause of actions is 'in ourselves.'[26]

However, even more prominent in Epicurean thought is the theme that determinism would render us *helpless*. When Lucretius describes the *libera voluntas* that the swerve snatches from the fates, he says nothing about responsibility, praise, or blame. Instead, *libera voluntas* is what allows each animal to go where pleasure leads it and the mind to move itself (*DRN* 2 257–260). Although Lucretius' later discussions of *voluntas* do not mention the swerve, they do confirm that it is *voluntas* that allows us to act as we wish to act – to visualize what we wish to visualize, to move our limbs as we desire, *etc.* (*DRN* 4 777–780, 877–880) So, if determinism threatens this *voluntas*, the implication is that determinism would render us unable to act as we wish to act, to move our limbs as we will, *etc.*[27]

A similar concern with fatalism lurks in Epicurus' discussion of the "fate of the natural philosophers" in *Ep. Men.* 133–134. Epicurus contrasts what is ἀνάγκη, which is ἀνυπεύθυνος – 'unanswerable' or 'beyond human control' – with what is παρ' ἡμᾶς, which is ἀδέσποτος – 'without master' or 'autonomous.' He then goes on to say that it would better to believe in the meddling Olympian gods than to be a 'slave' to the fate of the natural philosophers, since at least one can try to placate the Olympian gods, whereas the necessity of the natural philosophers is inescapable. In *On Nature* 25, the target of Epicurus' argument is a *fatalist*: this person

25 Alexander, *On Fate* 181, 13–182,20 (L&S 62G).

26 Diogenes of Oinoanda 32.1.14–3.14 (L&S 20G), Cicero *De fato* 40, *Ep. Men.* 133, *On Nature* 25 26–30 (L&S 20C).

27 See chapter 2, particularly section 2.3, for more discussion of Lucretius on *voluntas*.

denies that our decisions make any difference; what we do is not a cause or explanation (*aitia*) of what happens.[28] Finally, Cicero's discussions of the Epicurean and Stoic positions in the *De fato* show that a major concern of theirs was whether, if what will occur in the future has *always been true* and *always been causally determined*, the future is necessary in a way that makes all deliberation and action pointless.[29]

1.3 Epicurean ethics, Epicurean psychology, and Epicurean freedom

Now, before going through the texts, let's step back and ask: given Epicurus' ethics and his psychology, what sort of freedom *should* he be worried about? Epicurean ethics is egoistic and hedonistic. In every choice, one should strive to attain the 'goal of nature,' pleasure (*KD* 25). The problem with most of the traditional 'libertarian' interpretations of Epicurus is that they dissociate one's actions not only from external causation but *also* from being caused by the psychological states of the agent present at the moment of choice: his beliefs, desires, and character, since being causally determined by these states is incompatible with a robust ability to do otherwise than one does.

Let us leave aside, for the moment, the objection that a random atomic swerving in one's mind is an unpromising basis for the production of free and responsible actions, instead of random and blameless twitches.[30] Why should Epicureans be concerned to try to defend this sort of freedom of choice in the first place? If one has correct beliefs about the workings of the world and the limits of what is required for happiness, and one knows what one needs to do in the present situation to attain a pleasurable life, then having one's actions determined by these psychological states would not be ethically problematic – in fact, it is exactly what one would want to happen. This is the state of the Epicurean Sage. It is hard to see how having a 'two-sided' libertarian freedom of choice would help in the pursuit of *ataraxia*, or tranquility, which Epicurus maintains is the chief constituent of the happy life. And if this freedom would not help in the pursuit of *ataraxia*, it is hard to see why any good Epicurean should care about defending its possibility against the threat of determinism.

28 In chapter 4 I give further argument for this point.

29 *De fato* 17–38. See chapter 6, and section 6.1 in particular, for further elaboration of this claim.

30 As David Furley puts it, "the atomic swerve seems to be well adapted to produce unexplained, random, sudden, motiveless actions, but totally unsuitable to produce the deliberate actions which are typically liable to moral appraisal" (Furley (1967) 163).

A libertarian 'freedom of choice' would also be difficult to square with Epicurean psychology, which is hedonistic. Epicurus, it is reported, declares that pleasure and pain "supply the motives of desire and of avoidance, and the springs of conduct generally" (*DF* I 42), and even more strongly, they "lie at the root of *every act* of choice and avoidance" (*DF* I 23).[31] Lucretius gives a description of action-theory at the atomic level in which action seems to follow automatically from one's beliefs, desires, and the impact of atomic images.[32] Furthermore, cases of wrongdoing are explained, not by referring to the perverse will of the wrongdoer, but by saying that the wrongdoer has incorrect beliefs about what will bring him pleasure.[33]

Epicureans go to great lengths to defend this psychological hedonism. Torquatus, the Epicurean spokesman in *De finibus*, realizes that not all actions appear to spring from the desire for pleasure, and he gives a long and detailed account of how apparently disinterested actions by his ancestors, such as charging the enemy, really spring from self-interest (*DF* I 34–36). This *psychological* hedonism (and hence determinism) is so important to the Epicureans because it provides the chief argument for their *ethical* hedonism. They think that the good is "the end to which all other things are means, which is not itself a means to anything else " (*DF* I 9, echoing *NE* I 1, 1094a 17ff). Being good ethical naturalists, they believe that to discover what this end is, one ought to look at what creatures actually *do* pursue as the ultimate end of all of their actions. And what creatures actually do pursue as the end of all their actions is to attain pleasure and avoid pain. Torquatus advances this proof at the very beginning of his exposition of Epicurean ethics (*DF* I 30), and Cicero repeats it during his attack on Epicureanism.[34]

It might be objected that I am sliding much too quickly from "psychological hedonism" to "psychological determinism." I have been suggesting that Epicurus' psychological hedonism precludes a concern for libertarian

31 See also the rhetorical question in *DF* I 30 "What does Nature perceive or what does she judge of, beside pleasure and pain, to guide her actions of desire and of avoidance?" (Translations of the *De finibus* are from Rackham (1931).) Cicero repeats the Epicurean position on motives during his attack upon it, in *DF* 2 60ff. See also *Ep. Men.* 128: everything is done for the sake of being neither in pain or terror, which (according to Epicurus) is the most pleasurable state.

32 *DRN* 4 877–906. I will discuss this passage in more detail in section 2.3 to bolster this contention.

33 *KD* 7, 10, *SV* 16, *DF* I 32–33, 55.

34 The evidence for attributing both psychological and ethical hedonism to Epicurus is overwhelming; see O'Keefe (2001*b*) 273–276 for more discussion. See Cooper (1999) for an extended argument that Epicurus is only an ethical, and not a psychological, hedonist. However, even Cooper admits that, for Epicurus, what we all naturally pursue (and ideally would pursue, if not corrupted) is pleasure. And so, once we have correct beliefs about how to obtain pleasure, we should always act in accordance with them.

free will, a two-way power at the moment of decision. That is because, given that you desire pleasure, and you believe that doing *X* will bring you pleasure more effectively than any other available course of action, you'll do *X*. However, one might object that this implies psychological determinism only if we don't have control over what we believe brings us pleasure. But Epicureans *do* think that this is under our control, and so determinism does not follow. For instance, at the beginning of his anti-fatalist digression in *On Nature* 25, Epicurus says that how we develop depends on us (παρ' ἡμᾶς) and depends upon beliefs that are "from us ourselves " (ἐξ ἡμῶν αὐτῶν).[35]

I agree that Epicurus holds that our beliefs are under our control, but I think that we need to examine more closely *in what sense* they are under our control in order to discover the implications of this for Epicurean psychology.

We *can* imagine a case in which a person is 'controlled' by his desires in a way that would be worrisome to an Epicurean. Let us suppose that I was raised in a society where I developed deep-seated desires, via cultural indoctrination, to own a giant SUV, eat greasy Happy Meals, collect a complete set of Masters of the Universe action-figures, and the like. (Let us call the fictional country in this thought-experiment 'The United States.') Now, if my actions were controlled by these desires, and I were unable to modify them, then Epicurus would agree that this sort of 'enslavement' is bad: it leads to misery, because of the anxiety produced by worrying about whether I will be able to accumulate all of the action figures, have an unending supply of Happy Meals, *etc.* But, Epicurus thinks, we can modify such desires, by using our reason. We can discover, via reason, the limits of pleasure, and distinguish between natural and necessary desires, merely natural desires, and vain and empty desires (*KD* 18–22, 29–30). We can ask, of every desire we have, "what will happen if I get what I desire, and what will happen if I don't?" (*SV* 71). Using our reason, we can overcome hate, envy and contempt (*DL* 10 117) and even modify our congenital temperaments so that "nothing hinders our living a life worthy of gods" (*DRN* 3 288–322). Reason allows us to do this by showing us that certain desires, temperaments, and ways of life are not effective for getting us what we ultimately desire for its own sake, pleasure.

In this sense, our desires are under our control, and I believe that preserving this sort of reasons-responsiveness is at the heart of Epicurus' ethics and his worries about determinism. However, reasons-responsiveness

35 Arr. 34.26.3ff., L&S 20C1. I thank David Sedley for bringing up this objection.

is not at all the same thing as a libertarian two-way freedom of will; recent proponents of 'reasons-responsiveness' accounts of responsibility are explicitly compatibilist.[36] Libertarian freedom of choice requires that one's decisions not be causally determined by one's present mental dispositions, and since one's reasoning is itself a kind of mental disposition, one's decisions would be dissociated from that also. What I should want, consistently with Epicurean ethics, is the ability to reflect on my beliefs and desires and change them, using my reason, in order to be able to attain a pleasant life. Epicureans certainly would not be interested in having 'control' over one's desires in Sartre's sense.

Similarly, this sort of 'reasons-responsiveness' is quite different from the concern for 'ultimate origination' attributed to Epicurus in the internal cause interpretation. Bobzien rightly points out that having one's character be 'one's own' is important to Epicurus, and I agree that Epicurus wants our desires and beliefs to have an 'internal origin' in *some* sense. We do not want to have 'alien' desires and beliefs, implanted in us by Madison Avenue and a sick society, interfering with our pursuit of happiness. Instead, our beliefs and desires should be the result of our own correct reasoning about our nature and the nature of the world; only this can provide a secure basis for attaining the blessed state of *ataraxia*, or tranquility. But according to Furley and Bobzien, one's present character has an 'internal origin' because there are a few random causal breaks in the past that make it the case that one's present character cannot be fully traced to 'external' causes; instead, one's present character was at least partially caused by indeterministic atomic swerves in one's mind. Once again, it is difficult to see how being 'free' in this sense would help one at all in the pursuit of *ataraxia*, and so it is difficult to see why Epicurus would be concerned to preserve this sort of freedom.

I think that Epicurus is concerned with reasons-responsiveness as I have been describing it because of its connection with attaining pleasure, as follows: (1) we need to have our reason in charge in order to be able to deliberate about alternative courses of action and decide which one will most effectively bring us pleasure. (2) We need to be able to use our reason in order to investigate our needs and our desires, so as to be able to bring our desires in line with our rational judgments about which set of

36 See Fischer and Ravizza (1998). However, if one thinks that explanation in terms of reasons and causal necessitation are incompatible, as Malcolm (1968) argues, then a concern to defend reasons-responsiveness could lead to a denial of determinism.

desires will actually result in having a pleasant life. (3) Rational self-government can itself be a source of tranquility, since we don't have to worry about outside interference or outside control. If Epicurus thinks that determinism threatens the efficacy and rationality of deliberating about the future, this would give him a powerful reason to combat determinism.

Of course, I now need to show that the bivalence interpretation is supported by the texts dealing with the swerve and human freedom more strongly than are other interpretations of Epicurus' position. But at the very least, the bivalence interpretation ought to be given a serious hearing, since it responds directly to the problem Epicurus *should* be worried about, given his ethics and psychology.

CHAPTER 2

Lucretius on the swerve and voluntas

The natural place to look when trying to figure out the role of the swerve in free action is Lucretius' description in *DRN* 2 251–293 of why the swerve is needed to preserve our *voluntas*, and a great deal of attention has been lavished on this passage. So, in this chapter I will consider what we can learn about the Epicurean position from Lucretius. As far as the swerve itself is concerned, my conclusions will be mostly negative: Lucretius' description of the swerve tells us remarkably little about the role it is supposed to play in preserving our freedom. However, his descriptions in *DRN* 4 877–896 of voluntary action and in *DRN* 2 251–293 of the *voluntas* the swerve preserves both show what sort of freedom the Epicureans are concerned to defend against the threat of determinism. I will first examine *DRN* 2 251–293, and then *DRN* 4 877–896, and show that the *De rerum natura* undercuts the thesis that Epicurus' concerns are much like those of modern libertarians. Finally, I will turn explicitly to a consideration of the traditional interpretation, that every volition is constituted by a swerve, since the main textual support for this family of interpretations is *DRN* 2 251–293, and I will argue that *De rerum natura* actually gives us good reason to reject this interpretation of the Epicurean position.

2.1 DRN *2 251–293*

DRN 2 251–293 is the longest passage we have by an Epicurean that describes the connection of the swerve to free action. It occurs in the midst of an explanation of the causes of atomic motion. Earlier in book two, Lucretius establishes that atoms are constantly in motion, explains how they form compound bodies of various kinds through their collisions with one another, discusses the speed of atomic motion, and argues that all atoms naturally fall straight downwards. He then gives two arguments for the swerve. The first (which I discuss in chapter 5) is that the atoms must engage in a swerving motion to the side in order for the atoms ever to have collided with one another and to have formed compound bodies, as they evidently have. Then comes his argument that there must be a swerve in order for *voluntas* to exist, as it evidently does. Since I will be discussing his argument in some detail, let me quote the passage in full:

> Moreover, if all motion is always linked,
> and new motion arises out of old in a fixed order,
> and atoms do not by their swerving make
> some beginning of motion to break the decrees of fate,
> so that cause should not follow cause from infinity,
> from where does this free volition exist for animals throughout the world?
> From where, I ask, comes this volition wrested from the fates,
> through which we proceed wherever each of us is led by his pleasure,
> and likewise swerve off our motions at no fixed time
> or fixed region of space, but wherever the mind itself carries us?
> For without doubt it is volition that in each of us gives these things
> their beginning, and from volition that motions are spread through the limbs.
> Don't you see how also when at an instant
> the starting gates are opened, the eager strength of horses
> can nevertheless not surge forward as suddenly as the mind itself wishes?
> For all the mass of matter has to be stirred up throughout the body,
> so that stirred up throughout the limbs
> it may in a concerted effort follow the mind's desire.
> Thus you may see that the beginning of motion is created from the heart
> and proceeds initially from the mind's volition,
> and from there is spread further through the entire body and limbs.
> Nor is it the same when we move forward impelled by a blow,
> through another person's great strength and great coercion.
> For then it is plain that all the matter of the whole body
> moves and is driven against our wish,
> until volition has reined it back throughout the limbs.
> So do you now see that, although external force
> propels many along and often obliges them to proceed against their wishes

and to be driven headlong, nevertheless there is in our chest
something which is capable of fighting and resisting,
at whose decision the mass of matter
is also forced at times to be turned throughout the limbs and frame
and, when hurled forward, is reined back and settles down?
Therefore in the seeds too you must admit the same thing,
that there is another cause of motion besides impacts and weight,
from which this power is born in us,
since we see that nothing can come into being out of nothing.
For weight prevents all things from coming about by impacts,
by a sort of external force. But that the mind should not itself possess
an internal necessity in all its behavior,
and be overcome and, as it were, forced to suffer and be acted upon –
that is brought about by a tiny swerve of atoms
at no fixed region of space or fixed time.[1]

The overall form of Lucretius' argument

Lucretius' argument for the existence of the swerve follows a familiar pattern for the Epicureans. Its basic form is *modus tollens* (if A, then B. Not-B. Therefore, not-A). It involves starting from the *enargês* – what is clear or manifest, that is, something evident to perception – and from this inferring a conclusion about the *adêlon* – what is unseen or obscure, that is, something by its nature hidden from perception.[2] An example is the Epicurean argument for the existence of void. By its nature, void cannot be directly perceived, although we can get a sense of what it is by analogy with the so-called 'empty' space in rooms and the like. However, it is evident that there are bodies in motion. If there were not void space, bodies would be unable to move, and so we can infer that there is void. In

1 The translation (with minor modifications) is from Long and Sedley (1987). For ease of reference, I have taken the liberty of breaking the English text into lines that approximate Lucretius. (Note, however, that the text only *approximates* Lucretius' own breaks; in a few cases, particular words are "off" by one line from where they are in the Latin text.) For the Latin text, see the Appendix.

2 For much more on the Epicurean use of this argument form, see Asmis (1984) 83–224. Further evidence that the Epicurean argument for the swerve has this form is Diogenes of Oinoanda 32.1.14–3.14 (L&S 20G), who says that Epicurus brought the swerve to light, "demonstrating it from evident facts" (ἐκ τῶν φαινομένων δείκνυσιν).

this passage, Lucretius says that we cannot directly perceive individual atomic swerves, but the fact that animals are able to act freely, which we can see, shows that they exist:

(1) If the atoms did not have a swerving motion, there would not be *libera voluntas.*
(2) There is *libera voluntas.*
(3) Therefore, the atoms do have a swerving motion.

The passage follows the argument pattern closely. In the beginning of the passage, from lines 251–260, Lucretius tries to establish the first premise. In 261–283 Lucretius tries to establish the second premise. He gives two rather unclear examples that are supposed to show that *libera voluntas* exists. The main contrast the examples illustrate is between motion initiated by the mind itself, versus motion that comes about solely as a result of external blows and shoves, against the will of the animal. Then, from lines 284–293, he explicitly draws the conclusion: therefore, there is a third cause of atomic motion, in addition to impacts and weight, a swerving motion that allows us to act freely.

If all the passage establishes is that the swerve is a necessary condition for action initiated by the mind of the animal itself, and not solely as the result of external blows, this would leave entirely open *why* the swerve is a necessary condition for the existence of *voluntas* and how it figures into free action. We cannot justifiably assume from Lucretius' *modus tollens* argument alone that the reason the swerve is a necessary condition for *voluntas* is because *voluntas* is caused or constituted by it, any more than we should conclude that Epicureans think that motion is caused or constituted by the void, since the existence of void is a necessary condition for the existence of motion.[3]

However, several sections of *DRN* 2 251–93 have been taken to indicate a more direct relationship between swerves and volitions, so let me turn to a more detailed examination of Lucretius' argument.[4]

3 See Berryman (1997), who argues that no ancient thinkers believe void (actual or potential) has any mysterious "attractive power." The argument for the existence of void, based on the existence of motion, was first put forward by Leucippus, one of the inventors of atomism; see Aristotle, *On Generation and Corruption* 1 8 325a23–b6.

4 Many of the points I make below are similar to ones made in Bobzien (2000) 307–320, which I am indebted to for improving my understanding of the passage.

Premise 1, DRN *251–260: If the atoms did not have a swerving motion, there would not be libera voluntas*

In *DRN* 2 253–257, Lucretius asks, if "the atoms do not by swerving make some beginning of motion to break the decrees of fate . . . from where (*unde*) does this free volition exist for animals throughout the world? From where, I ask, comes this volition wrested from the fates . . .?"

It would be easy to interpret this passage in a way that supports the traditional interpretation, as follows: (i) Lucretius asserts here the swerve is that from which 'free volition' arises, and (ii) the most natural reading for why Lucretius asserts (i) is that 'free volition' come from the swerve because volitions simply are atomic swerves in the mind.[5] But both these steps are dubious. Lucretius does *not* say that volitions arise from swerves – he asks where volitions could arise from, if there were not a swerve, implying that they could not arise if that were the case. That is, the rhetorical question he asks implies only that swerves are a necessary condition for volitions and need not describe the relationship between swerves and volitions. Furthermore, even if one thinks Lucretius does assert that volitions somehow arise from swerves, this still leaves open the question of the sense in which volitions arise from swerves; it does not follow that volitions are identical to swerves.

In fact, *DRN* 2 251–257 actually provides as much if not more support for the bivalence and internal cause interpretations as it does for the traditional interpretation. It does not indicate that the swerve saves us from fate by being itself the origin of our actions; instead, it saves us from fate by breaking the chains of cause and effect that otherwise would stretch backwards into infinity.

In my quotation of Lucretius above, the passage that is hidden in the ellipses undercuts the traditional interpretation. Lucretius does not go directly from the clause "if the swerve did not exist . . ." to the question "from where comes our free volition," which might imply that the swerve is directly the cause of our free volition. Instead, the conditional is mediated, as follows: if "the atoms do not by swerving make some beginning of motion to break the decrees of fate, *so that cause should not follow cause from infinity,* from where (*unde*) does this free volition exist for animals throughout the world? From where, I ask, comes this volition wrested from the fates . . .?" This suggests that the real obstacle to our having freedom would be the infinite series of causes stretching

5 Purinton (1999) 257 interprets it in this way.

backwards, and that the swerve makes it possible for us to act freely by breaking this chain which otherwise would bind us, not by being a direct cause of our *voluntas.* So Lucretius' question is equally compatible with the internal cause interpretation, the bivalence interpretation, and the traditional interpretation. On the internal cause interpretation, swerves preserve *libera voluntas* by breaking the chains of cause and effect which otherwise would necessitate our character and actions, and on the bivalence interpretation, swerves preserve *libera voluntas* by maintaining the contingency of the future against the threat that what is going to occur has already been predetermined far in the past.

Similar considerations apply to the continuation of the passage just cited, *DRN* 2 257–260, in which Lucretius compares our ability to do what we want to do to the random swerving of atoms: "this volition wrested from the fates, through which we proceed wherever each of us is led by his pleasure, and likewise swerve off our motions at no fixed time or fixed region of space, but wherever the mind itself carries us." One could read this analogy in a way that supports the traditional interpretation: Lucretius compares our *voluntas* to the swerve of the atoms because the two are, at bottom, the same, and it is because our volitions are constituted by random swerves that our actions are likewise random, instead of being determined to occur at fixed times and places. But this is not the only way, or even the most plausible way, of taking the analogy.

I think that Bobzien's analysis of this passage is credible.[6] Lucretius talks about our *minds* carrying us, not volitions or swerves, and we are carried by our minds where we want to go because of our desire for pleasure. Because of this, any account of the role of the swerve that would undercut our ability to follow our desire for pleasure, as the traditional interpretation does (see section 2.3 for more argument for this contention), does not fit the text. The point of the analogy is not that our actions are totally *random, i.e.*, not determined at all, but instead that they do not occur at a *predetermined* time or place. That is, what we will do is not fixed from eternity, since such predetermination from eternity is not compatible with the mind moving itself as it wishes.

I do not think that the analogy forces Bobzien's reading, but it is compatible with her reading. Furthermore, the main point of all of *DRN* 2 251–293, it seems to me, is to make a contrast between voluntary motion, in which it is mind that moves itself because of its desire for

6 Bobzien (2000) 309–10.

pleasure, versus motion which is caused by something other than the mind, such as external blows or fate.[7] So Lucretius' analogy is compatible with any interpretation in which the swerve is needed in order for the mind to be able to move itself and not be subject to some sort of objectionable necessity that would *predetermine* what is going to happen.

And so, I conclude that Lucretius' attempt in *DRN* 2 251–260 to establish the first premise of his argument tells us little about the way in which the swerve underwrites our freedom, other than that it is somehow a necessary condition for *libera voluntas*; this is consistent with nearly every interpretation of the role of the swerve.[8]

However, as Annas (1992) 186 points out, this passage of Lucretius does seem to associate the swerve with the formation of *voluntas* and "not with any subsequent mechanism to carry it out." That is, Lucretius is here most naturally read as implying that the swerve must occur prior to or simultaneously with *voluntas*, in order for *voluntas* to arise at all, rather than that the swerve is utilized by the *voluntas* after it arises. This counts against interpretations, like the radical emergence interpretation, according to which *voluntas* arises without any previous swerves and then somehow uses swerves in order to produce action.[9]

7 Bobzien (2000) 310 also makes this point.

8 The only exception to this, I think, is Saunders (1984). Because the swerve is not mentioned in the case of walking which Lucretius uses to illustrate voluntary motion in book 4, Saunders concludes that the swerve is not involved in ordinary voluntary movements. Instead, it is involved only in those actions that require exceptional effort on the part of the agent, such as those (Saunders claims) in the examples Lucretius uses to show that creatures possess *voluntas* in *DRN* 2 261–283. The swerve is somehow exploited by the self, either to allow it to do things like "throwing a grand piano across the quad" (p. 44), which are physically difficult or even "barely possible for a human being to perform" (p. 45), or to help it to break out of habitual psychological patterns, or "grooves of activity" in the *animus* (p. 45), with action automatically following from stimulus. (Unfortunately, Saunders slides back and forth between these two very different possible functions without clearly distinguishing between them, sometimes in the course of a single sentence.) Saunders' account is inconsistent with *DRN* 2 251–260. Lucretius claims that the swerve is a necessary condition for the existence of *voluntas,* but on Saunders' reading, this is not true; it is a tool that the self needs to use only occasionally in unusual cases. (I also think that he misreads the significance of Lucretius' examples.)

9 Besides the radical emergence interpretation, other interpretations that view the swerve as a tool utilized by the *voluntas* after its formation include those contained in Saunders (1984), discussed in n. 8 above, and Englert (1987), which I discuss in section 3.3. I agree with Annas here, but I would not put too much weight on this consideration. After all, Sedley might be able to say that on his interpretation, if there were not swerves, there could not arise the *sort* of *voluntas* that Lucretius describes, *i.e.*, one that is able to move the animal around, since without the gaps that swerves provide for the *voluntas* to exploit, it would be causally impotent.

Premise 2, DRN *261–283: There is libera voluntas*

After asserting that the swerve is a necessary condition for the existence of *voluntas*, Lucretius next tries to show that *voluntas* exists; he thinks that its existence can be established by observing animal behavior. He illustrates this with two examples: the first is of eager horses bursting from the starting gates; the second is of a person fighting against some external force propelling him along. These examples shed a great deal of light on what sort of *voluntas* Lucretius thinks the swerve saves from the fates.

Both examples are meant to show that animals have an internal capacity to initiate motion, and that this capacity to initiate motion distinguishes animal motion from the way in which inanimate objects are simply shoved around by blows from outside. Voluntary motion has an 'internal source' in a quite literal sense for Lucretius: it is produced by the animal's mind (*animus*), which is an organ located in its chest.

The two examples show in different ways that animal motion has this sort of 'internal source.' In the case of the horses, it is (supposedly) shown by the slight delay between the external stimulus (the opening of the gates) and the resultant motion (the surging forward of the horses). It has been claimed that this delay is supposed to demonstrate that a swerve is directly involved in every voluntary action: we would expect the stimulus to immediately produce the effect of the body moving, since the horses are already eager. However, this does not immediately occur because, even though the desire has already been formed, the mind must wait for a swerve to occur in order for this desire to be translated into action.[10] But this is not Lucretius' point. Instead, the delay is supposed to show that there exists motion initiated by the mind, in which case it takes some time for the decision of the mind to stir together and move all of the matter of the horse in a coordinated manner. Motion caused by external blows, on the other hand, does not require the time for such internal processing: if a horse at the starting gate is plowed into from behind by another horse, it will be immediately shoved forward by this blow.

The second example, of a person fighting against external force, appeals not to a time differential between the two types of motion, but to our own experience of the two. We can imagine a person being carried down a river by its swift current against his will: perhaps he knows that there are sharp rocks downstream and that he will be injured if he is thrown against them. Unlike an inanimate object, such as a hollowed-out log, we need

10 Fowler (2002) 330–1, Englert (1987) 5, 68–9.

not allow ourselves to be carried along under such circumstances: we can fight against the current and swim for the shore in order to avoid the danger downstream.

The sort of internal capacity to initiate motion that these examples illustrate does not require that any causal indeterminacies be worked anywhere into the production of behavior, nor that an animal's mind, or its volition, be an unmoved mover in some mysterious way. As far as these examples go, a stuffed toy rabbit that has a little motor inside connected to its limbs that allows it to buzz along on its own, like the Energizer Bunny, would also have an internal source of motion in a way that most ordinary toy rabbits do not.[11]

It might be thought that, in order for the *voluntas* truly to be a 'beginning' of motion, as Lucretius asserts it is, *voluntas* itself could not be causally determined. But the Latin terms here translated as 'beginning' – *principium* in line 262, *initium* in line 269 – need not imply that these 'beginnings' be initiators of motion which themselves are uncaused. The Greek term Lucretius is here most likely translating from Epicurus is *archê*, 'origin.' Actions can have an 'internal *archê*' – an 'origin' internal to the agent – without any causal breaks. (Full substantiation of this claim will have to wait until chapter 3.) Likewise, I submit, volition can be an *archê, principium,* or *initium* of action – a beginning, or origin, or principle, or initiator of action, or however one wishes to translate – without any causal breaks in the production of volition. In any case, when Lucretius accounts for how *voluntas* arises and produces action in book 4 of *DRN*, he describes it in a way that implies that no causal breaks are involved (see section 2.2).

Finally, the sort of freedom that the swerve preserves is not a 'two-sided' freedom of choice between open options or the sort of ability to do otherwise that has featured centrally in current debates over free will and determinism. Lucretius establishes that there is free volition in animals by showing that the body follows the mind's desire (*studium*, 2 268), and Lucretius describes *voluntas* as that "through which we proceed wherever each of us is led by his pleasure" (2 258). The horses are not trying to decide *whether or not* to break from the gates, and a man caught in a current is not concerned with *whether or not* to swim for the shore.

11 Actually, this is probably not *quite* true, since an animal's *voluntas* prompts behavior in response to the animal's *desires*, which presumably is not the case in a toy rabbit. But this does not damage the main point, since there is no reason to think that for Epicureans intentional explanations of behavior require causal breaks. See section 3.3 for more on this issue.

Instead, as Lucretius portrays it, *voluntas* is what allows them to be effective agents, to move around in the world in order to obtain what they desire.[12] As I argued for above (section 1.3), this is the sort of freedom that we would expect to be important for Epicureans in any case, rather than a libertarian freedom of choice.

Conclusion, DRN *284–293: the atoms do have a swerving motion*

After establishing that *voluntas* exists, Lucretius ends his discussion of the swerve by asserting that, since we see that volition is a cause of animal motion, we must admit that the swerve is a cause of atomic motion. Lucretius draws an analogy between the three causes of atomic motion – collisions, weight, and the swerve – and three types of bodily motion – those due to external force, those due to 'internal necessity,' and those due to our *voluntas.* Lucretius writes that the weight of the atoms prevents all motion from being caused by external force and blows, and the swerve prevents the motions of the mind from being constrained by 'internal necessity.' He adds that since nothing comes from nothing, there must be some sort of motion responsible for our power of *voluntas,* and this motion is the swerve.

It is easy to see how this passage may seem to support the identification of volitions with swerves. The key interpretive question is what Lucretius means by the mind having "internal necessity in all its behavior," which will determine the way one thinks the swerve saves the mind from this sort of necessity and how strongly one reads the analogy Lucretius makes.[13] If Bailey *et al.* are right, the 'internal necessity' Lucretius refers to is having one's actions causally necessitated by the total set of one's present mental dispositions – one's beliefs, desires, *etc.* If the swerve did not exist, each action of ours would be forced by these dispositions. However, because all types of movement are to be explained in terms of atomic motion, and our actions are not to be subject to this sort of internal causal necessitation, there must be a third type of atomic motion that is uncaused, which

12 Bobzien makes this point (Bobzien (2000) 311). Lucretius' descriptions of *voluntas* in Book 4 also make it clear that *voluntas* is what allows us to do what we wish to do. If this is right, it undercuts one of the main apparent advantages of the traditional interpretation: if one thinks that Epicurus *is* concerned to defend a libertarian ability to do otherwise than one does, the traditional interpretation seems to answer this demand. Being identical with random swerves, volitions cause actions, without themselves being determined by previous states of the mind, so that the agent always has, at the moment of decision, the ability to act other than the way he actually acts. (However see section 2.3 for criticisms of this view of volition.)

13 Bobzien (2000) 316 makes this point.

is the cause of our actions.[14] So the analogy is meant quite literally: forced action is caused by the blows and reboundings of atoms; 'internally necessitated' action is caused by the weight of the atoms, and free action is caused by the swerve of the atoms.[15]

Unlike the earlier passages, I think that this passage, when considered in isolation, is most naturally read along the lines suggested by Bailey *et al.* However, it *need* not be read that way; Lucretius does not spell out what he means by 'internal necessity' and does not state how the swerve saves us from its threat. Bobzien suggests an alternate reading. She thinks that Epicurus' action-theory assumes that volitions are responses to environmental stimuli "determined by the agent's overall present mental disposition, with no independent decision-making faculty,"[16] so Lucretius cannot be trying to save our action from being caused by those factors. Instead, according to her, the 'internal necessity' Lucretius is discussing is best understood as the same sort of necessitation discussed in Epicurus' *On Nature* 25, which would involve the *development* of the mind being necessitated in an unacceptable way.

To decide between these understandings of 'internal necessity,' we need to look beyond this passage to see which one fits with other passages of *DRN*, other passages of Epicurus, and Epicurean philosophy overall. When looked at in this broader context, Bobzien's reading should be preferred. Lucretius' discussion of Epicurean action-theory supports Bobzien's contention that action follows automatically from the agent's present dispositions (see section 2.2). Furthermore, the sort of 'freedom' that Bailey *et al.* believe the Epicureans are concerned to defend does not fit in with Epicurean ethics and psychology (see section 1.3), and holding that actions are produced by random swerves would be a philosophical blunder and would not preserve the sort of freedom that Lucretius himself says the swerve is supposed to preserve (see section 2.3). On the other hand, making sure that our characters are 'up to us' and under our control *is* something that Epicureans should be concerned to defend (see section 1.3), and evidently something that they *did* worry about defending (see sections 4.2–4.2.3).

14 Or, at least, a type of atomic motion that is 'caused' only in the weak sense that the atoms have an inherent disposition to swerve occasionally at random times, so that there is some sort of explanation in terms of the properties of the atoms for why this *type* of motion occurs, but no causal explanation, and no causal necessitation, for why the atoms swerve at any of the particular times that they actually do.

15 Purinton (1999) 270–273 argues along these lines.

16 Bobzien (2000) 317.

One final cautionary note about this passage: despite initial appearances, Lucretius *cannot* mean for his analogy between different causes of atomic motion and different types of bodily motion to be taken entirely straightforwardly. After all, even forced motion caused by blows from external bodies is not caused *only* by blows and inertia, since the trajectories of those bodies is determined also by the weight of their atoms. And if we imagine animal bodily motion which is not entirely determined by external blows but in which the swerve is not involved – motion which would be subject to 'internal necessity' according to the traditional interpretation – it would not *at all* be only the weight of the atoms making up the animal's body and *animus* which allows the animal not to be just shoved around by external blows. What lets the animal move in the way it does is that the atoms constituting its body form a relatively long-lasting compound, because of their entanglements and mutual reboundings, while the fine atoms making up the *animus* are trapped within the rest of the body in such a way that they are able to engage in the 'motions of thought.' (cf. *DRN* 3 350ff) The explanation for this type of animal motion will therefore involve the weight of these atoms, their shape, their past trajectories and blows with other atoms, and their resistance, as opposed to the yielding of void. What exactly Lucretius *does* mean by his analogy is obscure,[17] but since he cannot be straightforwardly asserting that each type of macroscopic bodily motion he had discussed earlier is caused by one atomic phenomenon – that forced motion is because of blows, whereas 'internally necessitated' motion is because of weight – there is not much reason to think that he is asserting that voluntary motion is directly caused by atomic swerves.

2.2 *Epicurean action-theory in* DRN *4*

I have argued that *DRN* 2 251–293 shows that Lucretius' *libera voluntas* is not much like libertarian freedom of the will at all, that the passage gives us little information about how the swerve is involved in free action, and that it does not support the notion that swerves are somehow directly involved in the production of free actions. In *DRN* 4 877–96, in the

17 See Bobzien (2000) 319–20 for a possible reading of what Lucretius is trying to get at, with no implication that volitions are directly caused by swerves. Her suggestions are plausible, but I find Lucretius' discussion at this point quite opaque. I suspect that Lucretius may have simply been drawing a striking analogy for rhetorical effect, without too much thought about how exactly the terms of the analogy were supposed to be cashed out philosophically. Therefore, I am reluctant to read too much into it.

middle of his explanations of various psychological phenomena, such as mental visualization, images in dreams, hunger and thirst, and sleep, Lucretius explains how we are able to move our limbs as we wish, and how *voluntas* arises. This passage gives further confirmation to the thesis that *voluntas* is little like libertarian free will, and it undercuts the notion that swerves have any direct role in the production of free action: not only does Lucretius not mention the swerve, the way in which he discusses *voluntas* leaves the strong impression that it is caused by the reception of images by the *animus.* Again, let me quote the passage before discussing it:

> Now I shall tell you how it comes about that we can take steps forward
> when we want to, how we have the power to move our limbs,
> and what it is that habitually thrusts forward this great bulk
> that is our body – mark what I say.
> First, let me say, images of walking
> impinge on our mind and strike it, as I explained earlier.
> It is after this that volition occurs. For no one ever embarks upon any action
> before the mind first foresees what it wishes to do.
> (Whatever it is that it foresees, there exists an image of that thing.)
> So when the mind stirs itself to want to go forward,
> it immediately strikes all the power of the spirit distributed all over the body
> throughout the limbs and frame:
> it is easily done, because the spirit is firmly interlinked with it.
> Then the spirit in turn strikes the body, and thus gradually
> the whole bulk is pushed forward and moved.
> Besides, at that moment the body also expands its pores, and the air
> (as you might expect with something always so sensitive to movement)
> passes and penetrates through the opened passages in abundance,
> and so is distributed abroad into the very smallest parts of the body.[18]

18 The translation is from Long and Sedley (1987) and Rouse (1937). For the Latin text, see the Appendix.

Lucretius starts the passage by saying that he wishes to explain how we can move our limbs as we wish. He had earlier argued that our minds are constantly being bombarded by fine atomic simulacra of all types. When we walk, our mind is struck by an image of walking. After this, *voluntas* arises, says Lucretius.

DRN 4 881ff is a description of what goes on at the atomic level in the production of voluntary action: Lucretius talks about atomic *simulacra* striking the *animus*, the *animus* stirring the spirit (which in Epicurean philosophy of mind plays a role similar to the peripheral nervous system), *etc.*, down to details like air atoms being distributed through expanded pores into the smallest parts of the body, which allows small particles like those of the spirit to drive the whole body forward. Because of this, if atomic swerves did play some sort of direct role in Epicurean action theory, it ought to be mentioned here, and it is not.[19] This passage, then, gives *prima facie* evidence that the swerve does not play any direct role in Epicurean action-theory: the *voluntas* that initiates each voluntary action is not identical to a swerve, as the traditional interpretation maintains, and the swerve is not somehow utilized by the *voluntas* in each action, as Sedley and Englert believe.

It is only *prima facie* evidence, of course, since it is an argument from silence, though not a fallacious one. Nothing Lucretius says positively *precludes* the swerve from having a key role in the production of action.[20] Lucretius does not say "there is no swerving motion of the atoms at this point," nor does he say "*voluntas* is caused by the impacts of images and the state of the *animus*." He just says, in effect, "Let me explain how we are able to move ourselves as we wish to. First images strike the *animus*. Then *voluntas* arises, and it strikes the spirit, which in turn pushes the rest of the body forward." This leaves open the possibility that the *voluntas* invariably temporally succeeds the impacts of images on the *animus*, even though it is not caused by them, but is instead the result of an indeterministic atomic swerve in the *animus*, which Lucretius for some reason fails to mention in his description of what is occurring. However, unless other sections of *DRN* were to give us strong evidence that swerves are involved in this sort of way, I find this reading of the passage highly unlikely. *DRN* 4 877–96, then, seems to be giving a 'mechanistic' theory of action; *i.e.*,

19 *Pace* Purinton (1999) 279, who asserts that Lucretius does not bother mentioning the swerve that this point because he "trusts the reader who is interested in what is going on at the atomic level when the volition occurs to recall from *DRN* 2 251–293 that volitions are caused from the bottom up by swerves."

20 As Bailey (1947) 1287 points out.

one in which action follows automatically from the incoming stimulus and the state of the soul.[21]

Voluntas and desire

In addition to giving us evidence that swerves have no direct role in Epicurean action-theory, this passage also helps shed more light on the relationship between volition and desire. At the start of the passage, Lucretius reiterates that *voluntas* is what allows us to do what we want to do, such as walking. There are, I think, two opposing mistakes one can make when trying to work out the relationship between *voluntas* and desire.

One is simply to assimilate *voluntas* to desire. Fowler does this when he tries to explain why the swerve is not mentioned in *DRN* 4 881ff and says that "Lucretius is concerned in this passage with how we move when we wish to, not with how we come to wish to move; hence there is no explanation of how *voluntas* occurs."[22] Likewise, Purinton, in trying to

21 A few side notes: (1) I am concentrating on *DRN* 4 877ff, since this is the clearest discussion of action in Lucretius, and it is has received the most attention. However, a parallel argument could be given about *DRN* 4 777–817, where Lucretius explains how we are able to think of what we wish to think of; for example, how we can visualize a banquet when we wish to. This is also an example of engaging in a voluntary action, in which the mind moves itself, and here too, the swerve is not mentioned. (2) Images of walking cause the resulting *voluntas* only in a suitably disposed *animus, e.g.,* one that comes into the situation with a desire to walk. But this does not inject any sort of indeterminism into the process of the formation of *voluntas,* since where Lucretius does discuss how desire arises (*e.g., DRN* 4 858ff), it is the result of atomic interaction with no indeterministic element. (3) See Furley (1967) 210–226 for further argument, which I think is successful, that the action-theory in *DRN* 4 is 'mechanistic.' Furley notes extensive parallels between Aristotle's discussion in *MA* and Lucretius' in *DRN* 4; *e.g.,* the various stages of action given in both passages closely map onto one another, and the same example – walking – is used to illustrate an action in both passages. Furley then goes on to argue that there is not a single trace of any doctrine of 'free motion of the mind,' 'free will,' or the like, in either place. In fact, what is striking about both action-theories is that they seem equally 'mechanistic.' Given the incoming stimulus and the state of the soul, action follows automatically. The reason that Furley points out the parallel with Aristotle is that the lack of any 'free motion of the mind' or 'free will' is more clear in Aristotle's action-theory than in the *DRN* 4 passage. This is not because of any explicitly anti-mechanistic or indeterministic element in what Lucretius says, but because of how abbreviated the *DRN* 4 discussion is, which makes it more plausible to try to read in some implicit element of 'free choice' than it would be in Aristotle's case.

22 Fowler (2002) 329. Fowler has much more to say about the relationship between the swerve and the account of action given in *DRN* 4, in support of his distinctive twist on the traditional interpretation. Fowler's view is that volitions work "through a focusing of the mind," as Lucretius describes in *DRN* 4 802–17 (Fowler (2002) 441). When one decides to walk, for instance, making this decision involves the mind focusing on *simulacra* of walking, which produces an *imago* of walking, which in turn causes'one to walk. Fowler opens up many interesting issues regarding Epicurean action-theory, but I don't find his account convincing. I will not present those criticisms here, however; see O'Keefe (2003*a*) 464–6 for my doubts about Fowler's reading of the passage.

explain away the apparently 'mechanistic' formation of *voluntas* in *DRN* 4 883, says that the term *voluntas* as used by Lucretius is ambiguous. Sometimes, he says, it refers to desire (*e.g.*, wishing to walk), and it is this sort of 'desire' *voluntas*, which can be passively formed by the reception of images, which Lucretius is talking about here.[23]

However, Lucretius never uses the term *voluntas* to refer to a desire that is not acted upon; terms like *cupido* are instead used.[24] Epicureans recognize the difference between desiring something and trying to get something; *voluntas* is used for the latter. Not all desires are automatically translated into action. We need to believe that the occasion is right for acting to fulfill the desire; a hankering for Thai food may not result in any action if one is in rural Minnesota and no Thai food is in the vicinity. More broadly, using our reason, we can decide not to act on certain desires because we see that acting on them would be foolish for the purposes of attaining our ultimate desire for a pleasant life, *e.g.*, if one believes that desiring Thai food leads to dependency and anxiety.

However, it is equally mistaken to emphasize too sharp a break between desire and volition in Epicurean action-theory. Purinton does this, I think, with his distinction between two senses of *voluntas*: he claims that, in addition to the merely passive 'desire' *voluntas* (*e.g.*, wishing to walk), Lucretius sometimes uses the term *voluntas* to refer to volition (*e.g.*, the decision to act on this desire by walking), where the mind 'moves itself' and then stirs the spirit distributed throughout the rest of the body. (It is only this latter, 'active' *voluntas*, of course, that is identical to a swerve, a self-initiated atomic motion.) So I think it would be misleading to refer to *voluntas* as an 'act of will' or the like.

That is because I agree with Julia Annas that Epicurus' action-theory does not emphasize "deliberation or selection at the moment of action." Instead, Epicurus explains why a person acted in the way he did by referring to how the world appeared to the agent when he acted and to the agent's "overall state at that time, a state resulting from past choices and present endorsements of past developments."[25] So to posit, as

23 Purinton (1999) 279.

24 The only possible exception to this, *DRN* 3 174, does not disprove the general thesis. Lucretius is describing the interaction of mind and body in order to prove that the mind is something bodily. He describes the effects of a severe (but non-lethal) blow of a weapon, laying bare bones and sinews, on the mind. He says it often produces faintness, a turmoil of the mind, and a "hesitating (*incerta*) impulse to rise." The context does not make it clear whether this particular *voluntas* results in action, but this is obviously an exceptional case.

25 Annas (1992) 180–1.

Purinton does, a sharp distinction for Epicurus between the antecedent desire to do something and a subsequent moment of choice, whether or not to act upon that desire, is misguided. That is not to say, of course, that one is forced to act to try to get what one desires, or that there is not such a thing as deliberation or choice. But I think that most voluntary actions do not involve "moments of choice" but are simply elicited, without much conscious deliberation or choice, by one's beliefs and desires, and any action-theory that focuses on a discrete choice as a step in the production of each action thereby seriously distorts the phenomena of action. I do not believe that Epicurus' theory makes this mistake.

As Annas notes, when Lucretius uses the word *voluntas*, he seems to be translating some Greek term such as *hormê*, " impulse." Such an impulse is not the same as a desire – it would be odd to say that one decides not to act on one's *hormê* – but the two are closely connected: impulses always are impulses *toward* something, or strivings prompted by the desires of the animal. So it is not quite right to say that for Lucretius *voluntas* has two senses, which Lucretius (unfortunately) does not always mark clearly – sometimes referring to desires, sometimes to volitions. Instead, I submit, Lucretius uses *voluntas* univocally, to refer to a "volitional desire"[26] – an intentional impulse to attain the object of some desire. So, in *DRN* 883ff, Lucretius says that the impulse to walk arises when images strike a suitably disposed *animus*, and once this impulse arises, it causes the *animus* to bestir itself and move the spirit, which in turn causes the limbs to move.

2.3 *Assessment of the traditional interpretation*

I think that we are now in a good position to assess the traditional interpretation. Recall that, on the traditional interpretation, *voluntas* is the cause of our actions, but *voluntas* is not itself causally determined by the past states of the mind. It is a self-initiated motion in the mind constituted by a swerve.[27] Volitions are not separate events caused by swerves; instead, *voluntas* simply *is* the swerve of the atom. As Bailey puts

26 Of course, it does not follow that this is how it ought to be translated, since this would be intolerably awkward. In context, depending on whether the stress on that *voluntas* is a volitional *desire*, or a *volitional* desire, it would be sensible to translate it either as 'wish' or 'desire,' on the one hand, or 'impulse,' 'volition,' or 'will,' on the other. It does not follow from this that the term is ambiguous between two distinct senses in Lucretius.

27 This is the way it is stated in Fowler (2002) 330.

it: "the act of volition is neither more nor less than the 'swerve' of the fine atoms which compose the mind."[28]

Two of the standard objections against this interpretation, I think, are not decisive. The first is that, if we can simply identify swerves and volitions, then it would seem that every swerve is a volition. This, in turn, would seem to imply that "stones and trees ought to be enabled to act freely," since swerves – and hence, volitions – occur in them also.[29] However, this follows only if there is a type–type identity between volitions and swerves *tout court*. The traditional interpretation is better thought of as asserting merely a token–token identity between each swerve and the volition that constitutes it. This raises the further question, of course, of why only swerves occurring in minds are volitions. The most plausible answer to this would be that being indeterministic is necessary but not sufficient for an atomic motion to be a *libera voluntas*. That is because being such as to initiate action is part of our concept of what it is to be a volition. Since only swerves in minds are apt to act as self-initiated starts of *animal action*, only such swerves could be volitions.[30] Being undetermined lets these swerves be self-initiated motions, while occurring in minds lets them be causes of action. Although quite speculative, this sort of answer could be expanded upon as follows: Lucretius says that normally swerves have no discernable macroscopic effect but that this is consistent with there being such swerves. (*DRN* 2 246–250) One thing that Lucretius emphasizes about the *animus* (the mind), however, is how small changes in the fine particles that make it up can bootstrap up to large effects at the bodily level (*DRN* 3 177–207, 4 898–906). Therefore, Lucretius and Epicurus already have available to them the resources to explain why atomic indeterminacies would make a noticeable difference when they occur within an *animus* but not when they occur in a stone, similar to how quantum indeterminacies make no noticeable difference in a pencil, but can in the clicking of a Geiger counter.[31]

28 Bailey (1928) 320.

29 Annas (1992) 185.

30 This idea is inspired by a remark in Fowler (2002) 440–1. See O'Keefe (2003*a*) 463–4 for a fuller statement of the view and how it relates to Epicurean reductionism.

31 William James makes a similar argument about the nervous systems of more 'highly' developed creatures. He says that they are 'unstable,' and hence small changes at the neuronal level caused by these creatures' consciousness can bootstrap up to large behavioral changes. James thinks this allows these creatures to respond more flexibly to their environments than in creatures whose responses are more 'hard-wired.' (James (1890) chapter 5, "The Automaton Theory," pp. 138–43 in particular.)

The second objection is that there is no precedent in Greek philosophy prior to Epicurus for the notion of libertarian 'free choice' between open options, and so it is unlikely that he was advocating such a libertarian position, particularly since Epicurus is not the most original of philosophers. Furley complains that this view of human freedom would be unmotivated "by anything in the history of philosophy before Epicurus."[32] Some people have hailed this 'insight' of Epicurus', but Furley thinks that this novelty counts against the historical accuracy of the interpretation. This objection is more telling than the first. However, two replies are open to the defenders of the traditional interpretation. The first that it is not so implausible to suppose that Epicurus was the first to clearly draw out and try to overcome the unacceptable determinist implications of Democritus' atomism. After all, philosophers do sometimes come up with novel insights. The second is that there *is* precedent for Epicurus' doctrine of *voluntas* as a self-initiated motion in the mind: Asmis claims that this precedent is Aristotle's theory of voluntary motion, specifically his theory of *orexis* (desiring or striving). (See section 3.3 for a consideration of Asmis' claim.)

Even if these subsidiary difficulties can be overcome, however, there still remains what has long been recognized as the main objection to the traditional interpretation: having volitions constituted by random atomic motions is a particularly unpromising way of securing free and responsible action. Furley puts the problem in memorable terms:

> The stage is all set for someone to produce a rational, normal, decent action: he sees a friend in distress, his character predisposes him to help – then the swerve takes place, and instead he catches a No. 27 bus to Kew. And that – catching the bus – is a typically free action.[33]

Bailey admits that this is a problem and says that, if freedom is simply the result of the random swerving of atoms, then "the mind is really not self-determined, but is at the mercy of wholly undetermined movements inside itself, and free will after all its careful preservation turns out to be nothing better than chance"[34]

If a volition, or act of willing – or whatever one takes a *voluntas* to be – is simply *identified* with a random atomic swerve, then the swerve cannot undercut one's act of will, for obvious reasons. However, it does sever the connection between volitions and the preceding desires that prompt

32 Furley (1967) 164. 33 Ibid. 163. 34 Bailey (1928) 435.

volition. This can be seen particularly clearly in the case of Fowler's explanation of what happens in a typical free action. The horses at the starting gate that Lucretius describes are eager to run. But they do not start to run until the *animus* assents to this desire. The assent that initiates action is identical to a swerve, and so there is a delay in time between the desire and the initiation of action, while the horse waits for a swerve to occur. Fowler says that *usually* an animal will be able to do what it wants to pretty soon, since swerves probably occur fairly frequently. But, he admits, the delay time is unpredictable, and occasionally no atoms at all will swerve in the relevant period.[35]

There are obvious technical difficulties here. If the swerve is truly uncaused, then what exactly is the relationship between the preceding desire to run and the running that is caused by the swerve? Can the desire cause the swerve to occur? It seems not. Does the desire create conditions in the *animus* so that the possibility of a swerve is more apt to produce the sort of action desired, as opposed to actions that one does not desire to do? It is hard to see what sort of acceptable and coherent account can be given.[36]

The examination of *De rerum natura* above helps strengthen this objection to the traditional interpretation in two ways.

First, it shows that the traditional interpretation of the role of the swerve is even more inadequate philosophically within Epicureanism than is usually supposed. As discussed above, even if Epicurus were concerned to defend a libertarian notion of 'two-sided' freedom of choice as a necessary condition of moral responsibility, his supposed solution to this concern *via* the swerve is deeply problematic. I hope I have shown, however, that the *voluntas* the swerve is supposed to underwrite is not like this at all. Lucretius claims that it is evident that free volition exists because the body follows the mind's desire, and that *voluntas* is what allows each of us to go wherever we are led by our pleasure. But the swerve, on the traditional interpretation, makes us 'free' only by placing a potential roadblock between our desiring something and our doing it. The swerve, it seems, couldn't help us in our pursuit of *ataraxia*; the best we could hope for is that it does not get in the way too often. This sort of

35 Fowler (2002) 331–2.

36 *Mutatis mutandis*, this criticism also applies to Englert's interpretation, according to which the swerve is not identical of *voluntas*, but is a 'tool' used by it to initiate motion in an indeterministic way (see section 3.3).

freedom would be worse than worthless within Epicurean ethics, and it does not fit with Lucretius' description of the sort of freedom that the swerve is expressly said to preserve.[37]

Second, it helps block one common reply to the observation that Epicurus' theory is deeply flawed on this account: that this is a problem for Epicurus' theory, not the interpretation of Epicurus' theory. If I am right, the main text commonly used to support the traditional interpretation (*DRN* 2 251–293) does *not* strongly support it, and it is powerfully undercut by another passage in the same work (*DRN* 4 877–896). So considerations of charity should come in here, and we should reject the traditional interpretation, since it attributes to Epicurus a position that is manifestly inadequate on Epicurus' own terms.

2.4 *Lucretius on the swerve and* voluntas*: summary*

Here is what I think we should believe about what Lucretius says regarding the swerve and *voluntas*:

- The argument in *DRN* 2 251ff is a *modus tollens*: If there were no swerve in the motions of the atoms, we would not have *libera voluntas*, but we do have *libera voluntas*; therefore, there is a swerve in the motion of the atoms.
- The latter parts of the passage are meant to illustrate that *voluntas* does indeed exist. The main contrast drawn in Lucretius' examples is between self-initiated motion (the agent himself, or perhaps the mind itself, is the source of motion) and motion caused by shoves and blows from without, in which the agent is not the cause of his own motion.
- In the earlier description of our *voluntas*, Lucretius says that this *voluntas* is what allows us to go "where pleasure leads us." *Voluntas* is not a separate act of assent to the prompting of desires, or refusal to assent to it, but a sort of volitional desire, or intentional impulse. Lucretius' main concern seems to be to preserve the ability of the agent to use his mind to move himself as he wishes, so that he is able to get the pleasure that he desires. This is the sort of freedom that would matter within Epicurean ethics in any case (see section 1.3). So Lucretius is asserting that causal determinism would result in

37 Again, *mutatis mutandis*, this criticism applies to Englert's interpretation as well.

fatalism.[38] There is nothing in Lucretius to support the notion (and much to undercut it in his description of Epicurean action-theory) that he wishes to preserve a two-sided freedom of choice.

- However, Bobzien is right that a secondary concern for Lucretius seems to be avoiding "internal necessity" – that is, ensuring that we have some sort of control over the development of our own character.
- Nothing in the passage clearly spells out exactly why causal determinism is threatening to our freedom in these ways, or how the swerve is supposed to rescue us from this threat. Lucretius does seem to think that somehow the swerve saves us from fate by breaking the sequences of cause and effect that otherwise would stretch back infinitely into the past and bind us.

38 By 'fatalism,' I mean the sort of helplessness discussed above, which is implied by the traditional Greek notion of 'fate'. The Stoics, of course, deny that the fact that every thing is 'fated' implies anything of the sort. I discuss the notion of fate operative for the Epicureans in much more detail in chapter 6.

CHAPTER 3

Aristotle and Epicurus on the origins of character and action

A natural strategy to pursue when trying to understand Epicurus' position is to find a precedent in the works of previous philosophers in the light of which we can better understand how Epicurus thinks the swerve preserves our freedom. After all, it is more likely that the swerve was introduced by Epicurus as a reaction to a problem already placed on the philosophical agenda by his predecessors, instead of it being a radically new innovation without precedent. The predecessor most commonly enlisted to play this role since David Furley's influential study is Aristotle.

I am quite sympathetic to this way of approaching Epicurus' thought. In fact, I will be arguing (in chapter 6) that a key to understanding Epicurus' use of the swerve is to look back to Aristotle's arguments in *de Int.* 9, in which he contends that the unrestricted application of the Principle of Bivalence to all statements (including ones concerning contingent matters in the future) would have unacceptable fatalist consequences. In this chapter, however, I will be examining a different set of Aristotelian texts, particularly those dealing with voluntary action in *Nicomachean Ethics* book 3. In *NE* 3, Aristotle says that, in order for an agent to be responsible for what he does, the 'origin,' or *archê*, of his action and character must be within him. In *NE* 3 and elsewhere, Aristotle also talks about the way in which the agent himself must be the *aitia* – the cause or explanation – of what he does, in order for his action to be voluntary.

My conclusions in this chapter will be in part positive and in part negative. I will argue that Epicurus would be sympathetic to Aristotle's contention that an agent needs to be the origin of both her own character and her actions. However, nothing that Aristotle says in these texts helps us understand the role of the swerve. That is because nothing in Aristotle's discussions of agency need be interpreted in an antideterminist way. Scholars who have tried to understand Epicurus in light of Aristotle have thought that Aristotle introduced indeterminacies in order to help ensure that animals can be an 'origin' of action; I will argue that these interpreters misunderstand what is required, on Aristotle's view, for an animal to be an *archê* of action.

In the first section of this chapter, I will briefly examine the Greek terms *aitia* (cause or explanation) and *archê* (origin) and consider how Aristotle uses them. In the second section, I will turn to Aristotle's thesis in *NE* 3 5 that in order for the actions that proceed from one's character not to be necessitated, one's character must have its *archê* within the agent himself. I will argue, against the 'internal cause' interpretation, that one's character can have an 'internal origin' for Aristotle without any breaks in the causal nexus. In the third section, I turn from the origin of character to the origin of action. Some interpreters have taken Aristotle's claim that animals are 'self-movers' to mean that an animal's desire must be able to initiate action in a non-deterministic way so that it is not a mere 'domino' in a causal chain. Again, I will argue that nothing Aristotle says in this connection has anti-determinist implications. Instead, Aristotle's primary interest is to show that both an agent's character and actions are the result of that agent's choices, and that both are under the agent's rational control. This is similar to what I have argued above (sections 1.3 and chapter 2) and will argue subsequently (chapter 4) is Epicurus' primary concern regarding our freedom.

3.1 Aitia *and* archê

Aristotle's assertions that voluntary actions have their origin (*archê*) in us and cannot be referred back to other origins beyond those in ourselves (*NE* 3 1113b20–21), and that coincidences have no cause *(aitia, Meta.* 6 2–3), may already seem to have obvious anti-determinist implications. But whether they do or not depends on what Aristotle means by terms like *aitia* and *archê.* So before assessing Aristotle's claims about voluntary action and character in particular, let me first consider the import of these terms.[1]

Aitia in Aristotle is standardly translated 'cause,' but it has been argued that Aristotle's 'four causes' should really be called his 'four *becauses*,' since the term does not correspond very closely to the English 'cause.'[2] Whether

1 NB: most of the points I make in this section (particularly regarding the term *aitia*) are not at all original to me; I have drawn many of them from Vlastos (1969/1973), especially section 1, and Frede (1980). See the preceding plus Hankinson (1998) IV.2 for more on these issues and pointers to further discussion.

2 Vlastos (1969/1973) 79; Hocutt (1974).

or not this would be a felicitous translation, there is certainly something to the idea that motivates the proposal: each of Aristotle's four *aitiai* are ways of explaining why things are the way they are. As Vlastos puts it, "to say that X is the *aitia* of Y comes precisely to the same thing as saying that Y happened, or happens, or is the case, *because* of X."[3] Some of the things Aristotle calls *aitiai* seem like recognizable causes, *e.g.*, that the Persians invaded Attica because the Athenians had raided Sardis. But many of the things Aristotle is willing to cite as explanatory factors, and call *aitiai*, we would be reluctant to call causes: for instance, that a statue is heavy because it is made of bronze, that a man is taking a walk because of his health, and that a figure is a square because it has four equal sides and four equal angles. (These are, respectively, examples of Aristotle's 'moving' (or 'efficient'), 'material,' 'final,' and 'formal' *aitiai.*)[4] As Frede notes, the notion of explanation is given priority in Aristotle's conception of *aitia*; he will call *aitiai* "those items which have to be referred to in the account" of why things are as they are.[5]

This priority can be brought out by pointing to two differences between Aristotelian *aitiai* and what would typically nowadays be taken as causes. The first is that causation is now usually taken to be a relationship between events, whereas Aristotle will includes things like ends, forms, and the art of sculpture as *aitiai.* But the more fundamental difference is that, as Frede puts it, "though we may want to get away from such a notion, there is a strong tendency to conceive of causes as somehow active."[6] That is, causes are items which do something so as to bring about their effects. It is for this reason that the Stoic notion of cause, even though in some ways distant from most modern conceptions, still seems to be definitely a theory of *causation*: for the Stoics, causation is relationship between a body (such as a penknife) and a predicate (such as 'being cut') which it makes to be true of another body (such as the flesh above my knuckle).[7] In fact, the Stoics helped effect an important shift in the meaning of *aitia*: whereas the notion of explanation was previously central, *aitiai* came to be conceived of as active.[8] The former conception, which was Aristotle's, may be called an 'explanatory *aitia*,' the latter a 'causal *aitia*.'

3 Vlastos (1969/1973) 79.

4 The illustrative examples are akin to Aristotle's own, but not always exactly the same, and are drawn from Vlastos (1969/1973).

5 Frede (1980) 223–224.

6 Frede (1980) 218.

7 See Stobaeus *Anthology* I. 13. IC (L&S 55A), Sextus Empiricus *M.* 9.211 (L&S 55B). Hankinson (1998) VII.I is a good starting-place for more information.

8 See Frede (1980) for the story of how this occurred.

The two types of *aitia* are distinct, although there is obviously a great deal of overlap: one way to explain why something is the way it is is to cite its cause, for example, "he's bleeding because he slit his knuckle with a penknife while cutting a piece of summer sausage with it." Generally speaking, the category of explanatory *aitia* is much wider than that of causal *aitia*, but depending on how stringent one's standards are for a proper explanation, it is possible for something to have a causal *aitia* but lack an explanatory one, as we shall see.

A similar distinction can be made regarding the senses of the term *archê*, which is variously translated as 'origin,' 'beginning,' or 'first principle.' Here the distinction is between an 'explanatory *archê*' and a 'temporal *archê*.' Do the motions within the universe have an *archê*? Obviously, one's answer will depend on whether one is asking if there is some principle in terms of which one can adequately explain why the motions of the universe occur as they do or if the motions of the universe have a temporal starting-point.

In *Ep. Hdt.* 44, Epicurus claims that atomic motions, such as rebounds, have no *archê*. Here, Epicurus is using the term to mean temporal starting-point, since the claim comes in the middle of a discussion of how to explain why various types of atomic motion occur as they do. So for Epicurus, atomic motion has an explanatory *archê* but no temporal *archê*. (See sections 5.2 and 5.4–5.5 for further discussion.) On the other hand, Aristotle accuses Democritus of failing to give an adequate *archê* for motion and of falsely supposing that pointing to the fact that something has always occurred in some way is to give an adequate *archê* for it. Here, of course, Aristotle is not saying that Democritus should give a temporal starting-point to what always occurs; he is saying that Democritus has not given an adequate explanatory principle to account for why motion always occurs as it does. (See section 5.3 for further discussion.) And if one interprets the creation-myth of Plato's *Timaeus* literally, it holds that the motions of the *cosmos* have both a temporal *archê* (there used to be a disordered mass of material moving chaotically until the divine craftsman created the *cosmos* by imposing orderly motions upon the material) and an explanatory *archê* (the divine craftsman, being wholly good and free of jealousy, wished to make the perceptible world as orderly and good as it could be). (*Tim.* 28a – 30c)

Metaphysics Epsilon chapters 2–3 illustrate how Aristotle often uses *aitia* and *archê* to refer to explanatory factors. Sorabji has claimed that this part of the *Metaphysics* is extremely important for the controversy between libertarians and determinists, because in it Aristotle meets determinism head on and denies the causal determinist one of his favorite premises, that whatever happens has a cause.[9] That is because here Aristotle denies that the *sumbebêkos* (the coincidental)[10] has an *aitia*, and this is conjoined with the observation that the *sumbebêkos* must exist, for otherwise everything would be necessary, which it is not (*Meta.* 6 3 1027a29–b16). And in 1027b12–14, Aristotle discusses how a series of events may go back to some coincidental starting-point (*archê*), which itself does not have a cause (*aitia*). This might seem to suggest that certain events simply occur, or are "fresh starts" in the world, without themselves having antecedent causes.

When we look at the passage closely, however, Aristotle's claim turns out to be much less startling than that. Aristotle is saying that coincidences have no proper *explanation*, not that they have no *cause*. He talks about two different kinds of coincidences in *Meta.* 6. The first is a chance conjunction of items or events, *e.g.*, that a man who just ate spicy food happens to get killed at the well by muggers (*Meta.* 6 3), or that a baker's concoction happens to heal a disease (*Meta.* 6 2 1027a3–6). The second is the exception to a general rule, *e.g.*, that a freak snowstorm occurs in June (*Meta.* 6 2 1026b33–35).

In *Metaphysics* Epsilon, Aristotle is concerned with what sorts of things can be the subjects of a science (*epistêmê*), and he says that coincidences cannot be the subjects of a science, because they cannot be properly explained by appealing to the principles of various sciences. (*Meta.* 6 2 1026b3–10). For instance, that a house was built can be explained by appealing to a person's knowledge of architecture (*Meta.* 6 2 1026b6–7), and that it is hot in June can be explained by appealing to the climate in the area (*Meta.* 6 2 1026b34–35).

So, consider a person who eats spicy food, becomes thirsty, and goes to a well to drink. Some ruffians happen to be loitering there, and they smash him repeatedly on the head with a brick and kill him. Aristotle denies that this sort of event has an *aitia.* Obviously, he cannot mean that the man's death has no *cause,* as the term is usually used. (The man's skull was bashed in by a brick.) Nor does he mean that it can be given no explanation *whatsoever.* We can say, for instance, that the man went to the well because he was thirsty, that the ruffians were there to behold the

9 Sorabji (1980) 3–4.

10 *Sumbebêkos* is sometimes translated "accidental," but as Aristotle uses the term here, I favor the translation "coincidental," for reasons that will become clear once the content of Aristotle's doctrine has been laid out.

beautiful sunset, and that when the man showed up, they killed him because of their greed and callousness. However, it is just a coincidence that they all happened to show up at the well at the same time. There can be an explanation of event A, and of event B, but maybe not an explanation of the conjunction of events A and B.

The other examples that Aristotle uses reinforce this point. For instance, Aristotle says that the architect is not the *aitia* of all of the properties of the house that he builds, such as that it happens to be 2,272 miles away from the grave of Mao Zedong (*Meta.* 6 2 1026b7–11).[11] Obviously, there is no mysterious "fresh start" that makes it the case that the house has this characteristic. Aristotle is simply describing what sorts of things can be given a systematic explanation. We cannot give a good answer to the question, "why is this house exactly 2,272 miles away from the grave of Mao Zedong?" because it is just a coincidence.[12]

So, Aristotle claims that coincidences do not have an *aitia,* and, at 1027b12–14, even says that a series of events goes back to some starting-point (*archê*), which itself does not have an *aitia.* Aristotle certainly is not claiming that coincidences like the man being killed at the well are *uncaused.* All he means to say is that subsequent events, such as the grief of his family, can be explained by appealing to the coincidence – hence, the coincidence is an *archê* for those events – while the coincidence itself cannot be given a proper explanation – hence, it does not have an *aitia.*[13]

11 Aristotle actually says that the builder is not the cause of the building being pleasing to some and harmful to others, but these examples are quite unfortunate, since it is part of the *technê* (the craft) of architecture to make a building pleasing to onlookers (although some examples of modern architecture may belie this claim).

12 In the case of exceptions to general or 'for-the-most-part' rules, it is not quite as obvious that there are no 'fresh starts;' nonetheless, there is no reason to burden Aristotle with them in this case either. In June, we would not expect a snowstorm. But sometimes snowstorms do arrive in June. Aristotle presumably does not think that this freak weather has *no cause whatsoever,* and that the storm is a 'fresh start' in nature. He is simply saying that you cannot explain the snowstorm by saying, "Well, it's June in Central Texas" in the same way that one could say, in order to explain a different snowstorm, "Well, it's February in Western Minnesota." The June snowstorm is weird, but it does not require one to postulate 'fresh starts,' but simply to acknowledge that any explanations based on probabilistic principles will have exceptions.

13 So, *contra* Sorabji, the *Meta.* 6 thesis gives no aid or comfort to the libertarian. Sorabji himself distinguishes between 'cause' as explanation and 'cause' as necessitation, and correctly states that Aristotle's discussion focuses on explanation, not necessitation. What is needed for the libertarian case is not to show that coincidences are (in some way) inexplicable, but that human behavior can be explained in terms of personal agency (or something of that sort), without a person's behavior being necessitated. This section of *Meta.* 6 can be fruitfully compared to *Physics* 2 5 and its doctrine of luck and chance. Some causes are not explanatory, and coincidental events are not uncaused. For a more in-depth explanation of many of the points touched upon in this section, see Hankinson (1998) chapters 4 and 5, especially section IV.2 on coincidences and V.1 on the logical structure of Aristotelian explanations.

3.2 The origin of character

Nicomachean Ethics book 3, among other topics, is concerned with which actions are voluntary and which are not. The voluntary, Aristotle tells us, must be "what has the origin (*archê*) in the agent himself when he knows the particulars that the action consists in" (*NE* 3 1111a23). And so actions are involuntary for one of two reasons. Either they are due to force, such as a man being blown off a bridge by a strong wind, in which case the origin of the action is not in the agent himself, or they are due to ignorance, *e.g.*, a person who gives his wife a cup of coffee, not knowing that somebody else has poured rat poison into it, normally would not be held responsible for her death. But not all ignorance excuses, and even some forced actions are not entirely involuntary: Aristotle spends much of *Nicomachean Ethics* 3 refining his account and analyzing varieties of force and ignorance. The presumption, however, is that an agent is responsible for actions that proceed *from that agent*: from his character, desires, deliberations, and choices.

But in order for a person to be responsible for the actions that proceed from his character, it seems that he must also be responsible for his character. In *NE* 3 5, while looking further into what sorts of ignorance excuse an agent, Aristotle considers two exculpatory arguments based on *psychological* determinism. In the first, Aristotle starts by claiming that ignorance due to carelessness, such as not knowing the speed limit when it is clearly posted, does not excuse, because we assume that the person has the ability not to be ignorant and to take care. He then considers the objection that some people just are careless; they are simply the sort of people who are not going to take care. Aristotle admits this but thinks it does not excuse their wrongdoing:

> Still they are by their slack lives responsible for becoming men of that kind, and men are themselves responsible for being unjust or self-indulgent, in that they cheat or spend their time in drinking bouts and the like; for it is in activities exercised on particular objects that make the corresponding character.
>
> (*NE* 3 5 1114a4–7)

Aristotle later considers a more developed version of the same basic argument: what we do is based upon what appears good to us, while what appears good to us is not under our control, but is determined by our character. Thus, what we do is not under our control, and we cannot be held responsible for it. In reply, Aristotle grants that what we do is based upon what appears good to us, and that we must be responsible for who we are in order to be responsible for our actions, but he again denies that our character is beyond our control; we are responsible for who we are.

A repeated motif of *NE* 3 is that what is voluntary must have its origin (*archê*) in the agent, and it would seem that this applies both to actions and characters: "[if] we cannot refer [actions] back to other origins beyond those in ourselves, then it follows that whatever has its origin in us is itself up to us and voluntary." (*NE* 3 1113b20–21)

One way of understanding Aristotle's talk of the "*archê* being in us," which I do not accept, is what I will call the 'temporal *archê*' interpretation. On this reading, the agent must be the causal origin, at some point, of his actions, without this origin in turn being ultimately traceable to previous causes outside of the agent, *e.g.*, environmental and hereditary factors. For an action to have an internal *archê* in this sense would require Aristotle to think that there are 'fresh starts' in the world, breaks in the causal nexus so as to guarantee an internal *archê* of action. This is how Aristotle is understood by proponents of the 'internal cause' interpretation, who add that Epicurus accepts this doctrine of Aristotle's and that the swerve provides such a break in the causal nexus so as to guarantee an internal *archê* of action.

But both Furley and Bobzien, who advance this interpretation, think that it is anachronistic to attribute anything like the modern 'problem of free will and determinism' to either Aristotle or to Epicurus, and that neither Aristotle's action-theory nor Epicurus' contain any trace of a libertarian 'two-sided' power. Both have 'mechanical' action-theories; that is, ones in which the interaction of environmental stimulus with the state of the agent at the time automatically elicits the resultant action.[14] Thus, for Epicurus the swerve plays no direct role in the production of action. Only one swerve is required somewhere within the agent so that his character – and hence, his actions – cannot be entirely traced to antecedent causes outside of him.

The implausibility of this way of interpreting Aristotle and Epicurus can be seen by noticing how odd and philosophically unsatisfactory the resulting position is. If the internal cause interpretation is right, then according to both Aristotle and Epicurus, there are no causal breaks between the reception of stimuli by me, my reaction to those stimuli, and the

14 See Furley (1967) 210–226, discussed above chap. 2 n. 21; Bobzien (1998*b*) on Aristotle's action-theory, Bobzien (2000) 287–293 on Epicurus' action-theory.

resultant action that proceeds from my self.[15] However, there must be at least one internal break in the series of causes that *formed* my character, so that these causes cannot be traced outside of me. If this condition is satisfied, then the *archê* of my character, and thus my actions, is inside me.

But if there are no causal breaks from reception of stimuli to processing of stimuli to behavior, what conceivable ethical difference would it make whether my character is formed entirely by antecedent causes or whether there are some causal gaps in the process whereby my character was formed? Ethically – or in any other way – it seems all the same to me whether my character is formed by fully deterministic processes or by processes with some random causal gaps in them. In neither case is my character any more, or less, 'up to me' than in the other. In the form in which Furley and Bobzien present it, at least, the demand that the agent must be the *archê* of his action is arbitrary and inexplicable. The internal cause interpretation replicates in the *formation of character* the sort of philosophical problem that the traditional interpretation has in the *production of action.* Inserting random atomic motions in either the formation of character or the production of actions seems a promising way of inserting some arbitrary unpredictability into the process, but a horrible basis for the formation of something for which the agent can be held responsible.[16]

15 One caveat ought to be added. If the swerve is truly random, then Epicurus may think that there are occasionally causal breaks in some processes that lead to action, just as there may be occasional causal breaks in any process whatsoever. These breaks, however, are ethically irrelevant, and the process is in itself basically mechanistic.

16 Although I earlier drew a parallel between the internal cause interpretation and the position of some modern incompatibilists, such as Robert Kane, who wish to save one's character from causal necessity and make the springs of action the agent's own, I should here note a crucial difference between them. Kane draws an analogy between an indeterminate effort of will and a quantum event (Kane (1996) 128). Such indeterminate efforts of will paradigmatically occur when there are countervailing pressures for acting between various incompatible options (*e.g.*, a struggle between moral and prudential reasons for acting, with moral reasons indicating one should help a person in distress and prudential reasons urging one to run). Nonetheless, even Kane makes it clear that such efforts of will crucially involve an effort *by the agent*; they are not simply the production of states of character by quantum events unconnected with the agent, unlike the way in which Furley talks about swerves helping to bring about states of character. For Kane, the sequence that produces the effort of will – which he also calls a 'self-forming willing' – starts with the character and motives of the agent. The agent's character and motives explain *that* there will be such a willing, *e.g.*, a willing to act either on moral or on prudential reasons, but not *how* it will turn out, which is undetermined, so that the self-forming willing is not uncaused, but which way it will go is uncaused (Kane (1996) 124–151, ch. 8). Kane's 'self-forming willings' are still open to serious Humean objections, but he does at least try to show how these would make one's present character the 'agent's own' in a way Furley's position does not. (Bobzien's own position is more ambiguous. I have been treating it, and will continue to treat it, as primarily an extension of Furley's. However, at the end of her article on Epicurus, she sketches out two ways of developing her position, the second of which brings it more in line with Kane's. See n. 55 in chapter 6 for more on this issue. Insofar as Bobzien's position is developed in this second way, it would be subject to the same sorts of objections that she herself brings against the traditional interpretation.)

And so, when Aristotle demands that the agent has to be the *archê* of his actions and even his own character, I think we should look for an alternative to the 'temporal *archê*' interpretation. A more philosophically promising interpretation is available if we think Aristotle means that the agent must be an *explanatory archê* of both his character and action; this interpretation is also better supported textually.

In *NE* 3 5, Aristotle admits that some people are incorrigibly bad, because they have firmly fixed bad characters, and hence they cannot *now* control what appears good to them (*NE* 3 1114a15–22). Furthermore, he says that if we were simply born with certain ideals and character traits, which determined what we do, then both virtue and vice would be involuntary, because then having a good or bad character would be like having good or bad eyesight (*NE* 3 1114b3–10). Aristotle denies this, however, saying that, even if some people are incorrigibly bad *now*, at one time they had the ability to change their character, and hence they are still responsible for the base actions that flow from their character (*NE* 3 1114a20–30).

Given this context, I think that Aristotle does not mean in *NE* 3 that there cannot be antecedent causes that form our character. Instead, Aristotle is arguing against the notion that our character is entirely inborn and asserting instead that a person's character is up to the person himself. Aristotle believes that our natural make-up affects our development, but does not normally set it.[17] Hence, if we want to *explain* why a person has the character that he does, we cannot appeal simply to his original natural make-up, since people with the same natural make-up can develop quite different characters. Nor can we appeal to the person's parents or environment, since these too do not fix what one's character will be like. The best way to *explain* a person's character is by appealing to the sorts of actions that the person has performed, since there is a reliable link between a person's actions and a person's character. People who act viciously become vicious; those who act virtuously become virtuous. Thus, it is "up to us" what sort of person we become, because our character depends on our actions, and our actions *are* the *archê* of who we are. None of this, however, implies "fresh starts" or breaks in the causal nexus of any kind, since Aristotle's concern with *archê* in this context is with *explanation,* not *causation.* Aristotle wishes to assert that who we are

17 For example, at *NE* 6 13, 1144b3, 7 5, 1148b18, 7 8, 1151a18, 10 9, 1179b4–31, *Politics* 7 13, 1332a40–b11, 7 15, 1334b6, cited in Sorabji (1980) 231.

now has to be explained in terms of our own reasoning and our past actions, and he wants to deny that it can be entirely explained in terms of in-born propensities beyond our control, unlike having bad eyesight. Aristotle's ethics concerns itself with which states of character are necessary in order to attain a happy life and with how one develops these states of character. And so, Aristotle has good reason within his ethics to try to preserve this type of internal explanatory *archê* for our actions and character. On the other hand, he has no reason to preserve the sort of internal *archê* that the 'temporal *archê*' interpretation attributes to him.

The 'explanatory internal *archê*' interpretation of Aristotle is also supported by the very start of Aristotle's discussion of the voluntary in *NE* 3 1, in which he glosses what it would mean for an action not to have an 'internal origin':

> Those things, then are thought involuntary, which take place under compulsion or owing to ignorance; and that is compulsory of which the *archê* is outside, being a principle in which nothing is contributed by the person who is acting or is feeling the passion, *e.g.*, if he were to be carried somewhere by a wind, or by men who had him in their power.
>
> (*NE* 3 1 1109b35–1110a4)

Not having an internal origin is a matter of the agent not contributing anything, as the examples make clear. And having an 'internal origin' involves the person's passions, decisions, beliefs, *etc.*, being the items that produce the action and allow us to explain why it occurs.[18] There is no suggestion here that, in order for them to function as 'genuine' internal origins, these states of character, desires, *etc.*, cannot themselves have antecedent causes – in fact, it strongly suggests just the opposite. (It is worth noting that the way in which voluntary actions have an 'internal origin' for Aristotle seems quite similar to the sense in which animals

18 In the case of threats or other coercion, the picture is a little more complicated, but not fundamentally different. In the case of a person who tosses a treasure overboard in order to escape a storm, or betrays a secret because of a threat to his family, the action would have an 'internal origin' in *some* sense, unlike the cases Aristotle cites above. However, in these cases, the apparently vicious action would be inexplicable (assuming that the person is not profligate or unjust) until the coercive circumstances are factored in, since the agent has no desire to toss treasure overboard or betray the secret as such. Once these circumstances are factored in, however, so that the action *does* become explicable in terms of the agent's character, desires, *etc.*, the action often no longer reflects badly on the agent, and so he would receive pardon (or at least pity) for the act that normally would deserve censure (*NE* 3 1 1110a4–1110b9).

initiate their own motion in the examples that Lucretius uses in order to establish that *voluntas* exists; see section 2.1.)

The same considerations of charity which count against attributing the 'temporal *archê*' interpretation to Aristotle also count against attributing the 'internal cause' interpretation to Epicurus, absent strong textual evidence for it. The 'internal cause' interpretation, however, is largely based upon drawing parallels between what is said in the Epicurean texts and the 'temporal *archê*' reading of Aristotle, rather than any direct statement of the position in the Epicurean texts that we have. Therefore, if the 'temporal *archê*' reading of Aristotle is a *misreading*, this significantly undermines the internal cause interpretation of Epicurus.

Furthermore, there are two places where Lucretius and Epicurus do discuss our responsibility for our own characters, and these are places where we would expect the swerve to be mentioned if it were supposed to introduce breaks in the causal nexus so that our characters not be necessitated. Those two places are *DRN* 3 288 ff and *On Nature* 25, and in neither place is the swerve mentioned. In *DRN* 3, what allows us to overcome our inborn temperaments, unlike wild animals, and thus to achieve a blessed life, is not a random swerving in the soul, but instead the possession of reason. The passage of *On Nature* 25 is much more obscure, and I will discuss it in more detail later. (See sections 4.2–4.2.3.) However, swerves and random breaks in the causal nexus are not mentioned here either, and the most plausible reading of this passage also is that our reason is what allows us to shape our character and control our development. This emphasis on the role of reason is corroborated by other Epicurean sources and fits with concerns that Epicureans would plausibly have, given their ethics and psychology (section 1.3).

3.3 The origin of action

According to Aristotle, animals are 'self-movers,' unlike inanimate objects.[19] Furthermore, he says that both the animal's faculty of desire (*to oretikon*) and the desiring or striving (*orexis*) which forms the first stage of every voluntary action serve as internal *archai*, or origins, of movement and action.[20]

19 E.g., *Physics* 8 2 253a11–20, 8 5 255a6, 8 6 259b1–17. For a great deal more on Aristotle on self-motion, see Gill and Lennox (1994).

20 See *DA* 3 10 433a9–b30, *MA* 701a26–702a21.

These remarks of Aristotle's have been taken as inspiration for Epicurus' supposed use of the swerve in the production of each action. For instance, Walter Englert thinks that for Aristotle, if animals are really to be self-movers, and if the desire of an animal is to be in any special way an *archê* of its actions, then there cannot be sufficient antecedent conditions for what that desire causes. For Englert, the faculty of desire genuinely initiates motion; unlike a domino, it does not merely pass it along. He sees Aristotle as engaging in a 'delicate balancing act' between determinism and causal fresh starts, with the faculty of desire lying somewhere between being an uncaused 'beginning of motion' and a passive link in a causal chain.[21] According to Englert, what allows the faculty of desire to have this special intermediate causal status is its use of *sumphuton pneuma*, 'connate breath,' an element in virtue of which, Aristotle says, the faculty of desire initiates motion.[22] According to Aristotle, this element is "obviously well disposed by nature to impart movement and supply strength" (*MA* 10 703a18–19), and Englert says it is the 'tool' by which desire is able to move the body in special, 'active' way.[23] This supposedly parallels Epicurus' use of the swerve: swerves are not identical to volitions (unlike on the traditional interpretation), but swerves, as indeterministic atomic motions, can be exploited by a creature's *voluntas* in order to move the creature in an indeterministic way, thus allowing the creature's *voluntas* to genuinely *initiate* action.[24]

Likewise, Elizabeth Asmis tries to find precedent for the 'traditional' interpretation of Epicurus in Aristotle's doctrine that the *orexis* (desiring or striving) which forms the first stage of every voluntary action is a genuine beginning (*archê*) of action. Asmis says that Epicurus accepts this dictum, and so for *voluntas* to be a genuine *archê* there must be a swerve at the start of every voluntary motion. Asmis also suggests that Epicurus introduced the swerve in order to explain how there can be goal-directed action in a 'mechanical' universe. As Asmis puts it, "Epicurus removed teleology from the ordering of the physical universe; but he recognized it in the voluntary motion of animals. To prevent an animal's goal-directed striving from being a mechanical response, he posited a swerving motion at the beginning of each act of striving."[25]

21 Englert (1987) 85.
22 Englert (1987) 91–94.
23 Englert (1987) 93.
24 Englert (1987) 119–29.
25 Asmis (1990) 288.

But if my discussion of Aristotle's use of *archê* and the *Nicomachean Ethics* above is convincing, there is little reason to attribute to Aristotle any sort of indeterminism in his action-theory on the basis of such remarks, since he is most likely concerned in these passages with *explanatory archai*, not *temporal archai*. It would be profoundly foreign to Aristotle to think that being causally determined by past states of the soul would make desire or striving a mere 'link in a causal chain,' so that it would be unable to act as a genuine *archê* of action. No breaks in causation are required for something to be an *archê*. In 'practical inferences,' things like my belief that I must buy some cloth in order to make a cloak, or my desire for drink, can be *archai* of actions without themselves being uncaused. That is, they can be things to which we appeal when we wish to explain why an action occurs.[26] Sorabji points out that Aristotle often uses the word *archê* for one of several members of a casual 'chain,' *e.g.*, in *NE* 6 2, where deliberation and desire are the *archai* of deliberate choice (*prohairesis*) (1139a32–33), deliberate choice is the *archê* of deliberate action (1139a31, b5), and deliberate action is the *archê* of events like sea battles.[27] (I also suspect that using the notion of "links in a causal chain" in discussions of Aristotle is anachronistic.[28])

Once again, Aristotle's way of characterizing the sense in which the animal's desires and such can act as 'origins' of action parallels Lucretius' characterization of animals' internal capacity to initiate motion. For both, desires and character can act as 'internal origins' as long as they are the items which bring about the animal's actions, and having this type of 'internal origin' is what distinguishes animal action from the motions of inanimate objects, as well as from bodily motions simply caused by external shoves and the like.

In addition to the general philosophical objections to these sorts of interpretations of Epicurus pointed out above (section 2.4), let me briefly discuss some more particular shortcomings of Englert's and Asmis' use of Aristotle to understand Epicurus.

Englert's description of the role of connate breath is not warranted by the obscure comments on its role scattered in Aristotle's corpus. To say that *pneuma* is well-suited to producing movement no more implies some

26 See, for instance *MA* 701a7–701b1.

27 Sorabji (1980) 228. See also Furley's and Bobzien's discussions (n. 14 above) for further argument that Aristotle's action-theory is not indeterministic.

28 On the anachronism of applying the term "causal chain" to ancient discussions, see Hankinson (1996), esp. pp. 186–191. See also Sorabji (1980) chs. 1–3.

mysterious intermediate causal status than would the remark that fire is well-suited to warming things, especially since Aristotle says that the reason why it is well-suited to producing movement and giving strength is because it is heavy compared to what is naturally light.[29] In addition, the assimilation of the function of the swerve to the function of connate breath is ill considered. The swerve is a random motion, whereas connate breath is an element that Aristotle uses in various places to explain some of the capacities that animals have, such as sensation.[30] The obvious analog to this in Epicurus is the mysterious "unnamed element" that is responsible for sensation and thought.[31]

Asmis' suggestion that the swerve is "a way of accommodating goal-directed movement" in a 'mechanical' universe does not fit Epicurus, and Aristotle would be an unlikely inspiration for such a doctrine. Since the swerve would place a random, uncaused atomic motion between an animal's desires and its actions, it is difficult to see how it would help to accommodate rather than undercut goal-directed movement (see section 2.3). Asmis does raise an important philosophical question for any 'mechanistic' metaphysics – how does one account for the intentionality of mental states, action, language, and the like? – but there is no reason to think that the swerve is meant to solve this problem. To the extent that Epicurus does respond to such worries, *e.g.*, in the cases of the intentionality of language and perceptual states, he seems to give a dispositional analysis of their intentionality: what makes language and perceptual states 'about' the world is that they are apt to be the effect of certain causes and apt to be the cause of certain effects.[32] I think that

29 See the discussion in *MA* 10 703a4–28. I will not go into the issue of what *pneuma's* role *is* for Aristotle, since I do not have a definite view on the matter. None of the plausible suggestions as to its role, however, involve positing 'fresh starts' or Englert's intermediate causal status. A good overview of the literature on the topic can be found in Berryman (2002). Berryman's view is that *pneuma* allows animals to initiate locomotion in response to other kinds of change, and it is only in this sense that animals qualify as 'self-movers.' Another promising suggestion is in Furley (1994); he says that animals are uniquely involved in initiating their own motion because of the intentionality of desire.

30 *E.g.*, in *Generation of Animals* 744a3, cf. 736b29–737a1.

31 *Ep. Hdt.* 63, *DRN* 3 237–257.

32 See O'Keefe (1997) 126–34, esp. section 6, for a discussion of perceptual states: perceptual states are conceived of as effects of certain environmental causes, and (in part) what makes them all *alêtheis* – true or real – is that they are all like the objects which move the senses. For language, see *Ep. Hdt.* 75–6 and *DRN* 5 1028–90 (plus additional sources collected in Long and Sedley (1987) section 19). The basis of human language is certain instinctive utterances, akin to animal cries, in response to impressions and feelings. So if humans all cry out in a certain way when feeling cold, this cry means 'cold,' or 'I feel cold,' or something of the sort.

Epicurus would give a similar analysis of the intentionality of mental states such as desires, and the goal-directed movement of animals prompted by such desires.[33]

Aristotle too has no problem with thinking that the same phenomenon can be given both teleological and 'mechanistic' characterizations and explanations.[34] Aristotle says that anger can properly be defined both as blood boiling around the heart (from the point of view of the student of nature) and as the desire to hurt another in return (from the point of view of the dialectician). Likewise, one could also explain the actions prompted by anger in both 'mechanistic' terms (the blood boiling around my heart expanded, causing my pneuma to move, *etc.*, until my tendons flexed and muscles contracted in such-and-so a fashion) and teleological terms (my belief that my sister had poked me in the eye led me to kick her in the shins so that she too would be in pain), without the availability of one type of explanation obviating the possibility or the need for the other.[35]

And so, both Aristotle and Epicurus are concerned to defend the thesis that an animal's desires, thoughts, and other psychological states act as the origin of that animal's actions. But Aristotle's defense of this doctrine has no anti-determinist implications, and hence it sheds no light on the role the swerve plays in preserving our freedom.

3.4 *Aristotle and Epicurus on the origins of character and action: summary*

Trying to understand Epicurus' doctrines by finding plausible precedents and parallels in Aristotle is right-minded. Aristotle and Epicurus do share many concerns. For both Aristotle and Epicurus, preserving the ability of the agent to have control over the formation of his own character is

33 If this is right, Epicurus' materialist theory of mind would be similar in broad outline to the one given in Armstrong (1980), esp. pp. 16–31. To argue for this thesis would go well beyond the scope of the present book, but I submit that Epicurus cannot think that severing the connection between action and desire, via a random atomic swerve, is a good way of accommodating goal-directed movement.

34 Berryman (2003) correctly notes that it may be misleading to call ateleological explanations which appeal to things like atoms colliding or fire expanding and moving around 'mechanical' or 'mechanistic', since in the ancient world such explanations make no attempt to understand and explain the natural world by applying terms and ideas from the discipline of mechanics.

35 *DA* I 1 403a29–b9. To be fair to Asmis, this incompatibility is not one she ascribes to Aristotle himself; instead, it is (supposedly) the rejection of teleology in the natural world that leads the Epicureans to need to posit an uncaused atomic motion in order to accommodate Aristotle's doctrine that animals, because of their desire, are 'self-movers.'

important, as is preserving the agent's ability to be the origin of his own actions. The mistake that many interpreters make, however, is in thinking that, for Aristotle, being an *archê* of action requires causal breaks, either in the formation of character or in the production of action. The textual evidence does not support attributing such a position to Aristotle, or to Epicurus, for that matter. No causal breaks are mentioned to serve either of these purposes for either of these philosophers. For both Aristotle and Epicurus, what the texts support, and what would make sense in terms of their overall philosophy, is that an agent's character has to be the result of the choices that the agent makes, so that his character is under his rational control, not merely the result of environmental and hereditary factors beyond his control, and that the agent's actions must be the result of the agent's own beliefs and desires.

CHAPTER 4

Epicurus' reductionist response to Democritean fatalism

Other than Aristotle, Democritus is most often cited as the person Epicurus is responding to when formulating his position on freedom. Surely this is correct. For the most part, Epicurus appropriates his atomist metaphysics from Democritus.[1] However, the swerve is one of his major modifications to Democritus. The Epicurean Diogenes of Oinoanda writes that Epicurus 'discovered' the swerve, an atomic motion that Democritus did not discern, because Democritus failed to recognize that a swerving motion was needed in order for us to be free,[2] and Epicurus himself writes that Democritus' metaphysics, if true, would have disastrous consequences for our agency – consequences that Democritus himself did not see.[3]

Of course, it is one thing to say that Epicurus feels the need to modify Democritus' metaphysics because it has unacceptable consequences as far as our freedom is concerned, quite another to specify what those consequences are, why Epicurus thinks they follow, and how exactly he modifies Democritus' metaphysics to avoid them. I will make two related claims about Epicurus' response to Democritus. The first is that Epicurus objects to the consequences of Democritean *eliminativism*; in response, Epicurus tries to show how a reductionist atomism need not discount the reality and causal efficacy of phenomena like minds and reason. The second is that Epicurus primarily worries about the *fatalist* consequences of Democritus' eliminativism, not determinism as such. Let me briefly expand on these two cryptic claims.

1 Epicurus' ethics also owes much to Democritus, although this connection is less noted because our picture of Democritus' ethics is sketchy. Warren (2002) is the best place to look for information regarding how the ethics of Democritus and his successors shaped Epicurus' ethics; however, see O'Keefe (2003*c*) for some of my reservations regarding Warren's claims.

2 Diogenes of Oinoanda 32.1.14–3.14 (L&S 20 G).

3 In the main anti-fatalist argument of book 25 of *On Nature*, discussed in section 4.2 below.

Epicurus has a type–type identity theory of mind: the mind is a group of atoms in the chest, mental processes are atomic processes, and various mental capacities are explained from the "bottom up" by appealing to the intrinsic properties of the atoms constituting the mind and to their relationships to one another. Both Democritus and Epicurus are atomists. Democritus' ontology, however, is extremely parsimonious: Democritus declares that only atoms and void exist in truth, and that colors, tastes, and the like exist only 'by convention' (see *M* 7 135, DK 68 B 9). Epicurus thinks this eliminative materialism *vis-à-vis* sensible qualities has unacceptable skeptical consequences, and if consistently carried over to one's philosophy of mind, would have unacceptable consequences for our agency. Epicurus wants to resist these consequences, and so he rejects Democritus' eliminativism regarding both sensible qualities and the mind, in a way consistent with a reductionist atomism.

I have argued above (sections 2.1 and 2.2) that the sort of *libera voluntas* that Lucretius wishes to preserve has little resemblance to libertarian 'free will.' Instead, it is a matter of animals being able to initiate action in response to the promptings of their desires. Furthermore, I have argued (chapter 3) that the sense in which animals 'initiate' action or are 'origins' of action, for both Epicurus and Aristotle, has no anti-determinist implications. To deny that we can initiate action, in this sense, would be to render us helpless, and to make all action and deliberation pointless. Democritus' eliminativism, thinks Epicurus, would have these sorts of *fatalist* consequences, and it is to these consequences that Epicurus objects in his action-theory, not to determinism as such.[4]

This chapter has four main sections.

In the first, I start by setting out what I mean by calling Epicurus a 'reductionist' and why I think Epicurus' overall metaphysics is reductionist in this sense. I then argue that Epicurus has an identity theory of mind and that Epicurus' reductionism in his philosophy of mind is part of a broader reductionist program, including a *reductionist* response to Democritus on the ontological status of sensible qualities. Many 'anti-reductionist' interpretations of Epicurus are based upon confusing reductionism with eliminativism. Once this confusion is cleared up, it removes much of the philosophical motivation for anti-reductionist interpretations of Epicurus.

4 Let me make it clear that Epicurus *does* think that determinism has unacceptable fatalist consequences, and he posits the swerve to avoid these consequences. However, he thinks this because of arguments such as Diodorus Cronus' 'Master Argument'. I consider these arguments and Epicurus' response to them in chapter 6. Nothing in Epicurus' discussion of the development and causal efficacy of the agent considered here need be interpreted in an anti-determinist way.

In the next two sections I examine in depth some passages from book 25 of Epicurus' lost *magnum opus, On Nature.*[5] David Sedley has done a great deal of work to decipher this badly damaged papyrus, which has served as the main proof-text for anti-reductionist interpretations of Epicurus. In *On Nature* book 25, Epicurus is arguing against those, like Democritus, who say that everything occurs 'of necessity' (κατ' ἀνάγκην), and in his arguments he says many things that may appear to conflict with an identity theory of mind and causal determinism. For instance, he seems to claim that people develop psychological states which are not identical to the atoms of the soul, and that these states, and *not* the atoms, are then causally responsible for how a person acts. Further, this sort of state, once it acquires the 'cause out of itself,' transmits this to the 'first natures.' David Sedley says this is a claim that the self, as a 'radically emergent' phenomenon, exerts downwards causation on the atoms, in effect turning Epicurus into an interactionist property dualist.

The second section focuses on Epicurus' central anti-fatalist argument in *On Nature* 25. I contend that Epicurus' main thesis is that we cannot consistently argue against our conception of ourselves as rational agents, and it is our reason that allows us to reform ourselves, control our actions, and blame and praise one another appropriately. This is consistent with the 'reasons-responsiveness' account of freedom I have been arguing for in chapters 1–3. The third section deals with Epicurus' description of psychological development in *On Nature* book 25. I argue that this description is consistent with an identity theory of mind, and that Epicurus is trying to show how a reductionist can account for the causal efficacy of emergent phenomena like reason. In the final section, I argue that none of the various 'anti-reductionist' interpretations of Epicurus assign a philosophically plausible or textually supported role to the swerve in preserving human freedom.

4.1 *Epicurean reductionism*

Before we can address the question of whether Epicurus is a reductionist, we need to get clear on what exactly we mean by calling Epicurus either a 'reductionist' or 'non-reductionist.' The central text in disputes over

5 Book 25 of *On Nature* is not always referred to as "book 25 of *On Nature*"; it has also been known as book 34 and *liber incertus.* Simon Laursen has examined the papyrus and argues that the number of the book is likely 25 (Laursen (1987)). I will refer to the text as "*On Nature* book 25," but nothing hinges upon this.

Epicurus' reductionism has been *On Nature* 25. However, because *On Nature* 25 itself is so scarred with lacunae and jargon-ridden, we need to interpret its often murky passages in ways that make them harmonize with the rest of Epicurean philosophy. Thus, we first need to examine whether Epicurean philosophy overall, as well as the passages describing Epicurean philosophy of mind that are less obscure than *On Nature* 25, portray a philosophy that is in general reductionist or non-reductionist.

So first, I will describe what *I* mean when I call Epicurus a reductionist, and I will argue that many of the claims that are often cited in order to demonstrate that Epicurus is not a 'reductionist' do no such thing. Second, I will argue that the tenor of the rest of Epicurus' philosophy is reductionist. I will concentrate particular attention on what Epicurus has to say about sensible qualities, such as sweetness and whiteness. Epicurus' position on sensible qualities has been cited as support for a generally 'anti-reductionist' strain in Epicurean philosophy; I argue that it indicates just the opposite. Epicurus is showing how a reductionist can account for phenomena like colors, in order to resist Democritus' *eliminativism* about sensible qualities, which leads to unacceptable skeptical conclusions. Furthermore, Epicurus' response to Democritus in this area provides a valuable parallel to Epicurus' reductionist response, in *On Nature* 25, to Democritean eliminativism in the philosophy of mind. Finally, I will look at the strong textual grounds for ascribing a reductionist philosophy of mind to Epicurus.

4.1.1 In what sense is Epicurus a reductionist?

When I say that Epicurus is a reductionist, this amounts to the following: macroscopic bodies are not "irreducibly different" in kind from atoms, nor do they possess causal power beyond those of atoms. Epicurus describes macroscopic bodies as being nothing more than *sunkriseis* (compounds)[6] and *athroismata* (aggregates or collections)[7] of the atoms that

6 *e.g.*, *Ep. Hdt.* 40, 42, 54, 55, 62.

7 *Ep. Hdt.* 56, 62, 69. Because I will be concentrating on the term *athroismata* below, I should note that Epicurus uses the terms *sunkriseis* and *athroismata* interchangeably and views all compound bodies as aggregates; *i.e.*, Epicurus does not distinguish between compound bodies generally and a proper subset of them that are mere aggregates. In *Ep. Hdt.* 40–41 Epicurus says that all bodies can be divided into two types: "some are compounds *(sunkriseis)*, and some are those out of which compounds are made." Elsewhere in the letter, Epicurus uses the terms *sunkriseis* and *athroismata* indiscriminately when referring to macroscopic bodies, which suggests that he does not distinguish between them. That all compound bodies are aggregates – that Epicurus does, in fact, use the terms interchangeably – is clinched, however, in *Ep. Hdt.* 62, where he is discussing composite *(sunkriseis)* bodies in general at one point, and in the next sentence refers to this composite as an *athroisma*, an aggregate.

compose them. Furthermore, all of their properties can be explained in terms of the properties of and relations between these atomic constituents.

Aristotle's usage of the term *athroisma*, and his views about the relationship between parts and wholes, provide an instructive contrast to Epicurus. Forms of the word *athroisma* occur most frequently in Aristotle's biological works, and his pattern of usage is quite striking.[8] There are two main types of entities Aristotle will refer to as *athroismata*: groups of animals of the same type crowded together, such as a swarm of bees,[9] or accumulations of stuff, i.e., gatherings together of things that are mass items, such as the collection of milk in the breasts of the mother.[10] Aristotle always uses the word *athroisma* (and other forms of it) to refer to collections which do not have any essential unity, which are nothing more than the sum of their parts: for a swarm of bees to exist is simply for there to be to be a certain number of bees congregating together.

Aristotle restricts the term *athroisma* to such reducible entities because he does not think that *all* wholes could be reduced to their parts in such a way. For a swarm of bees to exist may be simply for there to be such-and-so many bees, gathered together in such and so a way. But this does not hold true for proper individuals, according to Aristotle, the main exemplar of which are biological organisms. A person is not just a certain number of human-parts, arranged in a certain way. The properties and actions of proper individuals cannot be explained in a "bottom-up" manner. That is, one cannot start by looking at the parts of an individual in isolation, and then, by "summing up" the properties of these parts, explain the properties and actions of the whole that they constitute.

Instead, the existence and behavior of these parts is posterior in the order of explanation to the existence of the animal. The various bits and pieces that make up a person can only be understood because they are part of the functional system that gives them their purpose.[11] Aristotelian explanations in the biological realm usually appeal to the functional

8 Some of these examples I am about to discuss use the noun form, to indicate that which has been gathered together, some use a form of the verb, indicating the process of collection.

9 *History of Animals* 9 40 625b12, 627a25. Other examples include a flock of pelicans (8 12 597a11), a herd of bulls (9 3 611a2), a shoal of dolphin (9 48 631a12), and a crowding together of crustaceans (8 2 590b30).

10 *Generation of Animals* 4 8 776b30. Other examples include the accumulation of ink in the cuttlefish (*History of Animals* 9 37 621b32), the collection of blood in the uterine region, (*Generation of Animals* 2 4 738b7), and the accumulation of fire in the body (*On Youth, Old Age, Life and Death, and Respiration* 5 469b28, b30).

11 As Aristotle says, a person has the parts he does because of his human form, which makes the possession of such parts necessary conditions of his existence (*Parts of Animals* 1 1 640a33–640a35).

organization of the animal as a whole in order to explain the various behaviors and properties of the parts that make up those animals. And this is the court of 'final' appeal, so to speak: the functional organization of the animal – its form – cannot in turn be given some reductive explanation in terms of the properties of the stuff that makes it up.[12]

Epicureans, of course, reject such irreducible immanent teleology. The parts of animals came into existence prior to their having a function and do not exist for the sake of fulfilling that function (*DRN* 4 823–57). The fact that animal parts presently happen to be well suited to serve various biological functions is the result of a process of natural selection (*DRN* 5 837–77 [L&S 13I], Simplicius, *On Aristotle's Physics* 371,33–372,14 [L&S 13J]). And Lucretius' explanations of various biological phenomena, such as sleep, always proceeds from the 'bottom up': by considering the properties of the atoms that constitute the organism and their relationships to one another, we can explain all of that organism's characteristics and behavior. (See *DRN* 4 for many such examples.)

For Aristotle, there is a clear demarcation between mere *athroismata* – reducible entities such as schools of fish – and non-reducible entities – such as the fish themselves. Aristotle would never use a term such as *athroisma* to describe an essentially unified subject. An especially informative example of Aristotle's usage occurs in *Generation of Animals*. When describing the imparting of form to the matter the female has provided, Aristotle calls the mass of stuff before impregnation an *athroisma* (730b2), but never refers to the developing fetus with such a term. Epicureans, on the other hand, do not make any such distinction.

If macroscopic bodies are nothing above and beyond the parts that constitute them, one would expect to be able to explain the features that macroscopic bodies exhibit in terms of the properties of the atoms that constitute them, along with their spatial relations, motions, *etc.* And indeed, examples of such reductive, 'bottom-up' explanations of the properties of macroscopic objects abound in both Epicurus and Lucretius. Epicurus and Lucretius give causal explanations of *why* these properties obtain in terms of the more basic properties, such that they can be completely understood in terms of the more basic atomic properties.

For example, in *DRN* 2 381–397, Lucretius tries to explain how some things can pass through different materials while others cannot by appealing to the sizes of the types of atoms that constitute a kind of

12 See, for instance, *Parts of Animals* 1 1 640b22–29.

thing: lightning-fire is made of smaller shapes than fire from torches, and thus can pass through more openings than fire from torches. Lucretius also explains the slower rate that olive oil passes through a colander than wine does by saying that either its atoms are larger, or that they are more hooked than wine atoms, and thus get entangled with one another more easily.

The liquidity of water will provide an excellent example of how properties of macroscopic bodies are given a reductive account in Epicureanism. In *DRN* 2 452–455, Lucretius gives a simple explanation of liquidity:

> Those others, the fluids which consist of liquid body, must be of elements smoother and rounder. Indeed you may scoop up poppy seed as easily as water, for the individual round particles are of no hindrance to each other; and when poppy seed is knocked over, it runs downhill just as easily.

So, a mass of water – let us say some water in a pitcher – is simply an *athroisma*, an aggregate, which is nothing above and beyond the atoms that make it up. This aggregate will have certain properties – for instance, if I pour it on a slanted desk, it will run down the desk and then drop to the floor. But this liquidity is not some irreducible property of the mass of water; it is simply for the aggregate of water particles – when considered as an aggregate, not individually – to act in certain ways (*e.g.*, flow down the desk), which behavior can be accounted for entirely in terms of the properties of its constituent atoms and their relations to one another. (Because such explanations will often involve *relationships* that hold among the atoms, there *will* be some 'emergent' properties – properties which can be predicated only of macroscopic bodies, not constituent atoms, and which come into existence because of the organization of the atoms that constitute the body – which will be invoked in explaining events. But as I explain below, admitting the existence of properties that are 'emergent' in this sense is compatible with Epicurus being a reductionist.)

Epicurus' philosophy of mind is consistent with his general reductionist view of objects and their properties. Like other macroscopic bodies, the mind is an atomic aggregate, and its properties and causal powers can be explained from the 'bottom up.' Mental processes (such as sensations) are identified with atomic processes.

In my later discussion of *On Nature* 25, I will often be claiming that what Epicurus is saying is perfectly compatible with a reductionist view of the mind. So let me here briefly set out what is, and what is not, implied by being a reductionist, as I am using the term.

1. *To assert that the mind is real does not entail that one is not a reductionist.* To explain something is not necessarily to explain it *away.* Nor does saying that the mind is nothing above and beyond a group of atoms entail that the mind is unreal; it entails just the opposite: if the mind is identified with a group of atoms, and the group of atoms is real, so too is the mind. The reductionist in philosophy of mind need not say dismissively that mental facts are 'mere appearances' of atomic facts; it is the eliminativist who does that.[13] To say something like "Pain is nothing but c-fiber stimulation" is to admit that there *is* something called pain, and to allow that it could be useful in explanations. That is quite different from saying that pain-talk is an outmoded theory, ascribes pain to objects that do not really have pain-states, and should therefore be eliminated, along with demon-talk, phlogiston-talk, *etc.*[14]
2. *To assert that the mind has properties and powers that individual atoms do not does not entail that one is not a reductionist.* The mind has many capacities that individual atoms do not. It can perceive, deliberate, and feel emotions. From this, some interpreters conclude that Epicurus is not a reductionist in his philosophy of mind.[15] But this inference is unwarranted. A reductionist can accept that wholes have properties that their parts do not. People can cry, while atoms cannot, but if crying is nothing more than the secretion of water from the tear ducts of a living organism, we can explain what crying is, and why people can cry while atoms cannot, in a way consistent with being a reductionist about crying.[16]

13 However, a reductionist bent *can* lead to eliminativism. If one thinks that anything that is real must be reducible to material entities, and that mental entities *cannot* be so reduced, then eliminativism results.

14 Annas often asserts that Epicurus is not a 'reductivist' in his philosophy of mind while using the term in a way that is much closer to what is meant by 'eliminativist.' For instance, she says that Epicurus' theory is not reductive, because "atomic theory [does not explain] away what we believe about ourselves" (Annas (1992) 204), and because, for Epicurus, "there are facts about atoms and facts about human agency, and each set of facts will be real; it will be wrong to treat the latter as the mere appearance of the former" (Annas (1992) 128). She then goes on to say that, "In particular, moral development is real . . . by reasoning the individual can overcome handicaps of inherited temperament" (Annas (1992) 129). Mitsis also seems to conflate reductionism and eliminativism; he says that Epicurus wants to save atomism from the "internal rot of reductionism," that is, "from an eliminative materialism that rejects the explanatory efficacy of notions such as desires, reasons, and intentions" (Mitsis (1988) 151).

15 For instance, Bailey says that the mind is more than a mere aggregate of atoms because it is a union of atoms in a complex, "which has a new individuality of its own in which it may acquire qualities and even powers which are not possessed by individual component atoms" (Bailey (1928) 435).

16 See Lucretius' mocking criticism of Anaxagoras, *DRN* 1 907 ff, in which he stresses the importance of appealing to the atoms' arrangement in order to explain the possession by the aggregate of qualities which the constituent atoms do not have. Lucretius says that if we were to suppose, along with Anaxagoras, that the constituent parts have the same properties as the objects that they constitute, we would have to believe that atoms sometimes cry or laugh.

3. *To use structural elements in one's explanations of the mind does not entail that one is not a reductionist.* Epicurus and Lucretius frequently avail themselves of the structural properties of bodies in order to explain their behavior. The types of atoms that make up a body, and the various spatial relationships, entanglements, *etc.*, that they have with one another, can all be taken into account when explaining the properties and behavior of that body.[17] A reductionist can happily utilize formal explanations *of a certain type*. A car engine can work only when the pieces are arranged properly. Change that arrangement, even in such a minor way as disconnecting the spark plugs, and the engine can no longer power the car. A reductionist can admit that we must take into account the pieces' arrangement to explain why the motor does or does not work.

If Epicurus can be a reductionist in his philosophy of mind while still thinking that (1) the mind is a real thing, (2) it can possess properties and powers which cannot be possessed by any of its constituents, and (3) one must often appeal to structural and formal elements in explanations involving the mind, what does it mean to say that he is a reductionist? Three things, I believe:

First, the mind is a real thing, but it is nothing above and beyond the atoms that constitute it. An example of this sort of thing would be a flock of sheep. A flock of sheep is a real entity, but it is nothing above and beyond the group of sheep gathered together. Second, although the mind has properties and powers which none of its atoms have, it has these only in virtue of the properties of and relationships amongst its constituent atoms, and the possession of the properties by the mind can be explained by reference to the properties and relationships of the atoms. Third, appeals to structural and formal elements are permissible, but only if they are ultimately reducible to relationships amongst atoms, *e.g.*, the tendency of a group of atoms to clump together because of the atoms' hooks getting entangled. Epicurus cannot appeal to *irreducible* form as does Aristotle.

4.1.2 Epicurus' reductionist response to Democritean skepticism[18]

Epicurus develops his view of sensible qualities in an attempt to work through the skeptical difficulties bequeathed to him by his predecessor

17 For instance, see *DRN* I 817–829.

18 A more detailed exploration of Democritus and Epicurus on the status of sensible qualities, including the impact of this issue on our understanding of Epicurus' dictum that "all perceptions are *alêtheis* (true or real)," can be found in O'Keefe (1997). For more on Democritus' position, including criticisms of O'Keefe (1997) on Democritus, see Ganson (1999).

Democritus. Epicurus takes his theory of perception largely from Democritus, but Democritus runs into severe skeptical problems as a result of that theory, problems Epicurus wishes to avoid.

Democritus has a detailed account of perception, trying to explain how the *pathê* (affections or sensations) associated with each sense arise as a result of the causal interaction of atoms with the sense-organs. For instance, the taste "bitter" is explained as a result of sharp atoms tearing the tissue of the tongue, "sweet" as the soothing action of round and fairly large atoms on the tongue.[19]

Democritus then notes that what sorts of sense-experiences someone will have will depend on his bodily condition: the same honey that appears sweet to most people may taste bitter to some other animal, and even among people, how some object will appear to them will depend on "their affections and their age." Because perceptual qualities seem to be relative to the percipient in this way, Democritus infers that none of them exist "in nature" (*phusis*) and these qualities are not part of the nature of the bodies we mistakenly think they belong to. Instead, they are merely affections of the senses as they are altered.[20] We may think that the honey is sweet, and somebody suffering from an illness may taste it and think it bitter, but "from the fact that honey appears sweet to some and bitter to others. . . Democritus deduces that it is neither sweet nor bitter, and for this reason utters the phrase 'no more' [*ou mallon*]. . ."[21]

Thus, Democritus is an eliminativist when it comes to sensible qualities, and this eliminativism leads him, at a minimum, to a deep pessimism about our ability to gain knowledge about the way the world is, and perhaps to a denial that knowledge is possible.[22] As Democritus puts it,

19 Our main source of information on Democritus on perception is from Theophrastus, Aristotle's successor as head of the Lyceum. For Theophrastus' discussion of the sense of taste, see *de sens.* 65–70. The Epicurean explanation of the sense of taste follows Democritus' very closely. See *DRN* 4 615–626.

20 *de sens.* 63–4. Not all interpreters accept that perceptual relativity is behind Democritus' eliminativism (*e.g.*, Wardy (1988)). See O'Keefe (1997) for a more extended discussion of this issue and objections to these interpreters.

21 Sextus Empiricus, *PH* 1.213. Translations of *Outlines of Pyrrhonism* are from Annas and Barnes (2000).

22 Whether Democritus thinks that knowledge is merely difficult or impossible to attain is a matter of some dispute. (See Hankinson (1995) 47–50 and (1998) 201–205 for an introduction to some of the reports and issues regarding Democritus' skepticism, and Curd (2001) for a recent argument that Democritus is not a skeptic and references to much of the literature on this topic.) Fortunately, the main thesis of this section does not depend on settling the question. Democritus certainly said many things that appear skeptical. He was interpreted as a skeptic by Epicureans (see *Adv. Colot.* 1108f), and Epicurus is interested in avoiding the skeptical difficulties that Democritus runs into by challenging Democritus' view on the unreality of sensible qualities, whether or not Democritus himself ultimately thinks that these difficulties can be overcome.

By convention sweet, by convention bitter, by convention hot, by convention cold, by convention color: in reality atoms and the void.

And he goes on to say:

We know nothing genuine about what there is, but what shifts in accordance with the condition of the body, and what enters it and presses upon it.[23]

For Democritus, there is a radical discontinuity between the properties to which we have access, and which must form the basis of all our knowledge, and the properties that exist in reality. Democritus says, "A person must learn. . .that he is separated from reality," and he most probably has in mind that the *pathê*, which must form the basis of all knowledge, are found not to be a part of reality, i.e., they are merely subjective.[24] In fact, almost all of the reports furnished by the senses (for instance, "The honey is sweet") turn out upon inspection to be false. We *think* that the honey is really sweet, but the sweetness is not in the honey at all – it is simply a change in our sense-organ.[25]

It is important to note that Democritus' abolition of sensible qualities does not follow directly from his reductionism. David Sedley notes, correctly, that Democritus' brand of atomism is a "bottom-up" theory, in which all things at the "macro-level" of ordinary experience are to explained in terms of the properties and interactions of the atoms that exist at the "micro-level." But then, Sedley thinks, Democritus infers sensible qualities like sweetness are unreal because they are "*nothing* over and above physical states."[26] This is to confuse reductionism with eliminativism. It is not from a belief that sensible qualities are nothing over and above physical states that Democritus infers that they are unreal. There *are* some properties of bodies that *can* be identified with properties of atoms, for example shape and resistance to blows, but it is precisely these properties that are *not* eliminated, but thought of as real properties

23 Sextus Empiricus, *M.* 7.135 (68 B 9 DK) (trans. Hankinson (1995)).

24 Sextus Empiricus, *M.* 7.137 (68 B 6 DK).

25 The complaint of the senses against reason shows that Democritus is well aware of the possibly self-stultifying nature of his philosophy: "Wretched mind, do you take your evidence from us and then try to overthrow us? Our overthrow is your downfall." (reported in Galen, *On Medical Experience* XV 8, 68 B 125 DK, trans. Hankinson (1995).) A painful irony lurks in Democritus' philosophy: his atomism is a response to the Eleatic philosophers, such as Parmenides and Melissus, who denied the reality of change and the phenomenal world. Atomism is supposed to provide an answer to the Eleatic challenge, as well as provide economical and comprehensive causal explanations for the features of the world. Democritus' atomism, however, threatens to undercut the authority of the senses as a source of information about the world, which in turn would lead to the collapse of reason, including the theories constructed by reason, such as atomism.

26 Sedley (1988*a*) 298–299.

of bodies. Rather, it is because sensible qualities *cannot* be identified with physical states that Democritus infers that they are unreal. No properties either of individual atoms or of atomic aggregates can be found with which we can identify things like 'sweetness' or 'redness.'

Epicureans think that it is unacceptable to abolish sensible qualities from one's ontology in this way, because the skepticism that results from such a position would make life impossible to lead.[27] Epicurus tries to avoid this skepticism and the resulting *apraxia* (actionlessness) by staunchly defending the reality of sensible qualities. His basic solution is to say that sensible qualities, although relative, are nonetheless *real.* Epicurus accepts the basics of Democritus' causal theory of perception. He also agrees with Democritus that sensible qualities like colors are not inherent in the nature of bodies. Instead they are "generated according to certain arrangements and position in relation to the sight," and in his work the *Symposium*, Epicurus concedes that there is a mixture of natures in wine such that a certain amount of it may affect one person one way, another person another way, and that wine is neither universally cooling nor universally heating.[28]

But it does not follow from this that wine is "no more cooling than heating," or that we are mistaken to say that the wine itself is cooling or heating, as long as we put in the proper qualifications: *for whom* the wine is cooling, and *under what circumstances.* The Epicureans defend the reality of relational and dispositional properties not only in the case of sensible qualities but in a host of areas. Lucretius includes among his list of accidental properties, "servitude and liberty, poverty and riches, war and peace. . ."[29] which, if they exist at all, must be relational and not intrinsic properties. Epicurus himself, in his discussion of justice, makes it clear that justice, although real, does not exist *per se:* "Justice was not a thing in its own right, but [exists] in mutual dealings in whatever places there [is] a pact about neither harming one another nor being harmed."[30] He elsewhere says that the same type of action can be just in some circumstances, unjust in others, or just at one time, unjust at another, as what is useful changes in accordance with the circumstances. Nonetheless, for as long as some law actually is useful, then for that length of time, at least, it is really just.[31] Polystratus, the third scholarch of the

27 *Adv. Colot.* 1108f. 28 *Adv. Colot.* 1109f–1110d. 29 *DRN* I 455–456.

30 *KD* 33. Unless otherwise noted, translations of Epicurus' letters, the *Principal Doctrines*, and the *Vatican Sayings* are from Inwood and Gerson (1997).

31 *KD* 37, 38.

Garden, explicitly defends the reality of relational and dispositional properties across the board. He writes that it is evident that some things are healthy, while others are fatal, and that the fact that the same thing can be nourishing for one creature but fatal for another does not make our beliefs about nutrition *false*: this sort of relativity is just what we should expect if we understand what it means for something to 'be nutritious,' and to think otherwise is naïve.[32] It may be true that cyanide is deadly poison for me, and not poisonous for some race of aliens. But that does not make cyanide 'no more deadly than not deadly,' in any non-relativized sense, of the sort which might make me skeptical about the deadliness of cyanide *for me*.

Epicurus shares with Democritus a causal theory of perception, where *pathê* are caused by the interaction of atoms with sense-organs, yet at the same time he wants to defend the reality of sensible qualities. He can accommodate both by thinking of sensible qualities as complicated dispositional properties that cause certain *pathê* within the percipient's mind when interacting with the percipient's sense-organs under certain conditions.

Allowing these sorts of dispositional properties into his ontology enriches it compared to Democritus' quite spare ontology, but doing so is still compatible with Epicurus being a reductionist, in the sense explained above. Experiences of bitterness, blueness, *etc.*, are not caused *merely* by bodies having the dispositional properties to cause such states, although it is true that they do have such properties. They have these dispositional properties in virtue of other complicated structural properties of the atoms and groups of atoms; *e.g.*, the taste bitter is caused by rough and hooked atoms tearing up the tongue. The various colors we see are caused by the arrangement and shape of the atoms on the surfaces of bodies.[33] Thus, these dispositional properties are tied systematically to complex structural properties of the atoms themselves and the bodies that are constituted by the atoms. Sensible qualities can be explained from the 'bottom up' by referring to the properties of the atoms that make up bodies and perceivers, along with the relationships these atoms hold to one another. It is precisely because Epicurus thinks he can explain these properties in this sort of reductionist manner that he is able to accommodate them within his metaphysics, rather than eliminating them as

32 Polystratus, *On Irrational Contempt*, 23.26–26.23.

33 Cf. the scholion to *Ep. Hdt.* 44, where Epicurus is reported to have said that the color of bodies is dependent upon the arrangement of the atoms.

Democritus does when he thinks he cannot identify such properties with any real feature of atoms or atomic aggregates.

Democritus and Epicurus, broadly speaking, have the same metaphysics and are both committed to a reductionist program of finding atomic explanations for all macroscopic phenomena.[34] Democritus, however, thinks that an outcome of this program is that sensible qualities cannot be reduced to any real qualities of bodies, with the result that they are eliminated. Epicurus thinks that this eliminativism is unacceptable, in part because it would be devastating pragmatically. In response, he tries to show how these sensible qualities can be accounted for and preserved within a reductionist atomism. The same basic pattern, I submit, holds in the case of agency. Epicurus thinks that Democritean eliminativism, if followed consistently in the realm of the mind, would have disastrous practical consequences. He wishes to show how a reductionist can preserve the reality and the causal efficacy of phenomena like human reason.

4.1.3 Epicurean reductionism in philosophy of mind

Epicurus' *Letter to Herodotus* and Lucretius' *De rerum natura*, the two most extensive and best-preserved sources on Epicurean philosophy of mind, talk about the mind in ways that strongly indicate a reductionist view of it.[35] Epicurus describes the mind as a body, composed of atoms (*e.g., Ep. Hdt.* 63 ff). And Lucretius describes mental processes in terms that seem to identify them with atomic motions; *e.g.*, while arguing that sensation is a property of the whole body, Lucretius says,

> Furthermore, if anyone denies that body can feel, and believes that it is the spirit mingled throughout with the body that takes on *that motion which we name feeling (hunc motum quem sensum nominitamus)*, he fights against things that are quite manifest and true.[36]

Lucretius often explains mental capacities from the "bottom up" by appealing to the properties of and spatial relations among the atoms that make up the mind. For instance, in *DRN* 3 177–207, Lucretius argues that

34 A good description of various varieties of reductionism, along with an argument (which I think is successful) that Epicurus is committed to a fairly robust reductionist program, can be found in Don Fowler's paper "What Sort of a Reductionist was Epicurus? The Case of the Swerve," appendix B in Fowler (2002). A discussion of Epicurean reductionism in general, to which I am indebted, is Barnes (1988), esp. pp. 287–294.

35 Purinton (1999) 253–254 also discusses texts that support a 'bottom-up' view of Epicurus' philosophy of mind. That Epicurus initially seems to be a reductionist is conceded even by those who think that he is not; see Long and Sedley (1987) vol. 1 p. 71, Annas (1992) 125.

36 *DRN* 3 350 ff. Unless otherwise noted, translations of Lucretius are from Rouse (1937).

the particles that compose the mind must be small, smooth, and round, because the mind can be moved so easily and quickly. He supports this argument by noting how poppy seeds, which are smooth and round, are easily moved by the wind, while rough ears of wheat are not. Lucretius explains the mind's ability to be easily moved by the make-up of its particles, and the analogy with poppy seeds points to an identification of mental processes with atomic motions, since otherwise the argument for the round shape of the atoms on the basis of the analogy would fail.[37] Also, Lucretius explains different temperaments by appealing to the types of atoms that predominate in animals' souls, *e.g.*, air atoms cause tranquility (*DRN* 3 288 ff), and the raving that accompanies epilepsy results from the soul atoms being tossed about like water boiling during a storm (*DRN* 3 487–495).

Furthermore, Epicurus' and Lucretius' proofs of the corporeality of the mind, based upon its causal efficacy, are difficult to square with viewing Epicurus as an anti-reductionist. Epicurus says it is evident that the mind moves the body, and that only bodies can move other bodies, so the mind must be a body.[38] This insistence on the causal efficacy of the mind confronts defenders of anti-reductionist interpretations of Epicurus with a dilemma about how to conceive of the relationship between emergent mental properties and the atomic complexes from which they emerge.

Either, as Annas holds, there are for Epicurus two different 'sets of facts' – facts about atoms and facts about minds – with the latter supervening upon the former, without being reducible to them.[39] On this view, only atoms and void exist *per se*; mental phenomena possess no causal independence from atomic phenomena, and facts about atomic phenomena are sufficient to determine facts about mental phenomena. Nonetheless, mental phenomena cannot be reduced to atomic phenomena. However, this position would not be acceptable to Epicurus because,

37 This sort of argument about the make-up of the soul could also be given by those who do not identify mental and atomic processes, *e.g.*, a functionalist or an epiphenomenalist, even though the functionalist would think that atomic events *realize* mental events, while the epiphenomenalist would think that atomic events *cause* mental events. However, Epicurus and Lucretius are neither functionalists nor epiphenomenalists, and so Lucretius' argument here points toward an identity theory.

38 See *Ep. Hdt.* 63 on the mind being a body, *Ep. Hdt.* 67 for the proof of mind's corporeality from its causal power.

39 If this is, in fact, her analysis. Her discussion is not entirely clear. She rejects Sedley's "radically emergent self" but says Epicurus is no "reductivist," since facts about minds are not just appearances of facts about atoms. However, she says that in the end, for Epicurus, "it is a truth of physics that I *am* atoms" (Annas (1992) 129).

on this view of the mind, all of the causal 'heavy lifting' is done entirely at the atomic level, and the supervening properties are epiphenomenal.[40] One of Epicurus' key concerns is to defend the causal efficacy of the mental.

Or one can propose, as Sedley does, that mental properties do *not* supervene on the base atomic properties; instead, they are "radically emergent" because they gain causal independence from the atoms that constitute the mind and exert "downwards causation."[41] This interactionist property dualism obviously does not render the mental causally inert, but it conflicts with Lucretius' proof of the soul's corporeality. Lucretius writes:

> . . . when [the mind] is seen to drive forward the limbs, to arouse the body from sleep, to change the countenance, to rule and sway the whole man, *and we see that none of these things can be done without touch [tactus],* and further, that there is no touch without body, – must we not confess that mind and spirit have a bodily nature?
>
> (*DRN* 3 161–167)

Like Epicurus, Lucretius believes that only bodies can act or be acted upon, but he adds that the reason for this is that all action and reaction must occur *by touch,* and that only bodies can touch and be touched. Lucretius thus specifies the type of causal interaction that bodies have, and it is exactly what we would expect in a universe composed of bits of stuff flying through space: the bodies bang into one another, bounce off one another, become entangled with one another, *etc.* All action is by means of touch.[42] On this theory, there would be no way for 'radically emergent properties' to 'reach down' and move individual atoms.[43]

I am glossing Lucretius' statement that a body cannot be moved *without touch* as saying that bodies must be moved *by means of touch.*

40 Noted by Sedley (1988*a*) 316 ff. The same sort of objection can be lodged against the version of anti-reductionism ascribed to Epicurus in Mitsis (1988) chapter 4 . I am here assuming that, for Epicurus, not only is the mind causally efficacious, but so are mental states and processes, such as desiring something, perceiving a nearby animal, *etc.* See Kim (1989) for an argument against supervenience theories on the basis that they render the mental causally inert.

41 Sedley (1988*a*) 320–322. He says that these mental properties reverse the normal "direction of causation," because, although they arise out of a certain atomic configuration, they "act upon the atoms" and are "genuinely free of antecedent mechanical causation," *i.e.*, how they behave is not determined by the states of the atoms.

42 'Touch' here also involves things *striking* one another; a piece of void 'touching' an atom is not 'touch' in this sense. Part of what makes atoms casually efficacious is their resistance to blows, contrasted with the yielding of void. See *Ep. Hdt.* 67. Void cannot act or be acted upon; it only allows bodies to move through it. See Berryman (1997), who argues that no ancient thinkers believe void (actual or potential) has any mysterious 'attractive power.'

43 See Purinton (1999) pp. 286–288 for a similar complaint against Sedley.

A different way of interpreting this passage is that he is asserting that there is no action at a distance – *i.e.*, that things that causally interact must be spatially contiguous. If this interpretation were correct, the passage would not damage Sedley's thesis of radical emergence. However, this reading is too weak. Even Plato's incorporeal soul could be in contact with the body with which it interacts, since Plato never makes lack of spatial location a defining feature of soul, unlike Descartes. And for Aristotle, an animal's soul has a location, although it is not a body, and thus its activity would not violate a "no action at a distance" dictum. Since Lucretius wants his argument to *exclude* such conceptions of soul, he must mean more by the phrase "we see that none of these things can be done without touch" than simply "there is no action at a distance."[44] This is further confirmed by his observation that there cannot be touch without body. Non-bodily things can be spatially contiguous, but cannot move things by means of touch. Within the Epicurean system, void would be an example of this.[45]

4.2 *Epicurus' main anti-fatalist argument in* On Nature *25*

If the argument of the previous section is successful, then our presumption when examining the arguments in *On Nature* 25 should be that Epicurus has a reductionist philosophy of mind, since the other texts we have, which are much clearer than *On Nature* 25, strongly indicate that this is Epicurus' position. Since Sedley's work, two long passages from *On Nature* 25 have received a great deal of scrutiny. In this section, I look at the passage that contains Epicurus' self-refutation argument against fatalism, and in the next, I examine the passage that gives an account of human psychological development and the relationship between psychological phenomena and the atoms that constitute the mind.

Any interpretation of *On Nature* 25 must involve a great deal of conjecture: the text is badly preserved and gappy. Also, it is full of contorted Greek and unexplained technical terminology. Fortunately, my view of the role of the swerve in preserving human freedom, and Epicurus' overall theory of freedom, is mainly based on other texts and does not depend crucially on wringing an exact meaning incontrovertibly

44 The dictum "no action at a distance" is a commonplace in ancient Greek philosophy, assented to by almost all thinkers who have any stance on it. The first philosopher to clearly dissent from it is the neo-Platonist Iamblichus. (See Simplicius *On the Categories* 9 302 28–303. 6 and Hankinson (1998) 428–429.)

45 Stephen Everson argues along similar lines about some of these passages; see Everson (1999) 550–552.

out of these obscure passages. All I need to show is that these sections of *On Nature* 25 can be construed quite plausibly along lines consistent with my overall interpretation. Finally, I should note that the swerve is mentioned nowhere in these passages. Anyone who wishes to insert the swerve into Epicurus' anti-fatalist argument or his account of human psychological development will, at best, be engaged in a speculative reconstruction based upon what seems to be plausible.

In book 25 of *On Nature,* Epicurus attempts to show that somebody who argues for the thesis that all things occur 'of necessity' (κατ' ἀνάγκην) refutes himself. This passage is sometimes called Epicurus' "anti-determinist" argument.[46] I prefer to call it his "anti-fatalist" argument, because this avoids prejudging important interpretative issues. The person who thinks that all things occur of necessity is contrasted with one who thinks that some things "depend on us." The target of this argument denies that our decisions make any difference: what we do is not an *aition,* a cause or explanation, of what happens. This position is better called *fatalism,* and it is a further question whether Epicurus in this passage is arguing that causal determinism entails fatalism.[47]

Here is the argument:[48]

[A] (1) From the very outset we always have seeds, some directing us towards these, some towards those, some towards these *and* those, actions and thoughts and characters, in greater and smaller numbers. Consequently that which we

46 For instance, in Long and Sedley (1987) vol. 1 p. 108.

47 cf. *Ep. Men.* 134, where Epicurus says it is impossible to fight the ἀνάγκη of the natural philosophers.

48 Arr. 34.26–30. This passage appears in Long and Sedley (1987) as 20C. The numbering is Long and Sedley's. The translation and supplements are largely Sedley's, but I have made a few changes:

(1) In Long and Sedley, κατ' ἀνάγκην is sometimes rendered as "necessitated." I translate it with the more literal (and vague) "of necessity." I believe the term "necessitated" has overtones of *causal* necessity, which I want to avoid, since in what follows I will be asking what it means to say that everything occurs κατ' ἀνάγκην.

(2) Sometimes Sedley translates παρ' ἡμᾶς as "up to us." I follow Annas and translate it with "depends on us." Annas notes that in this usage the preposition παρά is much weaker than ἐπί, and that Epicurus does not use ἐπί with the dative with the meaning "up to us," but commonly uses παρ' ἡμᾶς, *e.g.*, in *Ep. Men.* 133 (Annas (1993) 55–56 and n. 12). Annas thinks this use of παρά instead of ἐπί indicates that Epicurus wants simply to defend the "intuitive" idea that we are agents, and that he "seems not to want to defend a very strong and possibly unintuitive version of the idea" (Annas (1992) 129). I am not certain how strongly the use of παρά instead of ἐπί does suggest this. Insofar as it does, this usage is grist for my mill.

(3) The other phrases which Epicurus uses to say that certain things depend on us are δι' ἡμῶν αὐτῶν ("through us ourselves" or "arising from us ourselves") and ἐξ ἡμῶν αὐτῶν ("from us ourselves"). Sedley translates both as "our own agency," which I think has overtones of libertarian agent-causation in a way which Epicurus' own phrases do not. I have changed the translation

develop – characteristics of this or that kind – depends on us at some time absolutely (ἁπλῶς), and the things which of necessity (κ[α]τ' ἀνάγκην) flow in through our passages from that which surrounds us at one stage depend on us (παρ' ἡμᾶς) and depend upon beliefs of our own making. If against (?) the nature . . . *(Lacuna of approx. 60 words, a few fragmentary lines I do not include here, and another lacuna of approx. 12 words)* (2) . . .by which we never cease to be affected, the fact that we rebuke, oppose and reform each other as if the responsibility (τὴν αἰτίαν) lay also in ourselves, and not just in our original constitution (ἀρχῆς συστάσει) and in the accidental necessity (κατὰ τὸ αὐτόματον ἀνάγκηι) of that which surrounds and penetrates us. (3) For if someone were to attribute to the very processes of rebuking and being rebuked the accidental necessity of whatever happens to be present to oneself at the time, I am afraid that he can never in this way understand <his own behavior in continuing the debate> . . . *(lacuna of a few words)* (4) <He may simply choose to maintain his thesis while in practice continuing to> blame or praise. But if he were to act in this way he would be leaving intact the very same behavior which as far as our own selves are concerned creates the preconception of our own responsibility. And we would understand that the theory was altered <. . .> *(a few fragmentary letters, and another lacuna of approx. 45 words)* (5) <. . .> such error. For this sort of account is self refuting, and can never prove that everything is of the kind called 'of necessity;' but he debates this very question on the assumption that his opponent is himself responsible (δι' ἑαυτοῦ) for talking nonsense. (6) And even if he goes on to infinity saying that *this* action of his is in turn of necessity, always appealing to arguments, he is not reasoning it empirically (οὐκ ἐπιλογίζεται) so long as he goes on imputing to himself the responsibility for having reasoned correctly and to his opponent that for having reasoned incorrectly. (7) But unless he were to stop attributing his action to himself and to pin it on necessity instead, he would not even <be consistent . . .> *(lacuna approx. 30 words)* (8) <On the other hand,> if in using the word 'necessity' of that which we say arises from us ourselves (τὸ δι' ἡμῶν αὐτῶν) he is merely changing a name, and won't prove that we have a preconception of a kind which has faulty delineations when we call what's from us ourselves responsible, neither his own <behavior nor that of others will be affected. . .>. (*lacuna approx. 25 words)* (9) <. . .> but even to call necessitation empty as a result of your claim. If someone won't explain this, and has no auxiliary element or impulse in us which he might dissuade from those

accordingly, for example, translating τὸ δι' ἡμῶν αὐτῶν as "what's from us ourselves," at the expense of making it uglier, but I hope less tendentious.

(4) Laursen has made several small emendations to the text after further study of the papyrus (Laursen (1988)). I have incorporated most of these changes and altered the translation accordingly; see the Greek text in the Appendix for details.

(5) Sedley translates αἰτία as 'responsibility.' I retain this translation, but I want to note that αἰτία more basically means 'cause' or 'explanation,' and I think Epicurus is here primarily talking about ourselves being *causally* responsible for what we do, not *morally* responsible, although the two are connected.

The complete Greek text, in all of its badly-preserved, conjectural glory, is in the Appendix.

> actions which we perform, calling the responsibility for them 'what's from us ourselves' but is giving the name of foolish necessity to all the things which we claim to do calling the responsibility for them 'what's from us ourselves' he will merely be changing a name; (10) he will not be modifying any of our actions in the way in which in some cases the man who sees what sort of actions are of necessity regularly dissuades those who desire to do something in the face of compulsion. (11) And the mind will be inquisitive to learn what sort of action it should then consider that one to be which we perform in some way because of us ourselves but without desiring to. For he has no alternative but to say what sort of action is of necessity, <and what is not. . .> *(lacuna approx. 40 words)* (12) supremely unthinkable. But unless someone perversely maintains this, or makes it clear what fact he is rebutting or introducing, it is merely a word that is being changed, as I keep repeating.
>
> (13) The first men to give a satisfactory account of causes, men not only much greater than their predecessors but also, many times over, than their successors, turned a blind eye to themselves – although in many matters they had alleviated great ills – in order to hold necessity and accident responsible for everything. (14) Indeed, the actual account promoting this view came to grief when it left the great man blind to the fact that in his actions he was clashing with his doctrine; and that if it were not that a certain blindness to the doctrine took hold of him while acting he would be constantly perplexing himself; and that wherever the doctrine prevailed he would be falling into desperate calamities, while wherever it did not he would be filled with conflict because of the contradiction between his actions and his doctrine. (15) It is because this is so that the need also arises to explain the matter which I was discussing when I first embarked on this digression, lest some similar evil <befall us.>

This passage may usefully be divided into three main sections. First is a description of our responsibility for our own development (1). Next is the central self-refutation argument against those who deny that we are responsible for our own development and actions, instead saying that everything occurs 'of necessity' (2–7). Third, Epicurus considers a possible reply to the self-refutation argument (8–12). The end of the passage (13–15) makes it clear that Democritus is one of the targets of the preceding arguments.

4.2.1 Human self-development and wild animals

Sections (2)–(7) are the core of Epicurus' anti-fatalist argument. In order to understand it, however, we should look at the assertion in section (1) that the characteristics which we develop absolutely "depend on us." What does this mean, and what makes us able to control our own development? This may already seem to point towards some radically emergent faculty of will.

The contrast, I believe, is between humans, who can control their own development, and wild animals, which cannot. We have various potentialities, but how we develop is under our control. The clearest Epicurean statement of this doctrine is in Lucretius. Lions, Lucretius says, are naturally irascible because their souls contain many fire atoms, stags are timid because they have more wind atoms, *etc.* (*DRN* 3 288 ff). People also have natural temperaments: some tend to be easily moved to anger, while others are too fearful (*DRN* 3 307–319). These differences cannot be erased entirely, says Lucretius, but "so trivial are the traces of the different natures (*naturarum*) that remain, beyond reason's power to expel, that nothing hinders our living a life worthy of gods" (*DRN* 3 320–322). What allows humans to modify their natural temperaments is not some radically emergent self acting upon the atoms in a mysterious manner, but, Lucretius says, simply reason.

Other Epicurean authors also assert that it is our reasoning abilities that set us apart from animals. Hermarchus says that animals are not subject to justice because they do not have *logos.* We have civilization, he says, because we can reason about what is useful or follow others who can do so. People can calculate the outcomes of different possible courses of action, whereas animals have only 'irrational memory.'[49] According to Polystratus, animals are in general like people, but lack certain things: prudential concepts like 'healthy' and 'expedient,' ethical concepts like 'fine' and 'base,' and signs. He says that animals cannot take precautions before suffering something and cannot reflect on their lives as a whole and make them consistent.[50]

The doctrine that humans have reason (or certain types of reasoning) while wild animals do not is metaphysically neutral, however. To say that we can foresee various possible outcomes of our actions, can reflect on our character, and hence can shape ourselves in a way in which wild animals cannot, is consistent with any number of positions in the philosophy of mind.[51]

My thesis is that in section (1) of passage A, Epicurus states that our actions and characters are "absolutely dependent on us" because of our capacity to reason about the outcomes of our actions, and this capacity

49 Hermarchus, in Porphyry *de Abstin.* I 7–12, 26, 4.

50 These passages are discussed in Annas (1993) 66–69. My discussion of animal rationality follows hers.

51 Apart from eliminative materialism. That is, at least the proponents of these positions would themselves think that their position is consistent with humans having such abilities.

sets us apart from wild animals. An earlier passage of book 25 (here labeled [B]) helps corroborate this thesis.[52]

[B] If he, exactly because of the cause out of himself, goes in the direction of what is similar to the original constitution (ἀρχῆς συστάσει) which is bad, we occasionally criticize him even more – and not in the way in which we exonerate those animals which are wild by conflating their products (τὰ ἀπογεγε[ν]νημένα) and their constitution alike into a single thing, and indeed do not use either the admonitory and reformatory mode or the simply retaliatory mode.

This passage is discussing a person who has developed himself in the *wrong* way – in the direction of the "original constitution which is bad." The exact meaning of the phrase is not clear, but elsewhere Epicurus contrasts the 'original constitution' with the 'growing constitution' and the 'products' (ἀπογεγεννημένα – a key term which I discuss later). In humans, it makes sense to distinguish between our 'original constitution' (the temperament with which we are born), the way in which that constitution later grows, and the 'product,' which seems to mean certain types of psychological developments and which is key to moral responsibility. It is because humans are able to reason and change their characters ('the cause out of themselves') that we blame somebody who *fails* to develop properly and develops in the direction of the bad original constitution; *e.g.*, somebody who remains an impulsive hot-head. Conversely, we exonerate wild animals because we do not distinguish between their original temperament and what it develops into later, since they do not have the capacity to change their original constitution by reflecting on their own character.

Asserting that people are responsible for how they develop because they possess reason has neither anti-determinist nor anti-reductionist implications. Once we have the ability to use our reason to reflect on our congenital dispositions and modify them, this is sufficient on its own to save our current character from being 'internally necessitated' by our original constitution. *Pace* the 'internal cause' interpretation, having random swerves rearranging the atomic structure of the mind could not help make our character any more our own or any more reason-responsive.[53]

52 Arr. 34.25.21–34. It is printed in Long and Sedley vol. 2 as passage 20j; an updated text is in Laursen (1988), who includes some text not included by Long and Sedley. The translation is based upon Laursen's and Sedley's. The Greek text is in the Appendix.

53 See Bobzien (2000) 318–319. However, at Bobzien (2000) 325–7 Bobzien acknowledges that the efficacy of reason is central to this passage, without explaining how past swerves help preserve the causal efficacy of reason. See section 3.2 for more on the irrelevance of the swerve in this connection.

Nor is there any reason to think that causally determined reasoning is not itself causally effective or in some other way fails to be genuine reasoning.[54] Finally, nothing here implies that being able to give a physicalist account of human thought precludes giving an account of our development in terms of desires, the operation of reasons, *etc.*, especially since Epicurus identifies psychological states with physical ones.[55]

4.2.2 *The central anti-fatalist argument*

Thus, the way in which our characters 'depend on us' is compatible with a wide variety of positions about the relationship of the mind to the body. In (2)–(7) of passage A, Epicurus says that to offer an argument for the thesis that all of our actions are of necessity is self-refuting, because by doing so, the fatalist already presupposes the falsity of his thesis. Epicurus writes: "he debates this very question on the assumption that his opponent is himself responsible for talking nonsense. And even if he goes on to infinity saying that *this* action of his is in turn of necessity, always appealing to arguments, he is not reasoning it empirically so long as he goes on imputing to himself the responsibility for having reasoned correctly and to his opponent that for having reasoned incorrectly." The preconception of things being dependent on us, and not of necessity, is created by the practices of praising, blaming, and giving arguments. This may suggest to some that Epicurus believes, *à la* Kant, that notions of justified praise and blame already presuppose the falsity of determinism.[56]

But I think that this cannot be correct – after all, how would simply offering an argument for determinism presuppose that determinism is false? In section (1) of passage A, and in passage B, what makes things 'depend on us,' so that we have the 'cause out of ourselves,' is just the possession of reason. Epicurus is likely working with this same concept of how things 'depend on us' a few sentences later, when trying to refute the fatalist. When the fatalist says that our actions are of necessity, denying that the cause is 'in ourselves' (A 2), I take it that Epicurus believes such a position denies that our reasoning is efficacious. And to offer an *argument* which denies the efficacy of reasoning *does* seem self-refuting in a way in which offering an argument for determinism is not. The person who offers an argument must assume that he has *reasons* for his position ("appealing to arguments. . . he goes on imputing to

54 *Pace* Mitsis (1988) 150, 152.
55 *Pace* Mitsis (1988) 150–1.
56 *Grounding for the Metaphysics of Morals,* third section.

himself the responsibility/cause (αἰτία) for having reasoned correctly," A 6), and that his interlocutor has reason so that she can understand his arguments. Even if the proposition "human reason is not effective" is not self-contradictory – and even if to *assert* that proposition is not self-contradictory – to *argue* for it does seem to be self-refuting.[57] Epicurus' argument is like the following type of argument against eliminative materialism: to *offer reasoned arguments* for eliminative materialism, and to *believe* that it is superior to other theories, is incoherent, since the italicized folk-psychological terms are among the ones that are supposed to be eliminated, according to eliminative materialism.[58]

When Epicurus says that things 'depend on us' because our reasoning is causally efficacious, what this amounts to is still up for grabs: but the crucial point is that it still *is* up for grabs. Once again, Epicurus' argument is compatible with a wide variety of views about the mind. Annas puts this rightly: "We should note that this argument does *not* show that Epicurus is not a determinist. It shows that he thinks that, properly understood, determinism must be compatible with our commonsense understanding of ourselves and of the world."[59] Epicurus thinks it impossible to abandon our conception of ourselves as agents and be pragmatically consistent about it.[60] What we become is *not* determined by our natural temperaments, since we can reason about what is best and change ourselves. Nor is what we do determined by the environment, since how we respond to

57 For an interesting discussion of how Sextus Empiricus responds to such a charge, see McPherran (1987).

58 See Baker (1987), chapters 6 and 7, for an extended argument that denying our common-sense conception of the mental is self-defeating, and Heil (1992) 8–10 and Churchland (1988) 48 for brief summaries of this type of argument and different defenses of eliminative materialism against it. (Baker thinks that physicalism implies eliminativism, so by arguing against eliminativism, she is also arguing also against physicalism.) Lucretius gives a similar self-refutation argument against the skeptic in *DRN* 4 469 ff; see Burnyeat (1978) for a discussion of it. See also Llewellyn (1966) for an argument that it is incoherent to believe that 'pessimistic determinism' (basically, hard determinism) is rational to adopt; to adopt an 'objective attitude' (as P. F. Strawson puts it) towards all humans would be to abolish normative appraisals of them, but there is an inescapable normative element in thinking that people are justified in their beliefs, or that some beliefs are rational and others not. Epicurus may be making a similar point in *SV* 40: the person who ascribes all things to necessity has no grounds for criticizing the person who rejects that thesis, since his opponent's belief is itself (on this hypothesis) necessitated and hence not subject to censure.

59 Annas (1992) 128.

60 That is, it would be inconsistent if one thinks that this position can be justified by giving reasons in its favor, and that one can give reasons for behaving in one way rather than another. We can view Pyrrhonism as an attempt to show how we *can* consistently abandon our conception of ourselves as agents. See Burnyeat (1980) and Barnes (1982) for more on this issue.

the environment depends on our beliefs, and to this extent is up to us.[61] And to argue against this thesis already presupposes its truth.

4.2.3 *Is Epicurus' argument anti-reductionist, anti-determinist, or neither?*

The anti-fatalist argument from A 2–A 7, then, asserts only that it is self-refuting to argue against our conception of ourselves as rational agents. The key question is whether Epicurus believes that our *prolêpsis* (our preconception) of our own agency is incompatible with either reductionism or determinism. The argument from A 2–A 7 may be metaphysically neutral in itself, but it could still be part of an anti-reductionist or anti-determinist position if Epicurus thinks that the efficacy of our reasoning is incompatible with either reductionism or determinism.[62]

In passage A, Epicurus is responding to the supposed fatalist implications of Democritus' philosophy.[63] Although Epicurus does not make clear here why Democritus' philosophy has fatalist consequences, I believe that Epicurus thinks that it follows from Democritus' eliminativism. Many sources confirm that Epicurus thinks he needs to enrich Democritus' parsimonious ontology in order to avoid unpalatable skeptical difficulties. Democritus encounters these difficulties because he eliminates sensible qualities from the external world: we *think* that bodies have properties like sweetness and whiteness, but in reality, atoms and the void. Since sensible qualities are not real properties of bodies, he finds it hard to explain how the senses give us knowledge of the world (see section 4.1.2).

The situation is similar in ethics. Democritus thinks that, in reality, *only* atoms and void exist. Something like human rationality could not be admitted under his extremely restrictive ontology. We may *believe* that

61 And so, Epicurus' position on this matter is quite similar to Aristotle's on our character and action having an 'internal origin' (see sections 3.2–3.3). I believe that it is this sort of rational self-control that Epicurus is referring to at the end of A 1, when he says "the things which of necessity flow in through our passages from that which surrounds us are at one stage up to us and dependent upon beliefs of our own making." The Epicureans talk about the *epibolê tês dianoias,* the "focusing of the mind," to explain how we can respond differently to the information that we take in as compared to somebody else receiving the same information. For instance, Lucretius uses this to explain how we are able to focus on the image (*e.g.*, a person walking) that we need to in order to do what we want (*e.g.*, walking), out of the multitude of images constantly impinging on our mind.

62 For instance, Malcolm (1968) argues that having a complete neurophysiological theory which accounts for behavior would *exclude* explaining that behavior in purposive terms, because of the different logical natures of purposive and mechanistic explanations.

63 Although not mentioned by name, it is clear that the "first men to give a satisfactory account of causes, men not only greater than their predecessors but also. . .their successors. . ." (A 13–14) refers to Democritus and his followers.

our behavior is caused by our beliefs and desires, but, in reality, it is caused only by atoms interacting in the void. That the Epicureans think that Democritus' ontology had unacceptable consequences of this sort is supported by *Adv. Colot.* 1110e–f, in which Plutarch reports that the Epicurean Colotes accused Democritus of inadvertently excluding himself from his own ontology, hence making living according to his own philosophy impossible.[64]

Epicurus finds this conclusion unacceptable, and employs the argument in A 2–7 to show that the Democritean position (or any that would entail similar conclusions about our agency) cannot consistently be argued for. Epicurus does not think that Democritus himself drew these unacceptable consequences, nor, for my purposes, does it matter whether Epicurus is correct in supposing that Democritus' ontology entails an eliminativist philosophy of mind. What matters is that Epicurus *took* Democritus' ontology to have these consequences. Against Democritus, Epicurus wants to insist that human agency, human rationality, and moral development are all real. But Epicurus' objection to Democritus' eliminativism on ethical grounds is perfectly consistent with Epicurus being a reductionist about the mind and agency (see section 4.1.2).

We can put the Democritean argument that all human actions are necessitated as follows:

(1) Human actions are just movements of atoms.
(2) Movements of atoms are necessitated.
(3) Hence, human actions are necessitated.

As Annas explains, the Democritean argues that all human actions are really just motions of atoms, and thus are necessitated and not really 'up to us.' But Epicurus thinks that the Democritean's practice undermines his theory, and that one cannot consistently argue for such a conclusion.[65]

In passage A 8–12 Epicurus responds, in a revealing way, to a possible Democritean reply to his argument. I believe this response shows that Epicurus' argument is neither anti-determinist nor anti-reductionist. The

64 Plutarch agrees with Colotes, at 1111a and 1111e, that a consequence of Democritus' ontology is that mind (ψυχῆ) does not exist. See Purinton (1999) p. 287 n. 47 for more ancient sources on Democritus' spare ontology. However, this passage does not establish conclusively that Colotes thinks that Democritus' eliminativism excludes mind from his ontology, although that is how Plutarch reads him, and it seems to follow from Colotes' attribution to Democritus that "compound by convention." Colotes says Democritus would be unable to *conceive* of himself as a person. Thus, he might think that Democritus is unable to know this, given Democritus' skepticism.

65 Annas (1992) 127.

Democritean says that, because all of our thoughts and actions are ultimately atomic, what we do is 'of necessity.' Epicurus first tries to show that this position is self-refuting, because in the act of offering an argument for the fatalist position, the Democritean already presupposes its falsity. We praise, blame, and argue with others on the assumptions that we can reason, our interlocutor can reason, and we can change his behavior by offering arguments; all this is incompatible with fatalism.

The Democritean, however, seems to have an obvious counter-argument: just because our actions are necessitated does not imply that practices of praise, blame, and debate are ineffective. We may be the sorts of creatures who necessarily act in such a way that rational considerations can play a role in determining what we do. Epicurus' response is that this counter-argument misses the point – the relevant sense of 'necessity' in this context has to do with the distinction between actions that are under our rational control and those that are not, and has nothing to do with the general determinist hypothesis. As long as the fatalist does not challenge *this* distinction, he has not shown that what we do occurs 'of necessity.' We have standards by which we delineate which actions are of necessity and which ones depend on us. Epicurus says that we show this in our actions, since we try to dissuade one another from actions that 'depend on us,' while it would be pointless to do so for those that are of necessity (A 9–12). For instance, we can do nothing about the fact that we will die – it is necessary. What is not necessary is to fear death, since, through Epicurean therapy, we can come to understand death properly and no longer fear it. The former is not dependent on us, while the latter is.

Importantly, Epicurus nowhere in this passage says that, in order for an action to depend on us, it must not be antecedently caused. Nor does he say that, in order for an action to depend on us, it must not be subject to the necessity to which atomic motions are subject. He concentrates on the ways in which, because we are rational, we can say that certain things are 'under our control.' What if the Democritean admits that, in the ordinary sense, some things 'depend on us' but still wants to maintain that all of our actions are necessitated? Epicurus' reply here is the sort of reply offered by a compatibilist. As long as the Democritean does not challenge the ordinary distinctions that we make about certain things being under our rational control and others not, his thesis that everything is of necessity is empty. When we say that something is ἀνάγκη for us, we mean that we have no control over it. To say that something is ἀνάγκη for us but that we still have control over it is to misuse the term – to "call necessitation empty" (A 9). Our preconception of our own agency is formed by observing things like our ability to dissuade others from acting who desire to do something because they are being threatened (for example, persuading someone not to betray his friend even when he is being compelled to do so by threats) (A 10), and to do something without desiring to do it (so-called 'mixed actions,' as described in *NE* 3 1, *e.g.*, undergoing some pain now in order to avoid a greater pain in the future). In order to show that all of our actions are according to ἀνάγκη, the Democritean would have to show that things that we thought were under our rational control really are not – he would need to "prove that we have a preconception of a kind which has faulty delineations"[66] (A 8). I believe that it is this thesis – that nothing is under our rational control and that our reasoning is causally inert – which Epicurus calls "supremely unthinkable," and which "unless somebody perversely maintains this, or makes it clear what fact he is rebutting or introducing, it is merely a word that is being changed" (A 12).

In responding to this objection, Epicurus shows that he thinks that the Democritean argument fails because of an equivocation on the term "necessitated" in steps (2) and (3). Epicurus rejects the argument as invalid. Inferring that human action is all "of necessity" because all atomic motions are necessitated would be fallacious, so he has no reason to reject either the reductionist premise (1) or the determinist premise (2).

Thus, Epicurus can *grant* the Democritean thesis that all human actions are movements of atoms while still denying that all of our actions are subject to ἀνάγκη. Even if, in *some* sense, all actions are subject to ἀνάγκη, as long as our preconception of there being a distinction between what is under our rational control and what is not is not itself threatened (A 8), this would not undermine our conception of our own responsibility and show that everything is subject to ἀνάγκη in the *relevant* sense. In *Ep. Men.* 133, Epicurus says that what is ἀνάγκη is that which is ἀνυπεύθυνος – 'unanswerable' or 'beyond human control' – and he contrasts this with what is παρ' ἡμᾶς, which is ἀδέσποτος – without master' or 'autonomous.' This position is best compared to the 'ordinary usage' argument about human freedom advanced by, for example, A. J. Ayer. Ayer says that, in order to determine whether human beings are free, we must look at the ordinary usage of terms and phrases like 'freedom,' 'could have

66 Epicurus is here relying on his doctrine of προλήψεις, or "preconceptions." Some basic concepts, like 'person' and 'body,' must be the basis of further inquiry and not themselves require demonstration, on pain of infinite regress. See Asmis (1984) 19–80 for an extended discussion of the nature of προλήψεις.

done otherwise,' and the like, and to say that our actions are 'determined' or 'necessitated' is irrelevant to questions of human freedom, unless it can be shown how this conflicts with our ordinary ways of determining cases of free versus unfree action.[67]

And so, Epicurus' central anti-fatalist argument is neither anti-reductionist nor anti-determinist. To deny the reality of the mind and its properties, which the Epicurean Colotes claims is a consequence of Democritus' ontology, is not reductionist, but eliminativist.[68] So it is a mistake to think of Epicurus as a non-reductionist trying to resist the unpalatable epistemological and ethical consequences of Democritus' reductionism. The discussion of the nature of the mind in Lucretius and *Ep. Hdt.* shows that Epicurus is a reductionist in that he regards the mind as nothing more than a group of atoms (see section 4.1.3). But he is trying to find plausible ways of accounting for phenomena like colors (section 4.1.2) and reason (section 4.3) within his reductionist materialism in order to resist the unpalatable epistemological and ethical consequences of Democritean *eliminativist* materialism.

Epicurus does object to determinism. But in *this* context, Epicurus appears to be targeting Democritus' eliminativism, which is also well-attested, rather than his determinism. If Epicurus thinks that a result of Democritus' metaphysics is that the mind and reason are not real, it is obvious how this would have the unacceptable consequences he discusses earlier in the self-refutation argument, whereas it would not be clear how Epicurus would think fatalism follows from Democritus' determinism. But secondly, if my analysis above of Epicurus' reply to the possible Democritean objection is correct, this shows that here at least, Epicurus is not directly concerned with causal determinism as such.

4.3 Psychological development and freedom of action

Epicurus' central anti-fatalist argument in book 25 of *On Nature,* then, offers no support for the view that Epicurus is either anti-reductionist or anti-determinist. His insistence that we are rational agents who can control our own developments and are thus responsible carries little metaphysical baggage beyond the rejection of Democritean eliminativism. In fact, his answer to the possible Democritean response to his argument

67 A. J. Ayer, "Freedom and Necessity," in Ayer (1954) 271–284.
68 *Adv. Colot.* 1110e–f, 1111a and 1111e.

offered in A 8–12 appears more at home in a compatibilist than a libertarian theory of freedom.

This picture of Epicurus' philosophy of mind and action is confirmed – or at least, it is not disconfirmed – by another passage from book 25 of *On Nature,* which deals with psychological development. This passage is even more difficult to decipher than Epicurus' anti-fatalist argument. It is here that Sedley "clearly" discerns the notion of downward causation in Epicurus. Indeed, it contains several sentences that may initially seem to assert a causal independence of the self and its psychological states from the atoms, or at least their non-reducibility. However, when looked at closely, nothing that Epicurus says here conflicts with an identity theory of mind, or indeed with causal determinism. Instead, this passage, although difficult, is most plausibly interpreted as trying to show how the reality and causal efficacy of psychological states can be accommodated within a reductionist materialism. The passage follows:[69]

[C] (0) (not only. . .) coming about in accordance with the (atoms) thrust together, but also the (atoms) thrust together, evidently, in the same way. For they had the capacity, if thrust together, to produce such things and such . . . the same (atoms?) in accordance with the manner "from the same distance" (κα[τὰ] τὸν [ἀ]π[ὸ] τοῦ αὐτο[ῦ δ]ιαστήματος τρόπον) <. . .>*Lacuna of a few words* <. . .> come about in the aforementioned manner and be productive of the same things. (1) Many (products) capable of producing both this and that do not produce them, because of themselves (δι' ἑαυτὰ) and not because of the same cause in the atoms and themselves (οὐ διὰ τὴν αὐτὴν αἰτίαν τῶν τε ἀτόμων καὶ ἑαυτῶν). (2) These (products) are therefore a main target of our attacks and criticisms, because we . . . behave in accordance with the original disturbed nature (κατὰ τὴν ἐξ ἀρχῆς [τα]ραχώδη φύσιν), as is the case with animals as a whole. (3) For the nature of the atoms never did help them in any way to (perform) certain acts or to (develop) certain dimensions of acts and dispositions, but the products themselves were fully or for the most part responsible for these particulars (αὐτὰ τὰ ἀπογεγεννημένα τὴν πᾶσα[ν ἢ] τὴν πλε[ί]στην κέκ[τ]ητ[αι] αἰτίαν τῶνδέ τ[ι]νων), (4) and out of that (the nature of the atoms or the cause) some of the atoms move disturbing movements, not as a whole because of the atoms, but because of what comes in from the environment into the natural . . . the original constitution of the atoms being the cause . . . aggregate . . . out of the product itself unless . . . all . . .

69 Arr. 34.21. The translation is Laursen's, with minor modifications. The text and translation are in L&S 20B; however, Laursen examined the papyri and restored previously indiscernible pieces of text, so their texts differ, and the section numbered (0) here is not printed in Long and Sedley. The numbering otherwise follows Long and Sedley.

Lacuna of about 20 words

attacking and criticizing at the same time of the human beings, something that is in contrast to the cause in this same "necessary" manner. (5) Consequently, whenever something is produced that takes on some otherness from the atoms (ἑτερότητ[α τῶ]ν ἀτόμων) in a differential way (κατά τ[ινα] τρόπον διαληπτικόν), not in the way as from another distance (??) (ἀφ' ἑτέρου διαστήματος), it/he acquires the cause out of it/himself; (6) then it/he gives it on immediately (αναδίδωσιν εὐθὺς) until it comes to the first natures (τῶν πρώτων φύσεων) and in some way makes all of it (?) one (μίαν πως ἅπασαν αὐτὴ[ν] ποιεῖ). (7) Hence, clearly, those who cannot distinguish these things correctly put themselves in a winter storm as to the explanation of these causes, and in these same things we attack and criticize some more, some less.

The main subject of this passage is human psychological development, which is crucial for attributions of responsibility. The term ἀπογεγεννημένα is key here. Epicurus seems to be using it in a technical way. Since it is simply a participle of the verb (ἀπο)γεννᾶν, "to produce," Laursen translates the term as "products."[70] These "products" are the subject of praise and blame, and are also responsible for the particular ways in which a person acts and develops. The passage also refers to "the original nature" (ἡ ἐξ ἀρχῆς φύσις) and the "original constitution" (ἡ ἐξ ἀρχῆς σύστασις). As noted before, these seem to refer to the original dispositions that a person has. This passage describes somebody *failing* to overcome these dispositions. Laursen notes that the terms "original nature" and "original constitution" seem to be interchangeable.[71]

Two sets of questions about this passage need to be answered. First, in what sense are these products 'other' than the atoms? How should we understand Epicurus' claim that they are other in a 'differential way,' and how is this not the distinction 'as from another distance'? Are they distinct in a way inconsistent with an identity theory of mind? Second,

70 Laursen (1988) 10. Sedley translates the term as "developments." I follow Sedley (and most other interpreters) here and assume that the 'products' are mental states of some sort. Purinton argues (Purinton (1996) and Purinton (1999) 290–291) that the ἀπογεγεννημένα are *agents*. Purinton usually translates αἰτία as "responsibility" and argues that, since Epicurus attributes responsibility to the ἀπογεγεννημένα, the ἀπογεγεννημένα are probably agents, since "responsibility is more naturally predicated of agents rather than mental states or events." (Purinton (1996) 160). I am not convinced. It is not much of a strain to attribute responsibility to mental states; *e.g.*, "Hal's anger was to blame for his hitting Jim." Also, ἀπογεγεννημένα would be an odd term to use to refer to agents. (See section 4.3.2 below: my second reason for doubting that the phrase πρώτων φύσεων refers to atoms applies here, also.) In any case, I need not settle this dispute: everything that I argue for *vis-à-vis* the relationship between the products and the atoms that constitute the mind would apply just as well, *mutatis mutandis*, if one takes ἀπογεγεννημένα to be referring to agents.

71 Laursen (1988) 10.

what sort of causal power do these products possess, and how does this causal power relate to the causal power of the atoms that constitute the mind? Does anything Epicurus says here imply that the products gain some sort of causal independence from the atoms and even move individual atoms from the 'top down'? If my arguments above have been successful, our presumption when approaching this difficult passage should be to interpret it in a way consistent with a reductionist materialism: these psychological 'products' would be some sort of complicated atomic structure in the person's mind, which would allow him to do things he otherwise would be unable to do, but in a way explicable by referring to the atoms that compose the mind and their relationships to one another.

4.3.1 *The distinctiveness of the "product"*

Epicurus cryptically describes the relationship between the 'products' and the atoms in C 5 in the phrase ἐπειδὰν ἀπογεννηθῇι τι λαμβάνον τινὰ ἑτερότητα τῶν ἀτόμων κατά τινα τρόπον διαληπτικόν, οὐ τὸν ὡς ἀφ' ἑτέρου διαστήματος ("Whenever something is produced that takes on some otherness from the atoms in a differential way, not in the way as from another distance. . .") Epicurus talks both about the manner (*tropos*) in which the products do *not* differ from the atoms[72] – the manner 'as from a different distance' – and the manner in which they *do* differ–a 'differential' (*dialêptikos*) way. Let us deal with each in turn.

Purinton suggests that the manner 'as from a different distance' means being at different *spatial intervals*. That is, this manner of 'otherness' involves being at a different *location, e.g.*, the way in which two billiard balls differ.[73] Epicurus is saying that the products and the atoms do not differ in this manner, since the products and atoms *occupy the same space.* Purinton points to the beginning of the passage (C 0), which says that the atoms, when forced together, beget things "in a way which is from the *same* distance."[74] Purinton says this sentence is asserting, without the double negation, just what the phrase οὐ τὸν ὡς ἀφ' ἑτέρου

72 In fact, as Laursen (1988) 12 points out, it is not even entirely obvious from the text that the products differ *from* the atoms. The genitive of τῶν ἀτόμων can either be an ablative genitive of comparison, as Long and Sedley take it (and as I have translated it above), in which case the products differ *from* the atoms, or a simple subjective genitive, in which case the products differ *within* the atoms. Thus, Laursen translates this phrase as "whenever something is produced that takes on some sort of otherness *within* the atoms." The ablative genitive seems more natural here than the subjective genitive does, but either fits in with my understanding of the products' distinctiveness.

73 A good example of διάστημα being used to mean a determinate spatial interval is Aristotle, *De Caelo* 1.5 271b26–272a7.

74 Purinton (1999) 293.

διαστήματος is: the product of the atoms being squeezed together (as the fine atoms that compose the mind are, for instance, when confined in the container of the body) occupies the same location as do the atoms themselves.[75]

That simply says the way in which the product does *not* differ from the atoms, however, and still leaves open the question of how it *does* differ. Epicurus says that it differs in a *dialêptikos*, or 'differential' way. Sedley claims that it is tempting to translate *dialêptikos* as "transcendent," but the word considered on its own has no connotations of transcendence. It is simply the adjective formed from the noun διάληψις, which means "difference" or "distinction."[76]

I believe that a passage elsewhere in book 25 of *On Nature* specifies a way in which things can be distinguished which is perfectly compatible with a reductive materialism, and that it is this type of distinction between the products and the atoms that Epicurus is referring to in C 5. According to that passage: "We could talk about this particular thing not just *qua* (*hêi*) aggregate, but also *qua* atoms and *qua* moving atoms or aggregate, not speaking only of the moving itself."[77] Annas explains that the point is that we can discuss one and the same thing in different ways, and "if we use the *qua*-locution we shall not get confused."[78]

Thus, Epicurus recognizes that we can distinguish between different 'things' in thought which are in reality all aspects of a single thing. We *can* distinguish the product from the atoms that make up the product,

75 Sedley thinks that the phrase contrasts the way in which the self differs from the atoms with the way in which colors differ from atoms: colors differ only in the way of "viewing from a different distance." In the case of colors, individual atoms are not colored, but collections of atoms can be: that is the way of (viewing) from a different distance; it is only a difference "of scale, one between macroscopic and microscopic analysis." The self differs from the atoms in a more fundamental way, says Sedley; it is *radically* emergent, whereas colors and other accidental attributes are epiphenomenal (Long and Sedley (1987) vol. I 110). But this is extremely conjectural: the word "viewing" is supplied by Sedley, and absent clear evidence elsewhere that the phrase means this, Sedley reads too much into it.

76 Long and Sedley (1987) vol. I p. 110. The objection to this proposal is made in Purinton (1999) 294.

77 Arr. 34.11.1–7 The Greek:

οὐ μό-]
[νο]ν ἧι ἄθρο[ισ]μα τόδε τ[ι]
[ἂ]ν προσαγο[ρε]ύσαιμε[ν,]
ἀλλὰ καὶ ἧ͂ ἀτόμους καὶ
ἧι κινουμένας ἀτόμους
ἢ ἄθροισμα, καὶ μὴι μό-
νον αὐτὸ τὸ κα[τα]κινεῖσ-
θαι λέγοντα.

78 Annas (1993) 59. The translation of the passage is hers.

but this does not imply that the development is something non-atomic. Indeed, if Purinton is right, the phrase οὐ τὸν ὡς ἀφ' ἑτέρου διαστήματος specifically warns us against thinking of the product as another *thing* in a different location. Instead, to say that the product differs from the atoms in a *dialêptikos* manner simply means that we can focus on the specific features of the atomic aggregate that are distinctive of ἀπογεγεννημένα, such as rationality.

Epicurus' use of the phrase κατά τινα τρόπον διαληπτικόν supports this interpretation. The Greek word from which διαληπτικός is derived, διάληψις, can mean simply a distinction of parts,[79] but, as do many words that come from the verb λαμβάνω, to grasp, it often has overtones of some sort of *mental* grasp.[80] διάληψις can also mean "distinguishing in thought," "judgment," or "opinion." The way in which I interpret this τρόπος διαληπτικός closely parallels the way Epicurus uses the term διάληψις in *Ep. Hdt.* 69, where he says that the permanent attributes of a body can each be distinguished, even though they are not separable. When discussing the ontological status of the permanent attributes of a body (*e.g.*, size and shape), Epicurus says that they cannot exist *per se*, are not non-existent, and are not 'parts' in the way smaller bits and pieces are parts of larger bodies. He then adds, "These things have all their own individual ways of being focused on and distinguished (διαλήψεις), yet always in close accompaniment with the aggregate and in no way separated from it. . ."

Thus, the phrase ἐπειδὰν ἀπογεννηθῆι τι λαμβάνον τινὰ ἑτερότητα τῶν ἀτόμων κατά τ[ινα] τρόπον διαληπτικόν probably means that something takes on the sort of otherness in which we can distinguish between the product and the atoms in thought, even though the product is simply an aspect of the aggregate of atoms and, as Epicurus is careful to remind us, the two are not in different locations. I would translate the phrase as follows: "Whenever something is produced that takes on some otherness from the atoms in a (mentally) distinguishable way, not in the way as when things are at different spatial locations."[81]

79 For example, in *Progression of Animals* 705a25, where Aristotle claims that animals without parts are unable to move.

80 For instance, the Epicurean technical term *prolêpsis*, or "preconception," the Stoics' "kataleptic impressions," the supposedly infallible impressions that are the foundation for knowledge, and Epicurus' use of *perilêpsis* in *Ep. Hdt.* 40 to designate a kind of mental grasping or comprehension.

81 Purinton suggests another alternative that avoids radical emergence. He takes the phrase as being a verbal repetition with no significance in itself, *i.e.*, "It is different from the atoms in accordance with a certain way of being different" (Purinton (1999) 294). But because Epicurus means to

4.3.2 The causal power of the "product"

Three phrases in passage *C* discuss the causal power of the product. The most important occurs in sections C 5 and C 6, where Epicurus says, whenever a product arises that differs from the atoms in a differential way, "it/he acquires the cause out of it/himself; (6) then it/he gives it on immediately until it comes to the first natures and in some way makes all of it (?) one." The second phrase is in section (C 3): "For the nature of the atoms never did help them in any way to (perform) certain acts or to (develop) certain dimensions of acts and dispositions, but the products themselves were fully or for the most part responsible for these particulars." The third phrase is in (C 1): "Many (products) capable of producing both this and that do not produce them, because of themselves and not because of the same cause in the atoms and themselves." Let us look at each phrase in turn.

(1) The product and the "first natures"

The first phrase we shall examine is ...ἰσχάνε[ι] τὴν ἐξ [ἑ]αυτοῦ αἰτίαν· εἶτα αναδίδωσιν εὐθὺς μέχρι τῶν πρώτων φύσεων καὶ μίαν πως ἅπασαν αὐτὴ[ν] ποιεῖ. ("it/he acquires the cause out of it/himself; (6) then it/he gives it on immediately until it comes to the first natures and in some way makes all of it (?) one.") This phrase comes immediately after the description of the products taking on some otherness from the atoms κατά τ[ινα] τρόπον διαληπτικόν.

What does Epicurus mean here by the "first natures?" One proposal is that the "first natures" in question are *atoms*. However, I think it is much more likely that the phrase "first *natures*" is interchangeable with the phrase "first *constitutions*," and that both refer to the original, congenital dispositions of our souls which we can overcome through reason, which is the "cause out of ourselves," as discussed above. I have three reasons to believe this:

First, as Laursen says, the contrast made throughout this passage is between our original/first constitution and the later developments. The term σύστασις ('constitution') is often qualified by the terms ἐξ ἀρχῆς, πρώτη and ἐπαυξομένη (the 'original,' 'first,' and 'growing' constitution). Laursen notes that ἡ ἐξ ἀρχῆς σύστασις seems to be identical with ἡ ἐξ ἀρχῆς φύσις ('the original constitution' and 'the original nature'). For example, in C 2, Epicurus talks about how we especially criticize those

contrast the τρόπος διαληπτικός with the way of being in a different location, this seems unlikely, since being in a different location is a "certain way of being different."

who behave in accordance with the "original, disturbed *nature*," whereas in B 1–2 he says we especially criticize a person who "goes in a direction similar to the original *constitution* which is bad." Given the apparent interchangeability of the phrases ἡ ἐξ ἀρχῆς σύστασις and ἡ ἐξ ἀρχῆς φύσις, I think that the "first natures" are really the same as the "first constitutions," just as the *original* constitution and the *original* nature are interchangeable.

Secondly, the phrase "the first natures" is quite rare in Epicurus' extant writings. It occurs only twice other than in C 6. Both occurrences are also from *On Nature,* in passages that are too fragmentary for us to determine confidently what the referent of the phrase is supposed to be – in fact, in one case, it is far from clear that the phrase really is "first natures" (8 of the 12 letters are supplied by the editor).[82] If τὰς πρώτας φύσεις were a stand-in for "the atoms," we would expect it to appear more often, whereas if it is a piece of semi-technical terminology referring to "the first dispositions of the soul," then we would expect it only to appear in this section of *On Nature* and other similarly technical passages, just as the other numerous semi-technical phrases which occur often in this rebarbative passage but which are present very sparingly elsewhere in the extant writings of Epicurus (ἐξ ἀρχῆς σύστασις, πρώτη σύστασις, *etc.*).

Finally, the way in which Lucretius uses the word *natura* in a similar context supports this interpretation. As I pointed out before, the clearest parallel exposition of the process of psychological development that we have described in these three passages from *On Nature* 25 is Lucretius' discussion of the possibility of moral progress. When describing this possibility, Lucretius uses the plural of *natura,* the natural Latin equivalent of the Greek term φύσις, to name the various congenital

82 The passages:
Arr. 26.24.1–5

γωνιότη[τος]....α-
λει, ἀλλὰ τῆς καὶ πε-
ρὶ τὰ[ς] πρώτας φύσε[ις]
δυναμένης ἂν ὑπά [ρ-]
χειν.. ν. χ... ρο ....

Arr. 30.7.1–6

]ων περὶ τὰς π[ρώ-]
[τας φύσ]εις ὑπαρχόντω[ν]
[καὶ ἐξ] ὧν αἱ διάφοροι συγ-
[κρὶσεις γ]ὶνονται˙ τὸ δὴ μὴ
[παρέχειν τὴ]ν ὁμοιομέρει[αν]
].... νει – – – –

dispositions that reason can overcome: "so trivial are the traces of *natures* that remain *(adeo naturarum vestiga linqui parvola)* beyond reason's power to expel, that nothing hinders our living a life worthy of gods." (*DRN* 3 320–322) Earlier, Lucretius uses the plural of *natura* to describe how the various natures and habits of people differ (*DRN* 3 314-315). Given the parallel between Lucretius' subject in this passage to Epicurus' subject in *On Nature* 25, the fact that Lucretius uses of the plural of *natura* to refer to our congenital dispositions makes it likely that Epicurus is also using the plural of φύσις to describe our congenital dispositions.

Thus, Epicurus is saying that, once a product acquires the "cause out of itself" – which is reason – it is able to go as far as to reform one's congenital dispositions.[83] Normally, people exercise this capacity, but sometimes they do not. The "making it all one" would refer to a process of psychological integration, where one's temperament and desires are integrated with one's beliefs about how to achieve one's desires, as Lucretius puts it. Not all people succeed in doing this, however, and they behave in accordance with their bad congenital characters, rather than rationally. We blame such people, however, while we do not blame wild animals, because wild animals cannot reflect on their characters and change them, whereas people can.[84]

However, even if the "first natures" here are atoms, the phrase does not imply that the products are radically emergent, as Sedley claims. Even if, in some sense, the products do move the atoms, they need not move them by some sort of 'downwards causation.' Epicurus could simply be stressing that the products *do* have causal efficacy such that, once having arisen, the product will make a difference in the way that atoms move, as they would have to in order to affect one's behavior. If the products are simply certain aspects of the mind (itself a body), which the mind acquires when the soul atoms are arranged in a particular way, Epicurus could consistently maintain that these features of the atomic arrangement

83 One advantage of this interpretation is that it makes sense of Epicurus' remark that once the product has acquired the "cause out of itself," it immediately "gives it on until it comes to the first natures." On my reading, Epicurus means that one *imparts* reason as far as one's original dispositions, *i.e.*, even one's deeply rooted dispositions end up following one's reason and beliefs about how to attain pleasure.

84 The emended text (from [κ]αν[όνα π]ᾶσαν, printed by Sedley, to μίαν πως ἄπασαν by Laursen) is easier to understand if the "first natures" in question are psychological dispositions rather than atoms. If Epicurus is discussing a process of psychological unification, it makes sense to discuss unifying the first natures into "one thing," although the exact import is not clear. If the referent of the first natures is the atoms, little sense can be made of the notion of making all of the atoms somehow one.

do make a causal difference in the way the atoms of the body move, while denying that there is any sort of special 'non-atomic' causation going on. The mind, at a certain point in its development, acquires the ability to take in information from the environment and to respond to that information. This ability will make the mind act differently than it would if it did not have that ability, and thus it *does* affect the atoms, without there being any sort of non-atomic causation.[85]

(2) The nature of the atoms and psychological development

The second phrase which discusses the causal power of the products is οὐδὲν γὰρ αὐτοῖς συνήργηκεν εἰς ἔνια ἔργα τε καὶ μεγέθη ἔργων καὶ διαθέσεων ἡ τῶν ἀτόμων φύσις, ἀλλ' αὐτὰ τὰ ἀπογεγεννημένα τὴν πᾶσα[ν ἢ] τὴν πλε[ί]στην κέκ[τ]ητ[αι] αἰτίαν τῶνδέ τ[ι]νων. ("For the nature of the atoms never did help them in any way to (perform) certain acts or to (develop) certain dimensions of acts and dispositions, but the products themselves were fully or for the most part responsible for these particulars.")

This passage might seem to distinguish between the causal efficacy of the products and the causal efficacy of the atoms that constitute the mind, especially since Epicurus emphasizes that the nature of the atoms *never* helped the person to develop as he did. It is the products, and *not* the atoms, it appears, that are responsible for the particulars of action and development.

However, Epicurus does not say that the *atoms* do not help people to develop these potentialities; he says that the *nature* of the atoms did not

85 Consider a parallel example: wetness is a causally efficacious property of aggregates of water, not of individual water molecules, and this wetness makes the aggregate of water (and the molecules that make it up) behave differently than if the water were not wet. Nonetheless, wetness is not "radically emergent" (see section 4.1.1). On this interpretation of the passage, after stating that the products are only other than the atoms in a (mentally) distinguishable way, Epicurus wants to stress that these features of the atomic arrangement still *do* have a causal impact on how the atoms move.

Purinton tries to avoid Sedley's notion of 'downwards causation' by saying that in the sentence Epicurus is not concerned with psychological development, but that its subject is the fatalist, *i.e.*, the Democritean whom Epicurus shortly afterwards criticizes for not distinguishing causes correctly (c 7). Purinton asserts that Epicurus is saying that this *person* assumes that he has responsibility "from himself," and yet he *also* passes off that responsibility to his atoms. I do not find this convincing. Although Epicurus goes on to discuss the fatalist, the immediately *preceding* sentence (c 5) is talking about the 'products' in general, which is more likely to be the understood subject of this sentence rather than the confused Democritean who is introduced later. Also, in c 5 and the phrase in question, the subject is a neuter singular "something" (τι), while in c 7 the subject switches to the masculine plural (οἱ μὴ δυνάμενοι ...διαιρεῖν), so it is unlikely that Epicurus is implicitly referring to the confused Democritean in c 5.

contribute at all. I interpret this sentence as follows, given the context. Some people fail to develop in the way they should, and they behave in accordance with their original, disturbing constitution. For instance, some people, because they have an overabundance of fire atoms, are naturally quick-tempered and angry. Unlike lions, however, people have the ability to overcome this original tendency. Yet many people fail to do so. How do we explain this failure? We do *not* say that it is because of the nature of their atoms. After all, other people have just as great an original preponderance of fire atoms and yet manage to overcome this disposition. People who have the same basic atomic make-up develop differently, and it is because of these later developments that one person overcomes his natural anger and another does not. That is why, even though the "disordered motions" of anger *are* a result of the fiery nature of the person's atoms (C 4), we do not place responsibility for these disordered motions on the atoms, but on the person's inability to overcome this disposition. Although the text peters out soon after this, an important clue is located in the phrase that we do not place responsibility simply on the atoms, but on what enters the person from the environment. People are different from lions insofar as they are able to receive information from their surroundings and respond according to it in ways that lions cannot. That would help to explain why two people who have the same basic atomic nature develop differently – they respond to different inputs, to different environments, and hence develop differently. A person's character is malleable and flexible. This is, in part, why it makes sense to hold a person responsible for his quick-temperedness and not a lion – a person can change his hot temper while a lion cannot.[86]

This also explains why praise and blame are appropriate for people – they do respond to their environments, and hence praising and blaming them can be effective ways of reforming their characters, whereas, if their characters were set by the natures of the atoms that constituted their souls, this activity would be idle and pointless.[87] But what we do is also

86 Everson (1999) 556–557 develops a similar line of thought. Note the parallel between this interpretation of Epicurus and Aristotle's insistence on the malleability of our character, and the way in which one's present character must be explained by referring to the agent's past actions, discussed in section 3.2.

87 This makes the value of systems of praise and blame and the justification for blaming some people and exonerating others entirely instrumental. Thus, the Epicurean view about praise and blame would be similar to their view about justice. Justice is valuable because of its usefulness in maintaining society, and there can be justice only *vis-à-vis* animals that are capable of making agreements. However, justice is not merely conventional. *Mutatis mutandis,* similar

not entirely determined by the environment, since how we act upon the information we receive from the environment depends on our beliefs (A 1–2). Thus, neither our natural make-up nor the influence of the environment can be invoked on their own to explain why we develop the way we do.[88]

Annas notes that when Epicurus says that things have a nature to do so-and-so, he often uses 'nature' "in an intuitive way to imply that he is talking about the way a thing is, *as opposed to its non-intrinsic properties. . .*" (italics mine).[89] If Epicurus is using 'nature' in this sense, it supports my reading of this passage. We cannot explain why a person develops some potentialities and not others by referring to the *intrinsic* properties of the atoms, since there is nothing about the intrinsic properties of the atoms – their size, shape, and the like – that can explain why one person manages to overcome his anger and another cannot. Instead, we explain such things by referring to the way these atoms form 'products,' complicated atomic groupings and arrangements, which products are then responsible for certain potentialities developing and others not. This would parallel somebody saying today that we must appeal to things other than the properties of the subatomic particles that make up a person's brain in order to explain human mental development, even though everything that occurs is in accordance with the laws of physics, and the psychological

considerations apply toward the Epicurean conception of standards of praise and blame. I think this parallelism, and an instrumental regard for systems of praise and blame, count in favor of my interpretation.

88 Annas tries to sidestep any 'radically emergent' implications here by noting that the passage concerns *disordered* people, and thus is not an account of normal agency. (Annas (1993) 65 and (1992) 132–133.) However, this reply does not work. Even if it were *only* in disordered people that the atoms contributed nothing, this would still be a surprising development, which we would need to account for within Epicurus' philosophy of mind. Also, although this is an account of disordered people, there is little reason to think that it is only in the case of disordered people that the nature of the atoms 'contributes nothing' to their developments. What makes the people disordered is *not* that the nature of the atoms contributes nothing to how they develop; instead, it is that they behave in accordance with the "original, disturbing constitution." It is because the products themselves are the cause of these developments that we hold the products responsible for the way in which the person develops, attacking and criticizing it for developing wrongly. I assume that the same holds in the case of normal people.

89 Annas (1993) 57. (She cites *Ep. Hdt.* 40, 48, 68, 71, among other places, for this usage.) For instance, in *Ep. Hdt.* 68, Epicurus says that nature of body consists of its having attributes such as shape, which he contrasts with accidental properties, such as being enslaved. (The example of being enslaved is given in *DRN* I 455.) However, Annas also notes that Epicurus sometimes uses the "'the nature of X,' or 'the X nature' as a periphrasis for 'X'" (Annas (1993) 5, citing *Ep. Pyth.* 97, 133), and she believes that here Epicurus means by 'the nature of the atoms' just 'the atoms.' However, I think that reading the passage the way I propose allows us to give it a much more satisfactory interpretation.

properties of a person do not gain causal independence from the matter that he is composed of.[90]

(3) The products are the αἰτίαι, not the atoms

The last phrase which discusses the products' causal power is πολλὰ δὲ καὶ τῶνδε καὶ τῶνδε φύσιν ἔχοντα ἀπεργαστικὰ γίγνεσθαι δι' ἑαυτὰ οὐ γίγνεται ἀ[πε]ργαστικά, οὐ διὰ τὴν αὐτὴν αἰτίαν τῶν τε ἀτόμων καὶ ἑαυτῶν. ("Many (products) capable of producing both this and that do not produce them, because of themselves and not because of the same cause in the atoms and themselves.")

It is difficult to get any clear sense out of this phrase. I have two different ways in which it could be accommodated within the picture I've been sketching:

First, αἰτία can mean, not just 'cause,' but also 'explanation' or 'explanatory factor.' Above, I argued that we can understand how Epicurus could say that the nature of the atoms did not contribute to how people develop, but that they themselves are responsible for how they develop, in a way that is consistent with reductionism. This text could be saying something very similar. That is, to say that the products themselves have the αἰτία, and not the atoms, could just mean that we need to refer to these atomic products when explaining why people develop as they do, not just to the atoms that make up their soul.

Secondly, to say that something has the αἰτία for something also often means that it has the *responsibility* for it. Thus, Epicurus could be saying that it is the products which are *responsible* for the way in which a person develops, not the atoms that constitute the soul. We blame the products and rebuke *them,* just as today, a materialist could say that we blame the person, not his brain cells, even though (in some sense) the person's mind is identical to his brain.

4.3.3 Psychological development and freedom of action: summary

Passage C, then, although extremely difficult to understand, does not contain anything that supports attributing notions of 'downwards causation' or 'radical emergence' to Epicurus. We *can* distinguish between the product and the atoms that constitute the soul, but this way of being able

90 This interpretation helps us understand Epicurus' qualifier that it is the products that are fully "or for the most part" responsible for one's development. Although people's characters, desires, and reason might be the main factors that explain how they develop, it is not these *alone* that do so, since *e.g.*, the information that they receive through the senses will affect how they act.

to distinguish them does not imply any sort of 'radical emergence.' Epicurus recognizes that we can distinguish between different aspects of the same basic thing, concentrating on one or on the other. If Purinton is right about the import of the phrase οὐ τὸν ὡς ἀφ' ἑτέρου διαστήματος, Epicurus stresses that the product is *not* somewhere other than the atoms. Instead, it differs from them in a τρόπος διαληπτικός, a 'distinguishable manner.' This suggests that the product is one aspect of the aggregate of atoms, which we can distinguish in thought.

Epicurus is not concerned with gaining independence for the self from the atoms that constitute it, but in securing our ability, as rational creatures, to overcome our congenital dispositions (our 'first natures') and to control our own lives. We cannot explain why people develop the way in which they do simply by referring to the types and quantities of atoms that originally constitute their souls, since people, through reason, are able to determine their own development. Reason, however, is an ability that people possess in virtue of the organization of the atoms that make up the soul. Reason is real, causally efficacious, and predicable only to souls, not to individual atoms, without being thereby 'radically emergent.'

The central theme that runs throughout passages A–C, then, is not a stand *against* causal determinism or reductionism – it is a commitment *to* reason. Reason sets us apart from wild animals. Reason allows us to shape our own characters. Reason is the key to our practices of praise and blame, since these practices only make sense on the presupposition that people can respond to argument and reasons.

4.4 *Anti-reductionist interpretations of Epicurus and the swerve*

If my analysis of *On Nature* 25 is correct, this gives us good reason to reject the various anti-reductionist interpretations of Epicurus, since its passages constitute their main textual support, whereas Epicurus' and Lucretius' other writings on the nature of the mind, and their writings on metaphysics generally, provide strong *prima facie* evidence that Epicurus has an identity theory of mind. However, even if one were to accept the view that Epicurus is a non-reductionist, this still leaves entirely open the question of the role the swerve is supposed to play in Epicurus' defense of human freedom. None of the answers supplied by the anti-reductionists have any direct textual support. Instead, they are inferred on the basis of their philosophical plausibility, where interpreters first note that Epicurus (supposedly) thinks that the self is emergent and also that the swerve helps preserve our freedom, and then try to figure out what the swerve could be doing. However, the roles assigned to the swerve are not philosophically plausible, which gives us further reason not to accept the anti-reductionist interpretations of Epicurus.[91] The swerve can neither help secure the causal efficacy of the 'radically emergent self' (as Sedley claims) nor help block the reduction of intentional explanations to atomic explanations (as Mitsis claims). Let me briefly deal with each proposal.

Sedley asserts that Epicurus introduces the swerve, an antecedent causal indeterminacy, in order to secure the causal efficacy of the radically emergent self. Without the swerve, the radically emergent self would have no 'elbow room' in which to operate, because "if the laws of physics are sufficient to determine the precise trajectory of every atom within us," then the self could not be causally effective.[92]

But, *ex hypothesi,* when the 'radically' emergent self arises, there is an additional causal factor at work, and the laws of physics (at least, those that simply spell out how atoms move as a result of their weight, resistance to blows, and past collisions) would *not* be sufficient to determine the precise trajectory of every atom within us. The laws of physics do not 'ordain' how atoms ought to move. They are simply a summation of the effects of a number of causal factors that determine how an atom will move: for example its weight, past trajectory, and collisions with other atoms. If there really were a radically emergent self, that self would add an additional causal factor that could move the atoms. No antecedent indeterminacy like the swerve needs to be built into the other factors that cause atoms to move in order to ensure that the atoms can be moved by the self. All that is needed is that the atoms have a susceptibility to being moved by external forces – which they most certainly do have.

Mitsis, like Sedley, thinks that Epicurus is trying to fight reductionism in order to preserve the efficacy of the mental. He claims that the swerve preserves rationality at the macroscopic level of explanation.[93] The swerve,

91 I exclude Annas from the following discussion, since she has no theory about the role the swerve is supposed to play. According to Annas, once Epicurus has secured the impossibility of consistently denying our common-sense beliefs about our own agency, adding in an atomic indeterminacy on top of this seems utterly unhelpful and beside the point (Annas (1992) 182–183). She speculates that perhaps Epicurus didn't really have any clear idea of how the swerve was supposed to help underwrite human freedom, and later Epicureans tried to fill in his account in various ways, just as present-day interpreters do (Annas (1992) 188).

92 Long and Sedley (1987) vol. 1 p. 110.

93 Mitsis (1988) 163.

according to Mitsis, helps "guarantee the independence of intentional explanations" by preventing the aspiring reductionist from being able to give completely informative explanations of macro-level events in terms of atomic motions. That is because "such micro-level explanations will be underdetermined and never completely informative," which somehow implies that the reduction "can in principle never be completed."[94] I am not entirely clear how this is supposed to work, but my best guess is the following: for any particular motion in which the swerve plays a role (for macroscopic motions, these would be motions where the swerve 'bootstraps' up to macroscopic indeterminacy), we may be able to 'explain' the motion as the result of previous atomic motions plus an indeterministic swerve. But this explanation is not completely informative, since it still leaves unanswered the question of why this event occurred at the particular time that it did; this fact is 'underdetermined.'

If this is what Mitsis means, however, it is unsatisfactory. *Ex hypothesi*, if the swerve is truly a random motion, then no fully determinate answer can be given to the question as to why an atom swerved at exactly some particular time and not another (that is just what it means for the swerve to be random in this sense). But no interesting anti-reductionist results follow from this. For any particular effect of a swerve, we can say how it results from the swerve and the motions, spatial relationships, *etc.*, of the atoms in the vicinity of the swerving atom. We can also give explanations, of a certain odd sort, for why swerves occur – atoms simply have an inherent tendency, in addition to their natural disposition to fall downward, to swerve occasionally to the side by exactly one spatial minimum at random times and places.[95] Furthermore, we can even give type-level explanations of the following sort: *if* a swerve occurs under these sorts of circumstances (*e.g.*, in a suitably disposed *animus*), then this sort of result will follow. However, *if* no swerve occurs, then that sort of result will follow. Recent proponents of materialist identity theories of mind or of eliminative materialism do not think that the mere existence of indeterminacies at the quantum level poses any problem for their theories – nor should they think this.

94 Mitsis (1988) 165–6.

95 Purinton gives this atomic property the happy name of 'swerviness.' See Purinton (1999) 271–2 for more on the sense in which swerves can be said to have *some* sort of cause, even though the particular time, place, and direction in which swerves occur is not causally necessitated.

4.5 *Epicurus' Reductionist Response to Democritean fatalism: summary*

Epicurus' overall metaphysics is reductionist, and the descriptions of the mind in the *Letter to Herodotus* and *De rerum natura* strongly suggest that Epicurus has an identity theory of mind. Although the text is extremely hard to understand, Epicurus' assertion that fatalism is self-refuting and his description of psychological development in *On Nature* 25 fit in well with this picture. Epicurus' arguments in *On Nature* 25 are compatible with both reductionism and determinism. He can show that the mind is a real thing and possesses causal efficacy, even within a reductionist materialism. And when criticizing the Democritean fatalist, Epicurus says that what needs to be preserved at all costs are the ordinary distinctions that we make about certain things being under our rational control and others not, and that, as long as *this* is not challenged, to say that things are 'necessary' in some other sense is beside the point. We can hold people morally responsible for their actions because they are able to use reason to control their behavior, unlike wild animals.

CHAPTER 5

The swerve and collisions

Before I turn to the role the swerve plays in preserving human freedom, I wish to consider the other reason Lucretius gives for why there must be an atomic swerve: without the swerve, there would be no atomic collisions, and thus no macroscopic bodies, as there evidently are.[1] Compared to the extensive treatment of the anti-fatalist function of the swerve, the 'cosmogonic' argument for the swerve has garnered relatively little attention. Most treatments of Epicureanism either paraphrase Lucretius' argument in *De rerum natura* without giving any extensive analysis of whether the argument is cogent or simply dismiss it as inadequate.[2]

This disparity of attention is understandable. In connection with determinism, the swerve may ultimately be a mistake, but at least it opens up interesting questions about the relationship between causal determinism and free will. Lucretius' argument that the swerve is needed for atomic collisions, however, appears to rest on a simple misunderstanding – *i.e.*, that there needs to be a *start* for collisions – and once this misunderstanding is pointed out, the argument has, at best, some minor historical interest. In this chapter, however, I want to rehabilitate the idea that Epicurus had good reasons to think that the swerve was needed as an *archê* of collisions, and that the swerve – in this connection, at least – was not simply a blunder or a misguided oversight.

1 *DRN* 2 216–224. Cicero also reports and ridicules this function of the swerve at *De fato* 22–3 and *DF* 1 18–20.

2 Examples of the first approach include: Long, who asks, "Given that this fall is at constant speed for any atom, and in the same direction, how can a world be formed which consists of atoms in conjunction, atoms which have collided and formed compound bodies?" and then quotes Lucretius *in extenso* (*DRN* 2 216–224) without any analysis (Long (1986)); Zeller, who simply states that the swerve is needed "to render a meeting [of the atoms] possible" (Zeller (1962) 445–446); and DeWitt, who devotes one sentence on this argument (DeWitt (1954) p. 165). Rist has a very useful discussion of whether there is a temporal beginning to collisions, but he does not analyze in depth how Lucretius' argument is supposed to proceed (Rist (1972)). A good example of a brusque dismissal of Lucretius' argument is R. D. Hicks' discussion (Hicks (1962)). Long and Sedley (1987) contains a slightly more extensive treatment of the swerve. I discuss it below.

This chapter contains five main sections. In the first, I look at Lucretius' justification for the swerve and argue that, as it is usually understood, his argument is indeed deeply flawed. If the swerve is supposed to start a series of atomic collisions, then it must be assumed that an infinite series of collisions is impossible. Lucretius has no good reason to assume this. More significantly, this assumption contradicts what Epicurus himself says about atomic motion in the *Letter to Herodotus*; I argue for this in the second section of the chapter. In the third section, I turn to Aristotle's criticisms of Democritus' theory of atomic motion. Some of them are question-begging and depend on Aristotle's own theory of natural motion. Nonetheless, we can glean from Aristotle's writings legitimate, if not necessarily decisive, objections to Democritus' theory: in particular, that Democritus does not give any adequate explanation in terms of the nature of the atoms for why they move. In the last two sections I consider the swerve as an *archê* of collisions in light of Aristotle's criticisms of Democritus. I argue that the two major modifications Epicurus made to Democritus' theory of atomic motion – the swerve (section 4) and the natural downwards motion of the atoms (section 5) – both make sense if considered as responses to Aristotle, with weight and the swerve explaining why atoms move and collide, and thus being 'explanatory' *archai*, but not giving a temporal starting-point either to motion or to collisions.

Quite frankly, this topic is not essential to the main argument of the book, and impatient readers may skip ahead to the next chapter. The material is of intrinsic interest, however, and considering it will help round out my treatment of the swerve. In addition, the arguments of this chapter indirectly contribute to my overall case in two ways. First, some have denied that Epicurus had much acquaintance at all with Aristotle. But I argue that Epicurus is responding in the cosmogonic case fairly directly to Aristotelian worries, which he takes seriously. If so, this makes more plausible the supposition that in the case of human freedom Epicurus is also familiar with Aristotle's worries about fatalism and takes his concerns seriously. Second, I argue that both Aristotle and Epicurus wish to find an *archê* for motion in the sense of an adequate principle to explain *why* it occurs, not a temporal starting-point. If this is right, it somewhat supports my contention in chapter 3 that Aristotle (and Epicurus, insofar as he draws on Aristotelian concerns) wishes to make the agent's actions and character have an 'internal *archê*' in the sense of being explicable by referring to the agent himself and his decisions, not in the sense of his actions and decisions being the effect of 'fresh starts' somewhere in the agent's soul. This interpretation of 'internal *archê*' is not a piece of *ad hocery* designed to evade unwelcome indeterminist implications; instead, it is part of a broader pattern.

5.1 Lucretius' cosmogonic argument for the necessity of a swerve

Lucretius' cosmogonic argument for the swerve is brief. Lucretius first states his conclusion: that the atoms, although they are being carried straight downwards through the void by their weight, swerve just a little "at quite uncertain times and uncertain places."[3] He then argues for this, saying,

> For if they were not accustomed to turn aside, all would fall downwards, like drops of rain, through the deep void, and neither would a collision occur, nor a blow be produced among the primary bodies: in this way nature would have never produced anything.[4]

Next he handles one obvious objection – couldn't one atom overtake another, even if they all naturally travel in the same direction? – with a supplementary argument for why all atoms travel with the same speed.[5]

Once again, Lucretius' argument is a form of *modus tollens,* which goes from the *enarges* (evident) to the *adêlon* (unclear):

1. If the atoms did not swerve, there would be no collisions and no macroscopic bodies,
2. There are collisions and macroscopic bodies,
3. Thus, the atoms swerve.[6]

The crucial premise, of course, is the first. One way of reading this cosmogonic argument is parallel to *kalam*-type cosmological arguments for God's existence advanced by Islamic thinkers who think the world must have some temporal starting point: given that there are collisions, there must be some first collision in order to get the sequence of collisions started.[7] And given the Epicurean theory of the natural downwards motion of atoms at a uniform velocity, the only way for the sequence of

3 *DRN* 2 218–219. 4 *DRN* 2 221–224 (my translation). 5 *DRN* 2 225–242.

6 Actually, this conclusion may be a bit strong – perhaps it should read, "The atoms *did* swerve," at least on the traditional understanding of the argument, that there must be a swerve at some point in time in order to get the collisions started. Lucretius does not consider the possibility that the atoms (or an atom) did swerve at some point in the past and got the collisions started, but are no longer swerving. This possibility, besides leaving it open that the atoms could eventually get into a state where they all were moving in parallel, requiring another swerve, would not be satisfactory for the anti-determinist function of the swerve, and in any case (as I will argue later), if my interpretation of the force of the argument is correct, even the cosmogonic function of the swerve requires that the atoms *do* swerve, not merely that they *did.*

7 See Mackie (1982) 92–95 for a brief discussion of this family of cosmological arguments.

collisions to get started is for the atoms (or at least one atom) to depart from their usual motion and to bump into neighboring atoms. As Tony Long and David Sedley put it, "given the equal speed and natural downwards motion of atoms, how can collisions between them ever have started?"[8]

On such a reading, however, the argument appears pitifully deficient. Why think that there has to be a first member of the series of collisions and that the collisions have "to get started" – why can't there simply be an infinite series of collisions extending backwards in time? Any particular collision is caused by the velocities and directions of motion of the atoms that collide, which in turn are caused (in part) by the past collisions of those atoms, *etc.*, on down the line. This objection is particularly acute for the Epicureans, since they already believe that the universe is infinite both spatially and temporally. Worse – the atoms have *always* been moving, so the Epicureans cannot have some general principle that motion *as such* requires an initial temporal mover.[9] Thus, if the Epicureans are arguing that there needs to be a swerve so that there is a first collision to get collisions started, then they must believe that *motion as such* needs no first temporal cause, but *collisions* do – which would be an odd and arbitrary position.

In any case, the idea that a series of collisions requires a first member would probably be quite foreign to Epicurus. Democritus had already posited a series of collisions extending backwards infinitely in time, and among the various cosmologies that Greek philosophers devised, only Anaxagoras' gives motion a starting-point.[10]

5.2 *Atomic collisions in the* Letter to Herodotus

Unless Lucretius and/or Epicurus were incredibly obtuse, there is a final piece of evidence that clinches the argument that the swerve was not meant to give a start to a series of collisions: such an interpretation would

8 Long and Sedley (1987) vol. 1 p. 52.

9 *e.g.*, *DRN* 2 80–82, 2 89–94, *Ep. Hdt.* 43.

10 Plato may appear to be another exception, since his cosmology gives the universe a temporal starting point, instead of stretching backwards and forwards infinitely, but even in his case, the temporal starting-point of the world was the impression of form and orderly motions onto a pre-existing mass of stuff that was previously moving continuously and chaotically (*Tim.* 30a). Moreover, some Platonists interpreted the *Timaeus* story metaphorically such that it does not posit a temporal beginning of the cosmos. Other philosophers gave *this* cosmos a temporal starting-point. But thinkers like Empedocles, who gave this world a temporal starting-point, think that this is only one phase in a regular, endless cycle. Democritus himself thought that this cosmos was transitory, but that the atoms and void endured forever.

contradict Epicurus' statement in the *Letter to Herodotus* 44 that there have always been collisions. *Ep. Hdt.* 43–44 deals with different types of atomic collisions:

The atoms move continuously forever, and some separate far from each other, while others remain vibrating, whenever they happen to be locked in by interweaving or encased by atoms that tend to interweave.[11]

44. This is because the nature of the void separates each of them and is unable to provide resistance, and their actual solidity makes the rebound from the collision extend as far as the surrounding entanglement allows the return from the collision. *There is no beginning to these* [τούτων, *i.e.* these sorts of atomic motion, including rebounds], since the atoms and the void are eternal. (My translation, see the Appendix for the Greek text.)

The identification of the antecedent of "these" (τούτων) with types of atomic motion which include atomic rebounds is not entirely uncontroversial. It might be suggested that Epicurus is not saying that atomic *rebounds* have no beginning; he is simply saying that atomic motion *simpliciter* is everlasting. At the beginning of this passage, right before discussing the types of atomic rebounds, Epicurus states, "The atoms move continuously forever," and, it might be suggested, atomic motion as such is being referred to by the τούτων, and this might not include collisions. This gloss of the passage is compatible with the interpretation of Lucretius' argument just described, *i.e.*, the atoms have always been falling downwards in straight lines – thus, there is no beginning to atomic motion as such – yet there *was* a beginning to atomic collisions, which was caused by the swerve.

But this suggestion cannot be right. The phrase "ἀρχὴ δὲ τούτων οὐκ ἔστιν" immediately follows Epicurus' discussion of two different types of atomic motion: some atoms rebound a considerable distance, (αἱ μὲν εἰς μακρὰν ἀπ' ἀλλήλων διιστάμεναι) while others merely vibrate in place (αἱ δὲ αὐτοῦ τὸν παλμὸν ἴσχουσιν). The antecedent of the τούτων has to be either: (1) these two types of atomic motions, that both involve rebounds, or (2) atomic rebounds in general, which were being discussed in the sentence immediately preceding the τούτων. When Epicurus writes in *Ep. Hdt.* 43 that "the atoms move continuously forever," he almost certainly must include atomic collisions in this motion, since he discusses

11 The contrast here is between atoms that are actually entangled in other atoms, such as those that make up a solid body, and those that are merely encased by interwoven atoms without themselves being entangled, such as the atoms that make up the soul.

collisions right after making this statement, and the natural downwards motion of the atoms through the void has not been mentioned yet. Thus, Epicurus believes that there have always been atomic collisions and rebounds; there was no first atomic collision.[12]

Other passages in Lucretius confirm this. He writes that generation and destruction have always existed,[13] and that every possible combination of atoms has already come into existence, since the atoms have always been driven by collisions and their weight.[14]

Long and Sedley concede this point, but stick to the traditional interpretation of the argument for the swerve. The *Letter to Herodotus* was an early work, they say, which contained one solution to the problem of atomic collisions. The swerve was added later, and gave a different solution:

> When he wrote the *Letter to Herodotus*, at any rate, he was content with the more economical answer that, given the infinite past existence of atoms and void, there *was* no first collision. This raises the suspicion that it was his subsequent well attested concern about the autonomy of responsible agents that led him to the theory, and that it was then with hindsight grafted onto the existing cosmological system.[15]

I find this suggestion untenable, however. Even if we assume that Epicurus later introduced the swerve for the purposes of defending our autonomy, what possible reason would he have for using the swerve to explain the genesis of atomic collisions, if indeed he already had a perfectly economical, sensible solution, one which, moreover, fit in both with his own picture of the universe as infinite in both space and time as well as with that of most of his predecessors? Why would he have seen the

12 Inwood and Gerson (1997) translate the phrase ἀρχὴ δὲ τούτων οὐκ ἔστιν "There is no principle to these [entities], since the atoms and the void are eternal." But, given that the discussion is explicitly focused on atomic motions and the fact that the atoms move "continuously and forever," I don't see any reason to take ἀρχὴ in this context to mean "principle," instead of "beginning," or to think that "entities" (atoms and void?) is the antecedent of τούτων. Talking about the principles of the atoms and the void would be out of place in this section, since the preceding discussion is almost entirely about atomic rebounds, whereas saying that the atomic *rebounds* have no beginning would fit in perfectly well. To say that there is no "principle" to these *rebounds* also would not work as a translation. After all, in this passage Epicurus is giving an explanation, in terms of the properties of atoms and void, of why there occur these types of atomic rebounds, so that there *is* an explanatory principle to these rebounds, even if they do not have a temporal beginning.

13 *DRN* 2 569–580.

14 *DRN* 5 187–191. Both of these passages are cited and briefly discussed by Rist (1972) 50–51.

15 Long and Sedley (1987) vol. 1 p. 52; see also Sedley (1983) 13.

archê of collisions, on this view, as being a problem at all, much less one requiring a radical solution like the swerve?[16]

5.3 *Aristotle's criticisms of Democritus*

In order to discover why Epicurus thought that this was a problem, we should look to Aristotle's criticisms of Democritus' theory of atomic motion. Although many of Aristotle's criticisms of Democritus on this matter seem question-begging, I believe some of them raise genuine difficulties for Democritus, difficulties to which the swerve can be seen as a response.

In his discussion of Democritus' theory of motion, Aristotle lays great weight on the fact that, for Democritus, all atomic motion is forced, since all motions are simply the result of blows by other atoms, and no atomic motion is natural, since atoms have no natural direction of motion. Aristotle thinks that the absence of natural motion makes any motion whatsoever impossible:

> First, all motion is either forced or natural. But necessarily, if there is forced motion, there is also natural motion (for forced motion is contrary to nature, and motion contrary to nature is posterior to motion that is natural). Thus, if there isn't a natural motion for each of the natural bodies, none of the other motions will exist either.[17]

Aristotle goes on to argue that if there is void, there is no natural movement, hence no movement at all. At first, this appears to beg the question blatantly. According to Democritus, there is no natural motion of bodies as Aristotle thinks of it, and no natural place. Why should he be required to accept Aristotle's assumptions about such things? Aristotle's discussion of void as a cause of motion, which immediately precedes the just-quoted passage, also seems to miss the mark: "If there is some natural

16 Hicks presses this line of attack in particularly strong terms and thinks that Epicurus "comes off badly" in comparison with Democritus in this matter: "Leucippus and Democritus declined to give any cause of motion . . . [E]ach movement presupposes a preceding movement, and to seek for the beginning of an endless process is absurd . . .Epicurus seems to have argued that vertical motion in the determinate direction which we call downward is prior to the motion resulting from collision, impact and pressure, though why this is hard to see. . .Feeling bound to offer some explanation. . .he modified his premises in an arbitrary manner by the gratuitous assumption of an atomic declination . . ." (Hicks (1962) 259).

17 *Physics* 4 8, 215a1–13 (my translation). See also the discussion in *De Caelo* 3 2, 300b9–16, where Aristotle makes basically the same argument against Leucippus and Democritus: in order for there to be motion at all, bodies must have some natural motion, but all motion is by force, according to the atomists.

motion for each of the simple bodies (such as for fire upwards, and for earth downward and toward the middle), it is clear that the void cannot be the cause of these motions. So what will the void be the cause of?"[18] Void, however, is not *supposed* to be a cause of motion in the sense Aristotle wants natural motion to be a cause; it is simply the necessary condition of bodies moving.

I think that these two passages, however, make a legitimate point. Democritus cannot appeal to the void to explain why the atoms are moving, since the void is supposed to be simply the necessary condition for motion – void, as such, does not cause things to move. But Democritus also cannot appeal to the nature of the atoms to explain why they are moving, since atoms have no natural movement. Hence, *why do they move at all?* This may not be such a bad question after all.

It is important to note that Aristotle's dispute with Democritus is *not* primarily over whether Democritus can give an explanation for any particular motion in terms of previous motions, although Aristotle thinks that he cannot. Even if he could, however, this would not be adequate for Aristotle. Aristotle is not looking for an explanation of any *particular* motion, but for why there should be motion at all, and he sees no explanations forthcoming from Democritus. Aristotle points out that there is nothing about the nature either of the atoms or of the void that shows why the atoms move: "This is why some suppose eternal actuality – for example, Leucippus and Plato; for they say there is always movement. But why and what this movement is they do not say, nor, if the world moves in this way or that, do they tell us the cause of its doing so."[19]

Aristotle's demand that there be an *archê* for motion is not, of course, a demand for a temporal starting-point – he argues at length that a beginning of motion is absurd.[20] Rather, it is a demand that the whole sequence of motions be explicable by appealing to the nature of the things in motion – that such a sequence simply exists cannot be left as a brute fact, and to give an efficient cause of each of the members of the series is not the same as explaining the series as a whole:

Generally, it is wrong to assume that we can adopt, as an adequate first principle (*archê*), the fact that something always is or happens in this way. Now Democritus reduces the explanations of nature to showing that things also happened in the past as they happen now. But he doesn't think it worthwhile to

18 *Physics* 4 8, 214b13–17 (my translation).
19 *Meta.* 12 6, 1071b31–34.
20 *e.g.*, in *De Caelo* 1 10–12, 2 1, 279b4–284b5.

seek a first principle for this 'always.' He is right not to seek a first principle in some of these cases, but wrong to say that this applies to all cases.[21]

5.4 *The swerve as a response to Aristotle*

I believe that Epicurus introduced the swerve as a response to Aristotle's criticisms of Democritus. Of course, since the swerve appears nowhere in Epicurus' extant writings, any suggestions about why he introduced it are necessarily speculative. It has even been disputed whether Epicurus himself had a theory of the swerve. Its absence from the *Letter to Herodotus* is especially troubling, since the *Letter to Herodotus* was the summary of the whole system that his disciples were supposed to memorize.[22] There is also no mention of the swerve in Diogenes Laertius' account of Epicurus. But given Cicero's direct attribution of the swerve to Epicurus, its presence in Lucretius, and the later Epicureans' reputation for not making major innovations to the Master's teachings, it is extremely likely that Epicurus himself introduced the doctrine of the swerve.

If the swerve is Epicurus' doctrine, I think it would be best to employ the principle of charity when trying to decide what reasons he had for introducing it. This means that Epicurus' reasons for positing the swerve should: (1) not contradict what Epicurus says elsewhere, (2) fit with what Lucretius says about the swerve, (3) respond to concerns Epicurus might plausibly have had, given his own philosophy and those of his predecessors, and (4) actually address those concerns in a credible manner.

Since Epicurus derived much of his philosophy from Democritus, and lived in Athens shortly after Aristotle, I think it is quite likely that Epicurus was responding to Aristotle's criticisms of Democritus when he made his two major modifications of Democritus' theory on the motion of the atoms.[23] That Epicurus is responding to Aristotle is made even more plausible by the fact that Epicurus, in discussing the use of the words 'up' and 'down' in reference to atomic motions, very carefully spells out exactly what these terms mean and by what standard one can assert the existence of an 'up' and a 'down' without there being a highest and

21 *Physics* 8 1 252a32–b2 (my translation).

22 *Ep. Hdt.* 35–36, *Ep. Pyth.* 85. That the *Letter to Herodotus* was supposed to serve this function renders less likely Long and Sedley's claim that it is an early work.

23 Epicurus is reported to have paid at least enough attention to Aristotle to have abused him verbally (*DL* 10 8). And Epicurus' successor as Scholarch, Hermarchus, wrote a treatise "Against Aristotle." (*DL* 10 25)

lowest point.[24] This cautious discussion is most probably a response to Aristotle's assertion that the notions of 'up' and 'down' make no sense if the universe is infinite in size.[25]

Let us consider, then, how the swerve could be a response to Aristotle. As Epicurus states in the *Letter to Herodotus*, there is no beginning to atomic collisions. No 'first collision' is needed to get the series of collisions going. In this, Democritus was right, and Epicurus is not disputing the Democritean account on this matter. However, even if each individual atomic collision could be traced back to previous collisions, there is no explanation for why there are collisions *at all* – or, to put it another way, there would be no explanation for why there exist these *types* of motions, even if there could be an explanation for each collision-token in terms of previous motions. If the only natural motion of the atoms were straight down, we *would* expect that the atoms *would* fall straight downwards, like drops of rain in the night. There would be no satisfactory explanation in terms of the properties of the atoms – their extension, solidity, or weight – for why there are collisions at all. Once there is a swerve, however, we can appeal to a natural feature of atomic motion which would account for the existence of collisions. Of course, this explanation may be *ad hoc* and unsatisfactory, but it does give a reason why there are collisions that appeals to the properties *of the atoms,* instead of leaving the existence of the collisions 'dangling' without an explanation.[26]

The actual wording of Lucretius' discussion of the swerve is perfectly consistent with this interpretation. Lucretius does not say that there needs to be a beginning of collisions *at some point in time,* and hence the swerve. Instead, he says – to quote the passage again:

24 *Ep. Hdt.* 60. Other objections could still be brought against the notion of an absolute 'up' and 'down' in infinite space – for instance, in an infinite space with no center, isn't it rather arbitrary that one direction happens to be 'down,' when it just as well could have been any other? (I want to thank Bob Sharples for pointing this out.)

25 *Physics* 4 8, 215a6–10. Sandbach claims that Aristotle had almost no influence on Hellenistic philosophy. He concentrates on the Stoics in particular (Sandbach (1985)). Given the types of considerations discussed above, I find this extremely implausible. If there are no definite extra-philosophical reasons for ascertaining whether Aristotle influenced Hellenistic philosophy, then the best way of seeing if he did is to engage in the type of study being done here – do the arguments of Hellenistic philosophers make more sense if they are viewed in light of what Aristotle had to say, or do they display an ignorance of Aristotle?

26 The random nature of the swerve makes this more problematic than it would be if a law-like account of the swerve could be given. To what extent is the swerve really a feature 'of the atom' or a natural feature of atomic motion? Although the atoms swerve randomly and unpredictably, however, an occasional swerve is a regular feature of atomic motion, and hence it could be argued that there are two types of motion that are natural to Epicurean atoms – the constant downwards falling and the occasional, unpredictable swerve to the side.

For if they were not accustomed to turn aside, all would fall downwards, like drops of rain, through the deep void, and neither would a collision occur, nor a blow be produced among the primary bodies: in this way nature would have never produced anything.[27]

Notice the phrase: "if they were not accustomed to turn aside," (*quod nisi declinare solerent*). The focus is on the *nature* of the atoms: if the atoms were not such as to swerve occasionally from the straight and narrow, there would be no collisions – since, if my interpretation is correct, there would be no reason for there to be any collisions.

To go back to an earlier point: on the standard interpretation of Lucretius' argument, the conclusion ought to be, strictly speaking, not that the atoms *do* swerve, but that they *did* swerve – after all, this is all that is needed to get collisions started. Under my interpretation, however, Lucretius would be justified in concluding that the atoms *do* swerve now, since the type of *archê* that the swerve provides is not a temporal *archê,* but an explanatory *archê,* one that refers to the nature of the atoms and their motion.

5.5 Weight and natural motion for atoms

The very fact that Epicurus introduces a natural direction of motion to the atoms lends great support to the notion that Epicurus is heavily influenced by Aristotle in his modification of Democritus. Although I have been concentrating on the swerve, a similar argument, concerning the need for an explanatory *archê,* could be given for why Epicurus introduces weight as an intrinsic property of atoms.[28] The swerve would be an *archê* for the atomic collisions. But Aristotle's main criticism of

27 *DRN* 2 216–224.

28 Aëtius 1.3.18 and 1.12.6 say explicitly that Democritus denies that atoms have weight and that Epicurus added weight as a property of atoms. Aristotle, however, seems at points to attribute to Democritus the position that atoms have weight, when he says that Democritus believes that bigger indivisible bodies are heavier (see *On Generation and Corruption* 1 8 326a8, *De Caelo* 4 2 309a1–2). The usual way of reconciling these reports is that larger bodies are 'heavier' only in the sense that they have more of a tendency (when within the cosmic vortex) to move towards the center of the cosmos, and that atoms, as such, are weightless. (See Furley (1989*a*) 80–1 for a good summary of the texts and the literature.) Denis O'Brien argues at great length that weight is an intrinsic property of atoms for Democritus, inside or outside of the cosmic vortex (O'Brien, (1981)). However, the distinctive thing about "weight" for Democritus, according to O'Brien, is that it does *not* imply natural motion downwards, unlike weight for both Aristotle and Epicurus. Epicurus' innovation lies in giving atoms a natural motion (or motions, if the swerve is counted as a natural motion). (See Furley (1989*b*) for a summary of O'Brien and some pointed criticisms.) So both the usual view of Democritus and O'Brien's are compatible with the story I here tell.

Democritus did not have to do with collisions, but with the lack of an explanation for motion as such. Epicurus' attribution of weight to atoms would give an explanation for the existence of motion, as such, that appeals to the intrinsic properties of atoms. If the swerve were a later addition to Epicurus' theory, which occurred after the attribution of weight to the atoms by Epicurus, that fits in well with the story told here: the main Aristotelian criticism of Democritus that Epicurus needs to reply to is that there is no explanation for why the atoms move. Weight gives that explanation. Later it may have become apparent to Epicurus, however, that given his views on the equal velocity of atoms, the attribution of weight would give no explanation as to why there would be collisions amongst the atoms, and he then introduces the swerve to remedy that problem.

It may be objected that there is no need to concoct such a story, involving Aristotle's criticisms of Democritus, in the case of weight, since for a staunch empiricist like Epicurus, our experience would be enough to show us that there is a real up and down. No elaborate theoretical considerations are at work here.

Although this is plausible, I think that it is not decisive. Epicurus could very well have believed both that our daily experience makes it evident that the atoms have a natural motion "down," and that a natural motion down is needed in order for there to be an *archê* for motion. That is, the case for a natural downwards motion could be overdetermined. And a report in pseudo-Plutarch shows that weight *is* supposed to provide an *archê* for motion *simpliciter*: "It is necessary, says Epicurus, that the bodies [*i.e.* the atoms] are moved by the blow of their weight: for otherwise they

Furley argues, however, that atoms *do* have a natural motion downwards for Democritus, just as with Epicurus. Furley's main reason for thinking this is the principle of charity: without this supposition, Democritus would have no good explanation for the vertical fall of heavy bodies near the earth's surface; the usual explanation attributed to Democritus, that this is due to the cosmic vortex, is clearly inadequate (Furley (1989*a*) 78–81, Furley (1989*b*) 95–100). I do not find this particularly persuasive. Besides needing to dismiss Aëtius' reports, Furley's view is hard to square with Aristotle's criticism of Democritus, discussed in section 5.3, that Democritus fails to explain motion because atoms have no natural motion. Furley's main way of trying to deal with these passages is to say Aristotle would not regard atomic weight as a satisfactory *archê* of motion of the sort he is looking for, like the Prime Mover, or Anaxagoras' Mind (Furley (1989*a*) 88–89, Furley (1989*b*) 100–102). But this is strained. Aristotle says that there is no natural motion for each of the natural bodies, on Democritus' account. It would be grossly misleading to assert this if Aristotle knew that Democritus did think that atoms had a natural direction of motion, but he wanted to argue that Democritus had no ultimate explanation (*via* the Prime Mover or the like) for atoms having this natural motion. Furthermore, in the *De Caelo,* where some of these criticisms of Democritus occur, Aristotle himself does not feel it necessary to give any further explanation (*via* the Prime Mover) for the motions of the *cosmos* beyond the natural motions of its elements.

would not move."[29] If Epicurus introduced the natural downwards motion of the atoms only to account for our experience of things "naturally" falling down, he would not have made this sweeping statement, but something more modest, such as "If the atoms were not moved by the blow of their weight, they would not move in the manner they evidently do, but instead move randomly," or something of this sort. If Epicurus accepts Aristotle's criticisms of Democritus, however, and believes that there must be a natural motion of the atoms in order to give an adequate account for why motion exists at all, then the report in pseudo-Plutarch makes perfect sense.

5.6 The swerve and collisions: conclusion

Epicurus has three principles to explain atomic motion – weight, the swerve, and collisions, whereas Democritus has only one – collisions. One may think that Epicurus' additional principles are extraneous or even detrimental to his philosophy. Indeed, the cosmogonic argument that Lucretius gives for the swerve seems to be very weak, given the standard interpretation of it, since the swerve is *not* needed as a temporal *archê*, a starting-point, of collisions. But if, as I argue, both additional principles of motion are thought of as responses to Aristotelian objections that involve some sort of principle of sufficient reason, their introduction makes sense. And Aristotle's appeals to the principle of sufficient reason, if interpreted in a certain way, are the kinds of appeals that Epicurus would listen to. After all, events in the world are supposed to be explained by appealing to atomic properties – but under the Democritean metaphysics, there is no good explanation for the motion of the atoms. Democritus can account for each individual motion, but there are no resources within Democritean atomism to explain why motion exists at all, or to explain the particular types of motion that one encounters. Epicurus' modifications help to remedy this deficiency. The natural downwards motion accounts for there being any motion at all, while the swerve accounts for entanglements and collisions. Atomic weight is needed as an explanatory *archê* of atomic motion, while the swerve is needed as an explanatory *archê* of atomic collisions.

29 Aëtius 1.3.26, Usener 275.

CHAPTER 6

The swerve and fate

My argumentation thus far has been partly positive and partly negative. As far as how the swerve is supposed to help secure our freedom is concerned, it has been largely destructive: the swerve is *not* involved directly in the production of free action; it is *not* supposed to secure the agent as the *archê* of either his character or his actions; it is *not* needed to protect the emergent self from the threat of reductionism. Neither *De rerum natura*, nor supposed Aristotelian antecedents in the *Nicomachean Ethics*, nor *On Nature* 25 allow us to determine the role the swerve is supposed to play in protecting human freedom.

However, many important positive results about Epicurus' views on our freedom can be gleaned from these texts, as well as Epicurean ethics and psychology overall. Lucretius' discussion shows that *libera voluntas* is what allows us to act as we wish to act, and that it is a sort of intentional impulse. Somehow, if sequences of cause and effect stretched back infinitely in the past, we would not have this *libera voluntas*, and the swerve saves us from this. Insofar as Epicurus is picking up on Aristotelian antecedents in the *Nicomachean Ethics*, he would agree with Aristotle that it is crucial that an agent's character and actions have their origin in the agent himself. What allows our character and actions to have this sort of internal origin is the possession of reason, which lets us control how we develop and act, instead of having our character and actions being preset by accidents of environment or inborn temperament beyond our control. The central role of reason in allowing us to shape our development, control our actions, and praise and blame one another appropriately, is reinforced by Epicurus' discussion in *On Nature* 25, where he maintains that it is contradictory to argue against the thesis that we are rational agents. *On Nature* 25 also shows how Epicurus thinks he can account for the emergence and causal efficacy of phenomena like reason within an identity theory of mind.

Annas is correct, then, when she claims that the central point of Epicurus' theory is that we are responsible agents because we are rational.[1] Therefore, the questions facing us are why Epicurus would think that determinism threatens the efficacy of our reason, and how introducing an indeterministic atomic motion protects us against this threat. I think that Cicero's *De fato* does clearly describe the fatalist threat that Epicurus believes confronts him and the way the swerve is supposed to protect us from this threat.

The problem Epicurus faces and the solution he proposes are similar to the problem Aristotle faces and the solution he proposes in *de Int.* 9. Both believe that deliberation about what one should do would be idle if the Principle of Bivalence applied unrestrictedly to statements about what is going to occur in the future, since this would render the future necessary, and both deny the Principle of Bivalence in order to escape this threat. This similarity between Aristotle and Epicurus on the truth value of future contingents has been often noted before, but Cicero's *De fato* has had only a peripheral role in past discussions of the swerve; often the similarity is simply noted but the *De fato* otherwise ignored. One reason for doing so is because Epicurus thinks that "logical and causal determinism are interentailing," as Sedley puts it, and it is thought that Epicurus' concern about truth values is simply a trivial consequence of his more fundamental worries about causal determinism, which is what Epicurus thinks truly is threatening. If so, we would have to look elsewhere to find out why causal determinism exercises him so much. A different reason for ignoring the discussion of the swerve in the *De fato* is given by Bobzien. She thinks that for Epicurus logical and causal determinism are just separate issues, so Epicurus' concerns in the *De fato* do little to shed light on the role of the swerve or the way in which causal determinism threatens us. I think that both these maneuvers are mistaken. Once we see what fatalist worries Epicurus is confronting in the *De fato*, and how the swerve is supposed to solve these worries, we should conclude that this exhausts Epicurus' reasons for positing the swerve *vis-à-vis* our freedom. Furthermore, once we see what role the swerve plays, as shown in the *De fato*, this allows us to understand the other texts that mention human freedom and talk about the swerve.

1 Annas (1993) 70.

6.1 The fatalist arguments from bivalence Epicurus opposes

A large number of fatalist arguments were in the intellectual atmosphere at the time of Epicurus; most of them were probably fashioned by the 'Megarian/Dialectical' school. Some of them, such as the celebrated Master Argument, were simply supposed to establish Diodorus Cronus' modal definitions, but were taken to have fatalist consequences, while others, such as the 'Mower Argument' and the 'Idle Argument', were explicitly fatalist.[2] Trying to fix on the exact fatalist argument that Epicurus was responding to would be a mistake – there probably was not exactly one such argument, and Epicurus might not have been responding to a strictly formulated single argument. Rather, Epicurus was probably responding to a *type* of argument that can be presented in various ways. Nonetheless, from the various fatalist arguments and responses to them, I think we can do a reasonably good job of reconstructing the basic sort of argument Epicurus is worried about from these sources, without worrying too much about the details. Three of them – the 'Truth to Necessity Argument,' the 'Master Argument,' and the 'Idle Argument'—are recorded in the *De fato*, and it seems that Epicureans were concerned to rebut them all. A fourth argument, the so-called 'Mower' Argument, has a quite similar form to the 'Truth-to-Necessity' argument in the *De fato* and is more fleshed out, so it can be used to supplement our information on it.[3] I will also be drawing parallels to the determinist argument contained in Aristotle's *de Interpretatione* 9, since it often contains clearer statements of points presented more tersely elsewhere, and I will occasionally draw on other Epicurean writings about freedom to help understand what sorts of fatalist concerns motivate them.[4] Henceforward, I will speak of 'the' fatalist argument that Epicurus is confronting, but please keep in mind that it is something of a composite sketch.

2 See n. 5 in chapter 1 for further readings on Diodorus, the Megarians, and the Master Argument.

3 For more information on the sources and a detailed exposition of the 'Truth-to-Necessity' and 'Mower' arguments, see Bobzien (1998*a*) 76–81, and of the 'Idle Argument', see 180–193. However, Bobzien seems to assume in the way that she describes it that the 'Truth to Necessity' argument is a distinct fatalist argument. I think it is more likely that this 'argument' is simply a sketch of the type of general line of thought Epicurus wants to rebut, and that it thus subsumes many more particular and detailed fatalist arguments based on the truth-makers of statements about the future.

4 Although I will be using *de Int.* 9 to help illustrate Epicurus' position, my argument does not depend on the supposition that Epicurus is drawing directly on Aristotle. See section 6.2.1 for more on this.

Epicurus is reported to have rejected both the Principle of Bivalence (PB) – the principle that every statement either is true or is false – and the Law of Excluded Middle (LEM) – the principle that every statement of the form 'p or not-p' necessarily is true.[5] Most of the fatalist arguments that vex Epicurus start out with disjunctions of contradictory statements (*e.g.*, either Hermarchus will be alive tomorrow, or he will not be alive), and Epicurus rejects the thesis that such statements are true; that is, he rejects LEM, from which follows a rejection of PB. However, as Bobzien notes, Epicurus seems to be concerned with a 'semantic' version of LEM; that is, of every contradictory pair of statements, one or the other is *true*. With this understanding of LEM, PB and LEM are mutually entailing. So I do not think that too much hangs on whether one speaks of LEM or PB, and although the composite argument I am presenting will be in terms of disjunctions of contradictions, I will usually speak of the putative consequences of accepting the universal applicability of the Principle of Bivalence.[6]

5 See *e.g.*, *De fato* x 21ff, *De fato* xvi 37, *Academica* 2.97.

6 My discussion here is indebted to the excellent discussion in Bobzien (1998*a*) 76–86, although I disagree with her contention (p. 78 n. 43) that it makes much of a difference exactly which logical principle Epicurus took himself to be rejecting. Bobzien (rightly) says that Epicurus rejects a *semantic* version of LEM, because the principle he rejects is put in terms of one or the other disjunct in statement of the form (p or not-p) being true, *not* in terms of the statement as a whole being true. Using Bobzien's notation of T[*p*] for 'p is true' and F[*p*] for 'p is false,' we can formalize the principles as follows. (This follows Bobzien's own formalization on p. 77 n. 40, correcting a typo in her version of semantic LEM):
T[*p*] v F[*p*] (Principle of Bivalence).
p v ~*p* (law of excluded middle).
T[*p*] v T[~*p*] (semantic law of excluded middle).
From PB, the Principle of Non-Contradiction (PNC) [~(*p*&~*p*)], and the following obvious semantic principle: T[*p*] iff F[~*p*], semantic LEM follows. And indeed, given the standard understanding of the truth-conditions for a disjunction (at least one or the other disjunct is true for the disjunction as a whole to be true), Epicurus would be right, if he rejects PB, also to reject LEM. It is for this reason that Cicero pours scorn on those later Epicureans who reject PB but accept LEM for their pitiful ignorance of logic (*De fato* xvi 37–38) while grudgingly admitting that Epicurus is being circumspect in rejecting it. (*Academica* 2.97) However, even these later Epicureans would side with Epicurus in rejecting *semantic* LEM; the only difference would be on the question of whether all statements of the form (*p* v ~*p*) are true, even though in some cases both disjuncts are 'neutral' in truth-value, and these later Epicureans are reverting to Aristotle's position in *de Int.* 9.
Bobzien also mentions that in *De fato* 37 'we have a curious intermediate between Principle of Bivalence and semantic Excluded Middle,' *viz.*, (T[p] & F[~p]) v (F[p] & T[~p]). But I don't find this really to be that curious a principle; it follows trivially from semantic law of excluded middle, the principle of non-contradiction, and the obvious semantic principle cited above.
I think that the various fatalist arguments that depend on logical/semantic principles are formulated in terms of disjunctions of contradictory statements because that makes for a punchier presentation of their fatalist consequences, since deliberation is typically concerned with mutually exclusive alternatives, each of which we take to be possible, in *some* sense of possible.

In *De fato* 21, Cicero directly reports the sort of argument Epicurus was concerned to reject, saying "if either of two alternatives is true from all eternity, that alternative is also certain, and if certain it is also necessary. This, he thinks, would prove both necessity and fate." As it stands, this is obviously quite sketchy. Bobzien sticks in semantic LEM as a premise to reconstruct the line of thought as follows, calling it the 'Truth-to-Necessity' argument:[7]

(P1) Of every contradictory pair, either one or the other is true.
(P2) If one of every contradictory pair is true, it is also certain.
(P3) If it is certain, it is also necessary.
(C) Therefore, of every contradictory pair one is necessary.

Bobzien notes the striking similarity of the 'Truth-to-Necessity' argument to the so-called 'Mower' Argument, which has as its conclusion that the contingent – in particular, future contingency – is destroyed.[8] The fatalist argument Aristotle presents likewise has as its conclusion all events come about out of necessity, and that there is no contingency (*de Int.* 9 18b6–8).

Two questions about this argument sketch immediately present themselves: why would truth imply necessity, and what notion of necessity is operative here? Whatever the case, it must be a notion of necessity that is supposed to have the sort of unacceptable consequences for our agency that Epicurus fears.[9]

The key to understanding why truth implies necessity is that these arguments are assuming a 'tensed,' or time-dependent, notion of truth – statements are true at some time or other. Therefore, if one accepts PB, all

7 Bobzien (1998*a*) 79.
8 Bobzien (1998*a*) 80–1.
9 I will leave aside the question of how the epistemic notion of certainty and the modal notion of necessity are supposed to be related. (P3) asserts that one can be certain only of what is necessary, which initially seems quite unpromising. Even murkier would be trying to establish why all true statements are certain, and in what sense they are certain. Rather than thinking that there is some complicated theory about the relationship between truth, certainty and necessity implicit here, I would rather bypass certainty entirely in working out how one goes from truth to necessity in the fatalist argument. My guess (and it is only that) is that the talk of certainty has crept into the *De fato* and the sources reporting the 'Mower' argument because talking about infallible predictors (such as a Laplacean demon) knowing in advance exactly what is going to occur is a good way of illustrating the supposed fixity of truth-values possessed by statements about the future and the fatalist consequences flowing from that fixity, even though (as Aristotle says when using such an example while setting out his fatalist argument in *de Int.* 9 18b33–19a7), strictly speaking, actual predictors having knowledge of the future in this way are superfluous as far as the argument itself goes.

statements about what will occur in the future are now either true or false, and have been true or false "from all eternity," as it is put repeatedly in the *De fato*. What is especially problematic for Epicurus is the notion that what is going to occur has already been predetermined *in the past*, because all past truths are necessary truths.

Although we have no sources that attribute to Epicurus in so many words the thesis that all past truths are necessary, I think it is fairly clear that he accepted it. It is one of the premises of Diodorus' Master Argument, which was taken to have unacceptable fatalist implications, and if Epicurus had rejected this premise, this would have been sufficient for escaping the argument's conclusion. And in that case, Epicurus would have had no need to reject PB in order to escape this argument's conclusion, as Cicero reports he did. Furthermore, of those people who did consider the Master Argument (or similar arguments), the majority accepted this premise, including Aristotle, whose rejection of PB (on most interpretations of *de Int. 9*) makes his response to this sort of argument similar to Epicurus'.[10] Cleanthes and a few others were reported to have rejected this premise, but this is a minority position, which nobody attributes to Epicurus. But finally, and most tellingly, the way in which the past is described by Epicureans (or in reports on Epicurus) shows that they regard it as necessary in the sense of necessity pertinent to this argument (as I explain below), that is, the past is immutable.[11]

10 *De Caelo* I 12, 283b12–14, *NE* 1139b7–9, *Rhetoric* 1418a3–5, noted in Sorabji (1980) 105.

11 Cicero sets out the reason that the past is considered necessary by Diodorus and Chrysippus, and presumably by Epicurus also: "all things true in the past are necessary, as Chrysippus holds, as against his master Cleanthes, *because they are unchangeable* and because what is past cannot change from true to false. . ." (*De fato* vii 14) And, when Cicero is setting out Epicurus' fear of the results of fatalism, he refers repeatedly to things being "true from eternity," *e.g.*, "Epicurus is afraid that if he admits this [LEM] he will also have to admit that all events whatever are caused by fate on the grounds that if either of two alternatives are *true from eternity*, that alternative is also certain, and if it is certain it is also necessary. This, he thinks, would prove both necessity and fate." (*De fato* x 21. See also *De fato* ix 19–20, where Cicero reports that Epicurus worries about things having "fore-ordained causes" or being brought about by "everlasting causes," xii 28, where he speaks of "immutable causes, eternally existing," and the restatement of the Idle Argument in terms of what will occur being "true from all eternity." xiii 29. When describing the academic position, he says that it is fine to uphold that statements are "true from eternity," but *pace* the Epicureans, not subject to the "necessity of fate." xvi 37–38). See also Lucretius' emphasis on how it would be threatening for causes to be linked to other causes "from infinity." Bobzien also notices the importance of the tensed notion of truth in this argument, but she supposes that the problem is that it is true *now* what will happen in the future (Bobzien (1998*a*) 81–82). Although we can ask whether, given their other philosophical commitments, Epicurus and Aristotle should have been worried about the *present* truth of statements about supposedly contingent future events (and I think we can construct a good case that they should have been so worried), I do not think that the sources we have that report the fatalist arguments based on considerations of truth, and the responses to them, focus much on the question of *present* truth; instead, the focus is always on *past* truth.

The conclusion that the future is necessary is threatening to our agency because, as Aristotle says, we do not deliberate about what is necessary. For instance, we do not deliberate about mathematical truths or the celestial motions.[12] But by 'necessary' in this context Aristotle does not simply mean what is logically necessary (as are mathematical truths) or what is always the case (as are celestial motions), as he sometimes means by 'necessary.' Since even truths about particular changes happening to particular subjects in the past would be necessary, on the sense of necessary used in *de Int.* 9, *e.g.*, my getting a sunburn yesterday because of forgetting to put on sunscreen would be necessary.

In this connection, 'necessary' simply means what is inevitable or beyond our power to affect: mathematical truths, celestial motions and the past all cannot be changed by our efforts, and thus all are necessary. This immutability is also the reason Chrysippus gives (against Cleanthes) for why the past is necessary (*De fato* vii 14). When Peter van Inwagen gives a similar argument for the incompatibility of *causal* determinism and deliberation, he defines an 'inevitability' operator 'N' to capture this sense of necessity, as follows: "For any sentence *p*, the result of prefixing *p* with 'N' may be regarded as an abbreviation for the result of flanking 'and no one has, or ever had, any choice about whether' with occurrences of *p*."[13] This sense of necessity explains both the plausibility of the premise that the past is necessary – the past certainly seems beyond our power to affect – and the unacceptability of the argument's conclusion – if all future events are necessary, then they are all beyond our power to affect, rendering deliberation pointless.

The fatalist arguments that try to establish the fixity of the future do not concentrate on the fixity of what we are going to *do*; instead, they focus on the fixity of what is going to *happen* – often, what is going to *happen to us.* Aristotle speaks of there being a Sea Battle. In the 'Idle Argument', it is either inevitable that you will recover from an illness or inevitable that you won't recover. When he rejects LEM, Epicurus speaks

12 For Aristotle on not deliberating about the past, celestial motion and mathematical truths see: *Eudemian Ethics* 6 1 1139a13, 6 2 1139b7–9, 6 5 1140 a31–b1, 6 7 1141b10–11, 3 3 1112a30–31, with 3 5 1113b7–8, *Eudemian Ethics* 2 10, 1226a20–30, *Rhetoric* 1 2, 1357a8. We refrain from deliberation in such cases because they are necessary: *NE* 1139b7–9. Aristotle also says, in *NE* 1118b31–3, that if the determinist is right, why should we bother deliberating?

13 van Inwagen (1983) 93. He gives the following example to illustrate: "N All men are mortal" is an abbreviation for "All men are mortal and no one had, or ever had, any choice about whether all men are mortal." Like Aristotle, he asserts that all logical truths are beyond our power in this sense, so he asserts the following inference rule α for this operator: $\chi p \vdash \mathrm{N}p$

of it being either necessary that Hermarchus be alive tomorrow, or necessary he not be alive.

This leads, then, to the further conclusion that, if what is going to occur has already been set, then it is pointless to deliberate about it, *because what will happen, will happen regardless of what we do.* To put it in slightly different terms, if what is going to happen has already been *predetermined* and is true from all eternity, then it is pointless to strive to *make it the case* one way or the other. As Aristotle puts it, if the fatalist argument goes through, "there would be no need to deliberate or to take trouble (thinking that if we do this, this will happen, but if we do not it will not). For there is nothing to prevent someone's having said ten thousand years beforehand that this would be the case, and another's having denied it; so that whichever of the two was true to say then, will be the case of necessity" (*de Int.* 9 18b31–36). The Idle Argument, as restated by Cicero in terms of truth instead of fate, says that if it has been true from eternity that you will recover from an illness, then there would be no point in trying to bring it about, since it will happen no matter what you do.[14] Thus, the argument, if it goes through, would make futile not only deliberation, but goal-directed action generally.[15] This notion that

14 Although the first explicit response to the 'Idle Argument' itself is from Chrysippus (as recorded by Cicero), the probability is quite high that Epicurus also confronted an argument of this sort and responded to it along the same lines he responded to its sibling fatalist arguments. As Bobzien notes, the Idle Argument is strikingly similar to the Mower, and was probably developed as a companion piece to it (Bobzien (1998*a*) 189), and we can be fairly confident that Epicurus was familiar with the Mower because of its similarity to the fragmentary 'Truth-to-Necessity' argument that Cicero says vexed Epicurus, and both Cicero (*De fato* 29) and Seneca (*Natural Questions* II 37.3) give versions of the 'Idle Argument' in terms of the truth of statements about the future, instead of fate. Also, the way Cicero introduces the Idle Argument suggests that Epicureans were familiar with it and responded to it in a way similar to their responses to the other fatalist arguments. At xii 28, immediately after saying that PB has no fatalist consequences, and chastising the Epicureans for thinking that it does, and for denying PB, which is impossible, he says: "nor will we be hindered by what is called the 'Idle Argument.'" (*nec nos impediet illa ignava ratio quae dicitur.)* The use of 'nos,' which strictly speaking is not necessary since the verb indicates who the subject is, stresses the subject, like using ἐγώ in Greek. In his translation, Rackham indicates this by putting in a "for our part" after we: "Nor shall we for our part be hampered. . ." This is probably a bit of an overtranslation; perhaps a natural way in English of stressing the subject would be simply to put it in italics: "Nor shall *we* be hindered. . ." In any case, in context, this suggests that *we* (the academic skeptics) will not be hindered by this argument, even though our opponents (the Epicureans) *are* hindered by it, in the same sort of way that they get into trouble (denying a logical principle like Bivalence) because they falsely suppose (xii 27) that PB implies there are immutable causes, eternally existing, that forbid anything from turning out other than they do.

15 Cicero *De fato* 28–9, Aristotle *de Int.* 9 19a7–10. This also fits with Lucretius' discussion of the swerve and *voluntas* in *DRN* 2. Lucretius thinks that determinism is incompatible with the existence of *voluntas*, which is what produces animal action in general, such as the bursting of the horses from the stalls.

certain things will inevitably befall you, no matter what you do, fits in well with the traditional Greek notion of fate, as illustrated by Zeno's model of fate as a cart to which a dog is tied: the dog will be dragged along where the cart is going whether it is willing or not.[16] It is probably for this reason that Cicero repeatedly says that Epicurus feared that accepting LEM would establish the "necessity of fate."

6.2 *Epicurus' response to the fatalist argument*

Epicurus gives three sorts of reasons for rejecting the conclusion of the fatalist argument. The first is basically pragmatic: it would be impossible to live if one really believed the thesis that everything occurs according to the 'necessity of fate' and acted consistently with that belief. Epicurus gives this argument against the thesis that everything occurs 'of necessity' in *On Nature* 25, and Epicureans were fond of this type of argument. Lucretius offers an *apraxia* argument (literally 'inaction' argument, more colloquially 'idle' or 'lazy' argument) against skepticism in *DRN* 4 469–521, and the Epicurean Colotes actually argues against all philosophies other than Epicureanism on the basis that they make living impossible (Plutarch, *Against Colotes*). Such *apraxia* arguments might be problematic – after all, it does not follow from "believing *p* would make living impossible for the person believing *p*" that "therefore, not-*p*" – but they were quite common. Perhaps such arguments would be better viewed as trying to establish, not the falsity of *p*, but the rational unacceptability of *p*. In any case, the targets of these *apraxia* arguments did not respond by questioning the validity of the argument's form; instead, they denied the premise that their position (or lack of position, as the case may be) would entail *apraxia* if followed consistently.

A similar pragmatic point might be made the other way around, as it were – instead of saying that believing *p* would make life impossible, it might be said that a person's behavior shows that he does not 'really' believe *p*, or (slightly differently) that if he does believe *p*, his beliefs are inconsistent, since his behavior commits him also to believing not-*p*. Epicurus seems to be making this sort of point when he claims in *On Nature* 25 that Democritus' actions clashed with the fatalistic implications of his theory, although Democritus did not realize it. We may expand on

16 Hippolytus *Refutation of all heresies* 1.21 (L&S 62A). A similar idea is expressed by Cleanthes (quoted by Epictetus *Enchiridion* 53) when he says that he will follow Zeus whether or not he is willing.

his point slightly as follows: actions often manifest beliefs, for example, if I walk out the door, I manifest the belief that this is a better way of exiting the room than jumping out the window, which in turn depends on all sorts of other beliefs about the existence of the door, the way bodies behave near the surface of the earth, *etc.* Any person who deliberates, or even acts at all, shows that he believes that his actions can make a difference in the world. This contradicts the conclusion of the fatalist argument. Therefore, anybody who accepts the conclusion of that argument is doomed to be constantly contradicting himself whenever he acts. Since it is irrational to believe contradictory statements, and it is impossible for any agent to accept the conclusion of the fatalist argument without thereby being committed to believing contradictory statements, it is irrational to believe the conclusion of the fatalist argument.

Again, although I think that Epicureans advance this pattern of argument, I find it problematic. Skeptics, of course, will protest that actions need not manifest beliefs in the way Epicureans think they do.[17] More fundamentally, even if we were to grant to the Epicureans that anybody who accepts the conclusion of the fatalist argument is doomed to manifest constantly in his behavior beliefs that contradict that conclusion, it is unclear that the rational course is to reject the conclusion of that argument. That is because, from the premise "Acting manifests a belief that *p*," it does not follow that *p*. And if one really believes that some argument for *not-p* is sound, but that one is nonetheless inescapably committed as an agent to believing that *p*, then one would be reducing one's stock of true beliefs if one were to stop believing *not-p* in order to keep one's beliefs consistent. So it is not clear that, in this sort of case, it is actually epistemically preferable to give up the conclusion of the argument for *not-p* rather than to remain with contradictory beliefs.[18]

17 See, for instance, Carneades' skeptical criterion, reported in Sextus Empiricus *M* 7.166–84, and Sextus' description of the Pyrrhonian way of life, *PH* 1.21–4. Hankinson (1995) 108–115 and 293–308 is a good starting-place for discussions of the livability of skepticism.

18 My discussion in these past two paragraphs is heavily indebted to similar considerations advanced by van Inwagen (1983) 155–160. He thinks that deliberation manifests a belief that the various courses of action one is deliberating over are possible, so that anybody (like Baron d'Holbach) who acts and yet denies that there are such open possibilities thereby has contradictory beliefs. However, van Inwagen then goes on to say that this is *not* a good reason not to be a hard determinist, for the sorts of reasons I spell out above. Although I myself accept van Inwagen's objection to this sort of pragmatic argument, his objection probably would not have occurred to Epicurus or his opponents, since they would not have conceived of there being a gap between "I am inescapably committed to believing that *p*" and "*p*." As one of the anonymous reviewers of this book points out, that seems to be a distinctively modern move, associated with the 'insulation' of philosophy from ordinary beliefs, as it is put in Burnyeat (1997).

The final sort of reason for rejecting the conclusion is more straightforward. The way in which Epicurus describes the trichotomy of things which are due to chance, which happen of necessity, and which depend on us (*Ep. Men.* 133–134) makes it clear that, if all things did happen of necessity, nothing would 'depend on us.' And in *On Nature* 25, he asserts that our *prolêpsis* of what it is for certain things to 'depend on us' or 'be from us ourselves' – that is, what certain things 'depending on us' or 'being from us ourselves' really amounts to – is formed by observing our ability to shape other people's behavior through argument, to control our own behavior using our reason, and the like. Now, Epicurus thinks it is obvious that certain things do indeed depend on us in this sort of way; therefore, any argument for the conclusion that everything occurs 'of necessity' must be unsound. Similarly, when trying to show that not everything occurs according to the "decrees of fate" (*DRN* 2 254), Lucretius points to what is evident, the phenomenon that animals are able to initiate action in order to get what they desire. Aristotle gives the same reason for rejecting the fatalist argument he is examining: its conclusion is surely impossible, because "we see that what will be has an origin both in deliberation and in action."[19] To summarize the argument I take both Epicurus and Lucretius to be deploying, yet another example of Epicureans using a *modus tollens* in order to move from the *enarges* to the *adêlon*:

(1) If everything occurs of necessity, then we have no ability to initiate action or influence the course of events.
(2) We have the ability to initiate action and influence the course of events.
(3) Therefore, not everything occurs of necessity.

Once Epicurus establishes in this way that the fatalist argument is unsound, he avoids its conclusion by rejecting its premise that PB applies

It might also be urged that the sort of 'pragmatic' considerations I have been putting forward would be more compelling from within Epicureanism than I've been allowing. After all, like everything else other than one's own pleasure, philosophy and argument are valuable only instrumentally, because they are needed in order to help one attain *ataraxia.* Therefore, pointing out the disastrous practical consequences of the fatalist arguments would seem to be good reason to reject such arguments from within Epicureanism. However, thinking that argumentation is valuable only instrumentally is compatible with thinking that only cogent arguments are actually effective in promoting *ataraxia.* This seems to me to be the Epicurean attitude toward argumentation, and the arguments they advance are actually supposed to establish their conclusions. I do not see any evidence that Epicureans ever urge one to believe *p only* because believing *p* will make you happier, not also because there is good reason to think that *p* is true. (See O'Keefe (*2003b*) 54–55 for more on the status of argumentation within Epicureanism.)

19 *de Int.* 9 19a8–10. That the Epicureans and Aristotle consider this a refutation of the fatalist arguments makes it clear that they regard the conclusion of that argument as incompatible, not only with deliberation, but with effective goal-directed action generally.

to all statements, including those about the future. Instead, some statements about the future (such as ones about when Hermarchus will die) are neither true nor false. However, these statements change truth-value either to true or to false when the state of affairs picked out by the statement either obtains or is precluded from obtaining.

Since it is reported that Epicurus thinks that determinism is incompatible with justified praise or blame also, let me briefly discuss how the fatalist argument is connected with praise and blame. For both Aristotle and Epicurus, the class of actions liable to appropriate praise and blame is narrower than the class of actions generally. Children and non-human animals have *hormê* (*voluntas*, in Lucretius' discussion), since they initiate goal-directed action. However, only human beings with a certain level of development have *logos* and are able to reflect on their lives as a whole, calculate the outcomes of different possible courses of action, and use signs.[20] If my interpretation of *On Nature* 25 is correct, it is our possession of reason which allows us to have the 'cause out of ourselves' and be subject to praise and blame.

Lacking the necessary level of reasoning would exclude non-human animals from appropriate praise and blame for reasons similar to why they are excluded from considerations of justice. According to Epicurus, justice is an agreement "neither to harm nor be harmed" (*KD* 31), which is useful in social arrangements (*KD* 37) and which each of the parties enters into because of its benefits. There can be justice only where there is such an agreement, so that, for instance, no considerations of justice exist between states that have no agreements about how they should behave toward one another (*KD* 32). Because wild animals are unable to make agreements and thus cannot participate in the 'justice game,' there is no justice with regard to them. It would be nice if we could induce lions to agree not to attack us in return for our not attacking them, but since we cannot, we simply kill them off. In the same sort of way, it makes sense to praise and blame only those creatures which are able to participate in our socially useful practices of admonishing, warning, and encouraging one another to act in certain ways, and only creatures who are reasons-responsive can participate. Epicureans believe that we may *hate* destructive wild animals like lions, but we cannot properly *blame* them.[21] Possessing *voluntas* is necessary but not sufficient for being properly subject to praise and

20 See Annas (1993) 66–69 for a fuller discussion of animal rationality.
21 See Arr. 34.25.21–34, L&S 20j, discussed in section 4.2.1.

blame.[22] Since the fatalist argument abolishes *voluntas*, this would suffice to abolish justified praise and blame.

6.2.1 *Epicurus and Aristotle on the Principle of Bivalence*

I have been suggesting that the fatalist argument from PB that Epicurus is confronting and his response to it are quite similar to the argument Aristotle sets out in *de Int.* 9 and his response to that argument. In fact, I think it quite likely that Epicurus draws directly upon Aristotle in formulating his position, although my argument does not crucially depend on this supposition. However, there are problems with asserting this influence. Here, let me briefly lay out the similarities, give my reasons for thinking that Epicurus was influenced by Aristotle, and reply to the problems raised by this suggestion.

Like Epicurus, Aristotle confronts a fatalist argument that proceeds from the unrestricted application of PB to all statements, including statements about future contingents. The conclusions of the arguments are the same: that everything occurs of necessity, and hence that deliberation and taking care about the future are idle, since they depend on the assumption that the results of events depend on our actions (18b31–33). Aristotle thinks this conclusion unacceptable, because it is obvious that some things do depend on our actions, and so he rejects the premise of the fatalist argument that PB holds unrestrictedly. Statements about contingent matters in the future (*e.g.*, "There will be a Sea Battle tomorrow" or " 'Muskrat Love' will be re-released and become the no. 1 selling song of 2005") lack a truth-value.[23] However, even for statements about future contingents, the Principle of Bivalence does hold in a way: although they may *now* not be true or false, they will all *eventually* be either true or false.[24]

This understanding of *de Int.* 9 is somewhat controversial, although I think it is correct. I have been suggesting that Aristotle rejects a premise of the fatalist argument. After all, Aristotle says in several places in *de Int.* 9 that if it had been true all along that something was going to be the case, then it is necessary. He thus seems to accept the determinist's pattern of

22 So I disagree with Long and Sedley (1987) vol. II p. 113 that *DRN* 2 251ff shows that race-horses, because they have *voluntas*, are 'self-determining' in a sense strong enough to be subject to praise and blame.

23 *de Int.* 9 18a33–34.

24 Aristotle qualifies his denial of PB by saying that, of a statement and its negation, neither needs to be true or false 'yet' (*êdê*) (19a39).

inference from past truth to necessity.[25] I will call this interpretation of *de Int.* 9 the 'Anti-Realist' interpretation, because according to it not all statements about the future have truth-values. However, some people have thought that Aristotle rejects the validity of the fatalist argument. This is supposedly because Aristotle notices that the fatalist argument depends on a fallacious operator shift, going from the necessity of disjunctions of the form $\Box(p \vee \sim p)$ to the conclusion $(\Box p \vee \Box \sim p)$. This camp, the 'Realists,' claims that Aristotle accepts PB.[26] The interpretation of *de Int.* 9 was divided in ancient times, and continues to be divided today.[27]

To work through all of the scholarly controversies surrounding *de Int.* 9 and to come up with an original contribution of how best to interpret it in light of all of the previous scholarship would go well beyond the scope of the present work. Fortunately, to come up with an exact reconstruction of what *Aristotle himself* meant is not crucial for my purposes. The important thing, since I am concerned with what *Epicurus* is up to in light of the contemporary debate, is to understand what Epicurus took himself to be responding to. And how *de Int.* 9 was understood by Epicurus and the Stoics may not be the same as what the person who originally propounded the argument took himself to be saying. One constraint on this is that Epicurus' position should, at the least, be consistent with a plausible reading of the texts that we have. Happily, it is. Aristotle's immediate philosophical successors understood Aristotle in accord with the anti-realist interpretation, not the realist one, and the interpretation of the Master Argument and Aristotle's solution to it according to the anti-realist interpretation formed the backdrop for their own theories.[28] For

25 As Sorabji notes, "Aristotle seems repeatedly to say that the deterministic consequences follow if every affirmation and opposite negation is true or false (18a34, a37), or one true one false (b27–29), without giving any warning that he thinks the inference from premise to conclusion invalid" (Sorabji (1980) 94).

26 In my use of the terms "Realist" and "Anti-Realist," I am following Gaskin's nomenclature (Gaskin (1995) 12).

27 Rescher composed a summary of the history of the interpretation of *de Int.* 9, and put those of the Stoics, Epicureans, Ammonius, Boethius, M. Kneale, R. Taylor, C. A. Taylor, A. N. Prior and J. Lukasiewicz in the anti-realist school, and those of al-Farabi, Averroes, Abelard, Thomas Aquinas, Duns Scotus, Ockham, E. M. Edgehill, R. J. Butler, G. E. M. Anscombe, C. Strang and himself in the realist school (Rescher (1963), 45–46, quoted in van Rijen (1989) 106).

28 Sorabji notes some other sources on *de Int.* 9 which provide additional support for this contention. Aristotle was interpreted in an anti-realist fashion by the Peripatetics, according to Simplicius (Simplicius, Commentary on Aristotle's *Categories*, ed. Kalbfleisch, *Commentaria in Aristotelem Graeca (CIAG)* 407 6–13). An anti-realist position was also attributed to Aristotle by the Stoics, according to Boethius (Boethius, 2nd Commentary on Aristotle's *De Interpretatione*, ed. Meiser, Leipzig, 1880, 208) (Sorabji (1980) 92).

my purposes, this is sufficient, whatever the truth about what Aristotle himself might have meant to say in *de Int.* 9.

The second problem with asserting that Aristotle influences Epicurus in this way is that there is no direct evidence for such a linkage, and some, such as Sandbach, have denied that the Hellenistic philosophers were familiar with Aristotle much at all. I have given above my general reasons for being dubious about the plausibility of the Sandbach thesis. (See section 5.4.) If my argument in chapter 5 is successful, Epicurus is probably responding to fairly particular parts of Aristotle's technical work on motion when he formulates his doctrine of a universal direction 'down' and when he introduces the swerve as an *archê* of collisions. And Furley has convincingly argued that Epicurus' doctrine of minimal parts responds directly to Aristotle's criticisms of Democritus.[29] If this is right, the *prima facie* plausibility of Epicurus appropriating Aristotle's position in *de Int.* 9 – or at least a plausible reading of what that position is – is quite high. It is much higher than supposing that Epicurus came up with his response to the fatalist arguments, of denying PB, entirely on his own, with it simply being a coincidence that Aristotle earlier happened to come up with the same response to the same sort of argument.

That there is historical precedent for the sort of position I attribute to Epicurus raises its probability, since it is more likely that Epicurus would be developing his position against the background of concerns already on the philosophical agenda. Others have recognized this point and have tried to find precedents in past philosophers for the positions they attribute to Epicurus, but as I argued above (sections 3.2 and 3.3), these precedents depend on unlikely readings of the relevant texts.

In any case, everything I attribute to Epicurus, about the fatalist argument he confronts and his solution to it, can be found elsewhere; I need not assume that he draws directly on *de Int.* 9. Even if Epicurus does not draw directly from *de Int.* 9, my point still stands: there were many fatalist arguments that proceeded from principles like PB in the intellectual background while Epicurus was formulating his philosophy, such as the 'Master Argument' and its ilk. This makes Epicurus' use of the swerve more historically understandable on the Bivalence Interpretation than it would be on others.

29 Furley (1967) study 1, "Indivisible Magnitudes," particularly chapter 8.

6.3 *The Interentailment of logical and causal determinism, and the swerve*

Causal considerations are not present in the various versions of the fatalist argument Epicurus was responding to; the argument turns entirely on logical and semantic considerations. However, it is quite clear that, in order to escape the 'necessity of fate' that this argument would establish, Epicurus posited the swerve. For instance, right after setting out the Carneadean thesis that all statements about future truths are now true and cannot change their truth-value, Cicero adds, "nor, these things being so, is there any reason for Epicurus' standing in terror of fate and seeking protection against it from the atoms and making them swerve out of the perpendicular," and he later makes the same point, albeit polemically: "[Epicurus] confesses that he has been unable to withstand fate in any other way than by taking refuge in these fictitious swerves."[30] The clearest evidence that Epicurus posited the swerve in order to respond directly to the various logico-semantic fatalist arguments occurs in *De fato* ix 22. In the sentence immediately following the one where Cicero sets out the "Truth-to-Necessity" Argument, which Epicurus fears would prove both necessity and fate, Cicero says, "Epicurus thinks that the necessity of fate is avoided by the swerve of an atom."[31]

30 *De fato* ix 18, *De fato* xx 48. Translations of the *De fato* are from Rackham (1942) unless otherwise noted.

31 Thus, I disagree with Bobzien's assertion that Epicurus' denial of causal determinism *via* the swerve and his response to the fatalist argument are only loosely connected. (In Bobzien's view, the swerve is posited mainly to counter a very different sort of deterministic threat, that determinism implies that our characters are subject to "internal necessity." See section 4.2.3 for my reasons for thinking that there was no such distinct deterministic threat of that sort that Epicurus was trying to counter by the swerve.) Bobzien says, "We have no reason to think that the Truth-to-Necessity Argument involved causation in any way, and it is far from certain that it involved any concept of fate" (Bobzien (1998*a*) 83). However, even though that argument itself *can* be formulated purely in logical terms, I think Cicero's discussion in the *De fato* makes it abundantly clear that Epicurus' response to it *did* involve causation. (Fowler (2002) 338 also asserts that it is hard to see how the swerve and the denial of bivalence are connected, and "they may have been independent.")

Bobzien's reason for doubting that the argument and Epicurus' response to it involve 'fate' (despite the explicit mention in *De fato* that Epicurus thought this argument *would* confirm both necessity and fate) is that Epicurus himself *doesn't* "take 'to be necessary' and 'to be fated' as co-extensive" (Bobzien (1998*a*) 81). Instead, he distinguishes between fate (an all-embracing power the existence of which he rejects altogether) and necessity (which he admits is true of events that are neither due to chance nor dependent on us). Thus, Bobzien thinks, the mentions of fate are probably just Cicero's supplement, meant to make a connection between Epicurus' argument against necessity and Chrysippus' argument for fate from PB (Bobzien (1998*a*) 84). I don't find Bobzien's attempt to cast doubt on the reliability of Cicero's report convincing. Bobzien is right about the difference between fate, *qua* purposive all-embracing power, and necessity for Epicurus.

The reason Epicurus thinks that positing the swerve is relevant for responding to this argument is because of the tight connection between things being true from eternity and things being brought about by preexisting causes from eternity. As Long and Sedley put it, both Epicurus and the Stoics see "physical and logical determinism as two aspects of a single thesis. . . . [Epicurus'] conflation [of the swerve and the denial of bivalence] seems to rest on an assumed equivalence of 'true in advance' with 'determined by pre-existing causes.'"[32]

The *De fato* makes it clear that both Epicurus and the Stoics thought that logical and causal determinism were interentailing. From now on, I will call this the 'Interentailment Thesis.' Cicero records the Stoics as saying, "There cannot be things which are going to be true if they do not have causes of their future being. So things which are true must necessarily have causes" (*De fato* xi 26). Epicurus feared that, if every proposition were true or false, then everything would happen according to fate, because these propositions must then be true "in virtue of eternal causes derived from a necessity of nature" (*De fato* ix 19).[33] Similarly, in

But the sense of the 'necessity of fate' that Epicurus is clearly concerned with here is fate *qua* the thesis that everything is fixed in such a way that nothing depends on us, so Cicero, although he may be using his terms somewhat loosely, is not being that misleading or misguided when he says that Epicurus posits the swerve to avoid the 'necessity of fate.' In the places where Cicero needs to be more careful, in distinguishing between 'fate' and what we'd call 'fatalism,' and different sorts of necessity, in talking about Chrysippus, he is perfectly capable of doing so. Even Epicurus himself uses the term 'fate' in a similar way in *Ep. Men.* 134: "It would be better to follow the mythology about gods than be a slave to the 'fate' of the natural philosophers (τῇ τῶν φυσικῶν εἱμαρμένῃ): the former at least hints at the hope of begging the gods off by means of worship, whereas the latter involves an inexorably necessity (ἡ δὲ ἀπαραίτητον ἔχει τὴν ἀνάγκην.)." The 'fate' of the natural philosophers here clearly does not mean something like a purposive all-embracing power, but Epicurus still thinks it proper to call this sort of 'inexorable necessity' a type of 'fate,' precisely because we would be helpless before it, as in traditional Greek notions of fate. It is for this sort of reason that we properly call the sort of thesis Aristotle wishes to rebut in *de. Int.* 9 'fatalism.'

32 Long and Sedley (1987) vol. 1 p. 112.

33 Actually, Cicero does not directly attribute this to Epicurus, but the context makes it abundantly clear. He says that Epicurus has no need to fear fate if he concedes that PB applies to all statements about the future, because "it is not in virtue of eternal causes derived from a necessity of nature that the following proposition is true. . ." indicating that Epicurus *does* think that it is in virtue of eternal causes derived from a necessity of nature that the statement is true. Cicero goes on to say, "It is the case *both* that the statement 'Epicurus will die in the arconship of Pytharatus at the age of seventy-two,' was always true, *and* also that nevertheless there were no fore-ordained causes why it should so happen. . ." showing that Epicurus thought there would be foreordaining causes if he admitted that the statement was always true. Similar considerations apply to *De fato* xii 28: Cicero says "it does not immediately follow from the fact that every statement is either true or false that there are immutable causes, eternally existing, that forbid anything to fall out other wise than it will fall out," and in context, since he is discussing the shortcoming of the Epicurean position and the superiority of Carneades' emended position to it, Cicero indicates that the Epicureans thought that it *did* follow.

De fato 20–21, Chrysippus is said to prove causal determinism from PB using the following principle: if there were uncaused motion, then not every proposition would be true or false, since "anything lacking efficient causes will be neither true nor false," and Cicero states that Epicurus also accepts this principle, but (one person's *modus ponens* being another's *modus tollens*), uses it to disprove PB.[34]

Although I think that Long and Sedley's description of the Stoics and Epicureans on logical and causal determinism is basically correct, I do have one caveat. The way they describe the "conflation" of the swerve and the denial of PB, and an "assumed equivalence" between "true in advance" and "determined by pre-existing causes," might seem to imply that Epicurus (and perhaps the Stoics) simply confuse these theses, not seeing the differences between them. Although our evidence is somewhat sketchy on this matter, I think we can discern fairly reasonable semantic grounds, having to do with the truth-makers for statements about future states of affairs, for why Epicurus and the Stoics subscribe to the Interentailment Thesis, which do not involve simply confusing or conflating the denial of PB with the thesis that motion without a cause exists.[35]

In *De fato* xi 23–26, Cicero introduces Carneades' contribution to the debate between Stoics and Epicureans, which is supposed to be a sort of gift to the Epicureans, helping them to maintain their position against the Stoics without denying PB. According to Carneades, the existence of a "voluntary motion of mind" can be maintained without the swerve or "motion without a cause." Once there is such a voluntary motion, it has a cause (the nature of the mind itself), but no external and antecedent cause. Then, after setting Carneades' position out, Cicero asks,

This being so, what is the reason why every proposition is not either true or false, if we do not allow that whatever takes place is caused by fate? The reason is, says he [Epicurus], that future things that have not got causes *why* they will be in the

34 Therefore, Bobzien is incorrect when she states "we certainly have no reason to assume that Epicurus established a *direct* connection between the Excluded Middle and a chain of causes from eternity to the future event. It is not attested that Epicurus thought of fate as a series of causes, 'commencing' in eternity" (Bobzien (1998*a*) 84).

35 A modern view of the semantics of propositions regarding the future which comes reasonably close to the sort of view I attribute to Epicurus can be found in Tooley (1997); see chapter 5 in particular. Tooley, after arguing that one can make sense of a temporally-indexed notion of truth, defends the position that certain propositions regarding the future can have an indeterminate truth-value because *at that time* there is not yet a fact for the proposition (or its contradiction) to correspond to. Such propositions can later change their truth-value, as the facts to make them true (or false) come into being.

future cannot be true; therefore those that are true must necessarily have causes; accordingly when they have occurred they will have occurred by fate.[36]

Similarly, Chrysippus says (*De fato* x 20) "if uncaused motion exists, it will not be the case that every proposition. . .is either true or false, for a thing not possessing efficient causes will be neither true or false." And Sextus Empiricus says that, according to the Stoics, "true is that which subsists (ὑπάρχει) and is contradictory to something, and false is that which does not subsist and is contradictory to something" (*M* 8.10).

I take it that the point both the Epicureans and Stoics are making is that, since the future is not yet – it has not obtained – there is not yet anything there in virtue of which the statement about the future can be true, unless there presently obtain conditions to bring about the state of affairs described by the statement.[37] This might be mistaken, but it is not obviously wrong, and it is not based upon a confusion between causation and truth. We can spell out the principles about the truth-makers for statements about the future that underlie the Epicurean and Stoic acceptance of the Interentailment Thesis:

A statement *s* about the future is true at time *t* if and only if there obtains at time *t* sufficient conditions to bring about the state of affairs described in *s*, false at time *t* if and only if there obtains at time *t* sufficient conditions to preclude the state of affairs described in *s* from obtaining, and neither true nor false at time *t* if

36 When I speak here and elsewhere of Carneades' positions and arguments, I do not mean to imply that he himself is committed to any of them, rather than simply advancing them dialectically for the purposes of counterbalancing the arguments of others and inducing *equipollence* and hence suspension of judgment. For a purely 'dialectical' interpretation of Carneades' practice, see Couissin (1983). For an interpretation of Carneades as a moderate fallibilist, see Thorsrud (2002). An overview of these issues can be found in Hankinson (1995) chapters 5 and 6. None of my own argumentation hinges on which (if either) of these views is correct.

37 Precisely this point also seems to be made by Epicurean spokesman Boëthus in Plutarch's *The Oracles at Delphi (Pyth. orac.* 10, 398F–399A). Boëthus is considering what we should say about prophecies that turn out to be accurate, although they had no foundation (οὐκ ἔχοντας ἀρχὴν). Boëthus says that, at the time it was made, such a pronouncement had error in itself – *i.e.*, it was not true – because it told of things that were non-existent (τὰ μὴ ὑπάρχοντα), even though when the event that it predicted comes to pass, then it becomes true. Unfortunately, this report is muddied a bit by Plutarch. He takes the Epicurean argument to concern whether it could just be a coincidence that very vague, general predictions (such as "Athens will be overthrown") could be issued which, unsurprisingly, turn out to be made true by some specific event. Plutarch (or rather, the Stoic Sarapion within the conversation) grants that such vague predictions coming true does little to establish the reliability or value of oracles, but he retorts that it cannot be just a coincidence that many quite specific prophecies (of which he gives several examples) were correct (*Pyth. orac.* 11, 399B–399E). This, of course, is a quite different issue from the truth-value of the predictions made by oracles, and Plutarch conflates the two issues both in his presentation of the argument and his reply.

and only if there does not obtain at time *t* sufficient conditions either to bring about or to preclude the state of affairs described in *s*.[38]

Carneades questions the linkage that both Epicurus and Chrysippus make between the Principle of Bivalence and there obtaining sufficient causal conditions at present to bring about the states of affairs picked out by the statement. Carneades unequivocally accepts PB for all propositions, at all times: "from all eternity this proposition was true: 'Philoctetes will be abandoned on the island,' and this was not able to change from being true to being false. For it is necessary, when you have two contradictories. . .that one be true and the other false, though Epicurus disagrees" (*De fato* 37). He denies, however, that any deterministic consequences follow from PB, because the truth of a statement does not imply that there are "immutable eternal causes" that *make* it true (*De fato* 28). Instead, it is simply the fact that Philoctetes will actually be abandoned that makes the statement true.[39]

This, however, would not satisfy Chrysippus and Epicurus, who would ask in virtue of what *is* it now a fact that Philoctetes will be abandoned, without there being any presently obtaining cause to make it a fact that this will occur. In order to defend his position, Carneades appeals to the symmetry of the past and future: "For just as we call 'true' those past things of which it was at an earlier time true that they were being actualized, so we will call 'true' those future things that of which it will later be true that they are being actualized" (*De fato* xii 27). Just as something being true in the past does not depend on its having certain effects now, something being true in the future does not depend on its having certain causes now.

Therefore, Carneades thinks, logical determinism does not imply causal determinism. Carneades would reject the premise in the fatalist argument that 'every past truth is necessary.' If Carneades is right, then what I do now *can* have an effect on the past, in an attenuated sense. If the necessity of the past is tied to its irrevocability, then there *is* an asymmetry

38 To use an example to illustrate this thesis that is less contentious than putative free human choice: let us suppose that the Copenhagen Interpretation of quantum mechanics is correct, and that there are no 'hidden variables' that presently determine when *e.g.*, a particular atom will decay. Assuming that present conditions neither ensure nor preclude that atom *a* will decay at time *t*, then (at present) the statement "atom *a* will decay at time *t*" is neither true nor false.

39 cf. *De fato* ix 18: "If it were stated thus, 'Scipio will die by violence at night in his room,' that would be a true statement. For it would be a statement that what was going to occur actually was going to occur; and one ought to know that it was going to occur from the fact that it did happen." See Gilbert Ryle, "It was to be," chapter 2 of Ryle (1960), for a similar position, pp. 22–24 in particular.

between the past and the future, insofar as I can affect the future, and not the past. I can kill myself today or tomorrow; I cannot kill myself yesterday. However, by my present actions, I can make it *to have been true* that something was going to occur. Richard Sorabji has a very good analogy to make this point. If I commit suicide, I make my most recent birthday *to have been* my last. Similarly, if I choose to kill myself now, I make the statement "Tim O'Keefe is going to kill himself" to *have been true* in the past. As Sorabji puts it, both last and true are relational terms, one implying a relation to successors, the other to facts.[40]

In recent discussions of fatalist arguments, this point is made by drawing a distinction between 'hard facts' that are truly about the past (*e.g.*, that I spent my 35th birthday in Minnesota) vs. 'soft facts,' (*e.g.*, that it was always the case that my 35th birthday would be my last), with the former being beyond my present control, but not the latter.[41]

Once this distinction is made, however, then the fatalist argument that Epicurus fears can be restated in terms of causal determinism rather than logical determinism, and some people who reject the thesis that logical determinism implies fatalism accept that causal determinism does so. This is Carneades' position. When stated in terms of truth, the 'Idle Argument' is a sophism. However, if we instead state the argument in terms of everything taking place because of "antecedent causes" and "in a closely knit web of natural interconnection," we can validly conclude that nothing is in our power.[42]

Van Inwagen gives a clear exposition of this sort of Diodoran fatalist argument from causal determinism. He says that, if what is going to occur is the result of past states of affairs, which I can do nothing about, and the laws of nature, which I likewise can do nothing to affect, then the future is fixed by factors beyond my control in a way such as to render deliberation pointless. The past is beyond our control (that is, all of the 'hard' facts that are truly about the past), and if determinism is true, then from the (gigantic) proposition describing a total state of the world at some point

40 Sorabji (1980) 102. This might have been Cleanthes' point in his rejection of the first premise of the Master Argument, as Long and Sedley suggest (Long and Sedley (1987) vol. 1 pp. 234–236), but our evidence is too sketchy to decide this conclusively.

41 See Bernstein (2002) 71–4 for a brief synopsis of this distinction, as well as pointers to further literature on it.

42 Since my main concern at this point is Epicurus, and not Carneades, I will not spend time trying to reconstruct here precisely how Cicero thinks the argument is supposed to go, and what exactly he means by things being "in our power." However, I do take it that the conclusion of the argument *is* supposed to be fatalist, in the same sense in which Epicurus thinks the arguments he confronts have fatalist results, since Cicero presents it as a tightened-up version of the 'Idle Argument'. See the epilogue for more on Carneades and his influence on the subsequent debate.

in the past, plus the laws of nature, any true proposition about the future follows. He then proposes the following rule of inference, β, about his 'inevitability' operator N: $N(p \supset q)$, $Np \vdash Nq$. This is reminiscent of Diodorus' premise that the impossible cannot follow from the possible, but using the 'inevitability' operator: the consequences of what is unavoidable are themselves unavoidable. But since all truths about the future (put these in place of *q* above) are consequences of the conjunction of statements describing some past total state of affairs plus the laws of nature (put this conjunction in place of *p* above) if determinism is true, it follows that what will happen in the future is unavoidable for us, if determinism is true.[43] And, since deliberating about what is unavoidable is futile, it follows that if determinism is true, deliberation is futile.

6.4 *Epicurus' mistakes*

Let me briefly recap the argument that Epicurus confronts, and how he uses the swerve to respond to it: If logical principles like LEM and PB apply to all statements about the future, it follows that what is going to occur has been fixed all along, from eternity. And, because of the Interentailment Thesis, it follows that what will occur in the future is fixed by chains of cause and effect that stretch back indefinitely into the past. If this is true then, since we can do nothing to effect the past, the future would be fixed in a way that would render deliberation and action pointless. But this conclusion is unacceptable, both for pragmatic reasons, and because it is evident that deliberation and action are *not* pointless. Therefore, we must reject the argument's premise that PB and LEM apply to all statements about the future. Because of the Interentailment Thesis, this also involves rejecting the thesis that there are 'eternal causes' in the past that determine everything that is going to occur in the future. The swerve, a non-deterministic atomic motion, ensures that not everything is determined by pre-existing causes, which also renders PB and LEM false, at least for some statements regarding the future. This allows us to avoid the 'necessity of fate,' as Cicero puts it.

43 Van Inwagen (1983) 93–105. Van Inwagen thinks that his argument proves that nobody has the sort of ability to do otherwise necessary for free will, and it is this aspect of his argument, which is a contribution to the 'traditional' problem of the compatibility of free will and determinism, via PAP (see section 1.1), which has attracted the most attention. However, van Inwagen also thinks that this argument establishes that, if determinism is true, then there are not 'open possibilities' in the future in a way that precludes effective deliberation and action (van Inwagen (1983) 153–161). It is this aspect of his position that I concentrate on, since it is the part that closely parallels Epicurus' argument.

I think that the *De fato* does clearly attribute the above line of thought to Epicurus. However, this line of thought is problematic. In his arguments for the swerve, Epicurus makes three mistakes, which are subsequently exposed by Chrysippus and Carneades. Let me describe each in turn.[44]

(1) The interentailment thesis. I think that Carneades is right that 'logical' determinism need not imply causal determinism. Let us adapt a line of argument Cicero gives (*De fato* xii 27–8), using an example from quantum mechanics. Suppose (for the sake of argument) that an indeterministic interpretation of quantum mechanics is true (there are no 'hidden variables'), and we cruelly set up a version of 'Schrödinger's cat' thought-experiment, so that whether Fluffy lives or dies depends on whether an atom decays in the course of an hour, and there are no sufficient conditions prior to an atom decaying or not decaying for whether an atom decays during that time.[45] Let us suppose that Fluffy is not killed. Then, Carneades would say, if I had stated the day before the experiment, "Fluffy will not be killed in our diabolical experiment," I would be stating something true, since Fluffy actually was not killed. Fluffy's not being killed is what makes my statement to have been true all along.

Carneades also appeals to the symmetry of past and future: what makes a statement about some *past* event true is that the event described in the statement occurred as described, not the present effects of that event. We can imagine, especially in an indeterministic world, certain past events whose effects are 'washed out' over time, *e.g.*, some atom decayed far in the past, at time t, and the present state of the world is compatible with that atom decaying either at that moment or at time t+.001s. We wouldn't then say that there used to be a determinate truth about what time the atom decayed, but that since then it has become indeterminate whether the atom decayed at time t or not.

(2) Causal determinism implies fatalism. A more serious problem with Epicurus' line of reasoning is exposed by Chrysippus' response to the Idle Argument, where he shows that causal determinism does not make the

44 I cannot here establish *conclusively* that all three of these are mistakes, since all three 'mistakes' rest upon quite substantial philosophical theses that are still disputed, and to establish that these theses are mistaken would probably each require its own book. But for my purposes, I do not need to establish that each of these are mistakes. I will simply point out why *I* think they are mistakes, which should be enough to bring out more clearly some potentially problematic presuppositions that Epicurus makes.

45 I am leaving out the observer-dependence aspect of the thought-experiment, which is the main point of it, since for my purposes all I care about is the indeterminacy of the event.

future inevitable in a manner that renders action or deliberation futile (*De fato* xii 30). Let us slightly modify Chrysippus' example. If I am bitten by a poisonous snake, and it is causally determined that I will not die as a result of the bite, it does not follow that injecting myself with the anti-toxin that I have stored in my backpack is pointless, since it is my action of injecting myself with the anti-toxin that will bring it about that I recover from the snake bite. 'Genuine open options' are not required for actions to have some point; all that is needed is for actions to be causally efficacious, so that the following sorts of statements are true: "If you take the anti-toxin, you will not be killed by the snake bite, and if you do not, you will be killed." For many of our actions, I think that we can believe that what we are going to do is causally determined, and we can even know *what* action we will take (so 'self-foreknowledge' is not a bar to acting), without rendering that action pointless or our deciding to act as we do irrational. For instance, if I am bitten by the snake, I may perfectly well know exactly what I am going to do (I am going to inject myself with the anti-toxin), and I may believe that this action of mine is causally determined by my brain states that realize my beliefs about the anti-toxin, my desires not to suffer horribly and die, *etc.*, and none of this would have the slightest bit of impact on the rationality of my deciding to inject myself. Since the vast majority of our actions do *not* involve deliberating among options, we can imagine somebody who always acted in this way. Thus, I think that van Inwagen is wrong to assert that "a man who didn't deliberate would either move about in random jerks and scuttles, or would withdraw into catatonia."[46] This assertion is plausible only if one conflates purposive actions generally with actions that are the result of deliberating.

I also think, *pace* van Inwagen, that even deliberation does not presuppose that the courses of action one deliberates about are 'possible' in the sense that each of them is still *causally* possible. Deliberation can be viewed as a matter of gathering more information about my situation, or of exploring the ramifications and implications of the information I already have, so that I am in a better position to act than I was before I deliberated, instead of a matter of standing poised between two open options and simply 'going' for one. Deliberation presupposes a sort of epistemic openness–one can deliberate about various actions only when one does not already know which of them one will do – but need not

46 van Inwagen (1983) 163.

presuppose causal openness. In the case of deliberation, if one accepts the principle that "one deliberates only about courses of action that one believes one can do," which is plausible, I think that *this* sense of "can do" is subject to the sort of conditional analysis that 'classical' compatibilists subject the "could do otherwise" condition of free will to. A simple example of such an analysis would be "*a* can do *d* iff, if *a* decides to do *d*, *a* does *d*." On such an analysis, I presently can scratch my nose (even if it is causally determined that I will not do so), whereas I cannot jump 20 feet in the air.[47] Once "can do" is subject to such an analysis, the principle about deliberation would read something like the following: "one deliberates only about courses of action that one believes are such that, if one decides to do them, one will do them."[48]

An example might help to make this clearer. Let us suppose that I am deliberating about whether or not to buy a particular house. It makes sense to do so only if I believe that, if I do decide to buy the house, I'll be able to buy it. If I thought that somebody else had already contracted on the house, it would be pointless to deliberate about whether to try to buy it. I need to believe that what will occur is contingent on the decision I will make. Furthermore, if I already knew which decision I was going to make, it would (for conceptual reasons) be impossible to deliberate about *what* decision to make – deliberation requires that I be ignorant of what I am going to do, so that the options are *epistemically* open to me. And so, I go through the pros and cons of buying the house, thinking of the neighborhood, cost, and other factors, before coming to a decision, because I think that going through this process will help me secure an outcome that is more likely to be to my liking than if I simply make the decision on impulse.[49] But all of this is compatible with me believing that it is causally determined which decision I am going to make, although I do not *know* which one I will make.

47 See Berofsky (2002) for more discussion of this issue.

48 This is a little *too* simple. There are complications. For instance, if I knew that I had a crippling psychological condition that made me incredibly phobic of petting cats, I would not deliberate about whether to pet a cat, even if I believed that I would pet the cat if I decided to do so, because I would know that I could never bring myself to make that kind of decision. And I may not need to believe that I *will* do what I decide to do; probably it would be good enough to think it quite likely. Tweaking my overly simple version of a conditional analysis of 'can do' in order to handle all such complications, however, would take me too far afield and is not necessary for my basic point.

49 Of course, because of time constraints, this process must be terminated at some point, and it is not *always* rational to be more reflective. See Dennett (1984) chapter 5 for much more on deliberation, with which I agree and to which I am indebted.

If the preceding is correct, it shows that van Inwagen's inference rule β, $N(p \supset q), Np \vdash Nq$, is invalid if one has an interpretation of 'no one had any choice about' that is relevant for issues of the futility of action and deliberation. An operator like 'logically necessary that' might be closed under entailment, but an 'inevitability' or 'unavoidability' operator such as van Inwagen's 'N' is not. I have no choice about what has occurred in the past, and propositions describing past states of affairs plus the laws of nature might entail what will occur in the future. However, it does not follow that what is going to occur in the future is inevitable in a way such that deliberating about whether to bring about some outcome *o* or *not-o* via my actions would be irrational.[50]

(3) Using an indeterministic atomic motion to secure the contingency of the future. Even if Epicurus were right to think (*pace* Chrysippus) that there is an incompatibility between causal determinism and effective action and deliberation, Carneades' criticisms of the swerve are cogent. If the problem is that there is an incompatibility between causal determinism and the effectiveness of *our decisions*, the solution needs to show how *our decisions* can be effective while not being determined. Epicurus thinks that there is an incompatibility, and he tries to solve it by simply banishing determinism. Carneades agrees that, if causal determinism were true, nothing would be in our power (*De fato* xiv 31–32). However, since Chrysippus had already spelled out a compatibilist account of the sense in which things might still be 'in our power,' if one thinks that this sense is inadequate, one must be willing to develop an incompatibilist account of how thing can be 'in our power' in a more robust sense. According to Cicero (*De fato* xi 23–25), Carneades at least gestures at this sort of account, which is reminiscent of later doctrines of 'agent-causation.' (I cause the 'voluntary movements of my mind,' i.e., the impulses that generate my free actions, without that voluntary movement being causally determined by any events or states of the universe prior to my moving myself in this way.)[51] Once we start addressing this problem, however, we should see that simply positing an indeterministic atomic motion to

50 I will leave aside questions about the sort of "freedom to do otherwise" or "having a choice about something" that some people think is necessary for deontic appraisals or moral responsibility, and whether β is valid for *that* sense of 'having a choice,' since I am not concerned about those issues here, and neither was Epicurus. (This, of course, is distinct from questions about the appropriateness of praise and blame, which Epicurus *was* concerned with.)

51 I realize that this characterization of Carneades' position is terse and might be controversial. I think that the point I am making about Carneades exposing shortcoming of Epicurus' position does not depend on accepting my exact characterization of what Carneades is saying. However, I will expand on and defend this point somewhat in the epilogue.

render determinism false will not suffice to put our actions 'in our power' in a robust incompatibilist sense.

6.5 *The swerve's limited role and the principle of charity*

Despite the philosophical shortcomings identified above, I think that we can understand Epicurus' use of the swerve within the context of the debate over various fatalist arguments that proceed from logical principles like PB. Because he accepts the Interentailment Thesis, positing the swerve gives Epicurus grounds to deny one of the premises of the argument. My interpretation puts the swerve in the midst of a debate that was going on at the time, and therefore makes the introduction of it more understandable. There is little reason to think that Epicurus was the first figure to stumble upon the problem of free will and determinism and give it a libertarian solution. He is not a likely candidate to do so, for reasons given above (section 1.3), and ancient sources do not paint him as the first to come upon this problem. According to my interpretation, Epicurus was not a radical innovator. Instead, he is contributing to a debate that he has good reasons to be concerned about.

If Epicurus uses the swerve in order to circumvent the fatalist implications of the Master Argument, Idle Argument, *etc.*, I think it likely that the swerve has little impact on the rest of Epicurus' philosophy. The swerve is a specific mechanism – perhaps an *ad hoc* one – designed to address two specific problems, the explanation of collisions and the contingency of the future. Thus, the swerve, by defeating the threat of necessity as posed by the Megarian fatalist arguments, provides a necessary condition for other things that matter within Epicurean ethics – it saves us from the necessity of the physicists, against which there is no appeal, it allows us to deliberate and to act efficaciously in the world, which would not be possible if all things happened of necessity. Beyond playing these specific, though important, functions, the swerve has no impact on Epicurus' general metaphysics, philosophy of mind, or action-theory.

Drawing parallels to Aristotle might help here. In *de Int.* 9, Aristotle is concerned to address a particular problem that he thinks logical determinism poses to our agency. If everything that is going to happen is predetermined, this would have disastrous consequences on our ability to act. That is because it makes sense to deliberate only about what is contingent, whereas, if everything is predetermined, the future is necessary. In order to overcome this threat, Aristotle simply denies that the Principle of Bivalence holds for statements about future contingents.

However, once he has overcome this threat, he feels free to develop an action-theory in which the agent's actions are simply the result of the "overall disposition of the person's mind at the time of forming the volition,"[52] with no trace of libertarian free choice in his action-theory.[53] I believe that the situation is quite similar for Epicurus. He is responding to the same sort of problem, but once he has overcome it and secured the possibility of us using our reason in order to make decisions and move about in the world, he then feels free to discuss how we act in terms of the way the world appears to an agent interacting with the state the agent is in at that time,[54] as Lucretius' discussion in *DRN* 4 shows (see section 2.3).

Bobzien says her interpretation is 'minimal,' since the swerve is supposed to work only in the formation of character (to make one's character non-necessary), and has no direct role in Epicurean action-theory.[55] It would be fair, then, to characterize my interpretation as 'ultra-minimal,' since on it, the swerve has no direct role anywhere in either the formation of character, the formation of the *voluntas*, or the execution of the decisions made by the *voluntas*. Instead, it simply helps to secure the openness of the future against the threat posed by the arguments of the dialectical/Megarian school, which, if successful, would render the future fixed, where the fixity of the future in this way would be incompatible with effective action.

I take this ultra-minimacy to be an advantage of my interpretation. Now, it may be objected that it is a *disadvantage*. After all, it may be thought that it would be awfully odd for Epicurus to posit an indeterministic atomic motion and think that it is vital for securing our freedom,

52 This is how Bobzien characterizes the "whole-person" model of agency that she attributes (I believe rightly) to both Aristotle and Epicurus (Bobzien (1998*b*) 291).

53 See Furley (1967) 215–225.

54 As Annas (1992) 180–181 notes.

55 Bobzien (2000) 335–336. Actually, she says that *one* way of developing her position is 'minimalist,' a way that aligns it more closely to Furley's position: random swervings in the *animus* are a necessary condition for preventing one's character from being necessitated by hereditary and environment, but this need not have any connection to a person's decisions or use of reason to shape his character. On the second way of developing her position, swerves somehow correlate to or constitute the conscious efforts to change one's mental dispositions. This development, as Bobzien notes, would bring her view much more in line with the traditional interpretation, but with the difference that the stress is not on one's ability to do otherwise at the moment of each choice, but that one's present character be at least partially the result of decisions that were not causally determined, so that 'springs of action' in this way are genuinely the agent's own. This latter way of developing Bobzien's position would also bring it much more in line with the position of those like Kane, where who one is must be at least partially the result of 'self forming actions' – see n. 16 in chapter 3 for more on this issue.

even though it has *no* direct role in the formation of character or the production of action. It should fit in there *somewhere*, it might be urged, if it really is supposed to be somehow relevant to our freedom.

Now, I agree that there is something odd here, but I deny that it gives us any reason to reject the bivalence interpretation. That's because I think that it is well documented that the various fatalist Megarian-dialectical arguments were much discussed around Epicurus' time. It is also well documented, I think, that Epicurus thought that unacceptable results followed from these arguments if their premises were accepted (whereas I think that the proper response to them is to dismiss them as invalid), and that he blocked such arguments simply by denying one of their premises, the Principle of Bivalence. Furthermore, it is well documented that Epicurus accepted the Interentailment Thesis: he thought he needed to give a physical basis for his rejection of the Principle of Bivalence, and the resultant fixity of the future, and the swerve was his means of doing so.

The assorted fatalist arguments, however, operate entirely at the level of various high-level logical (or perhaps semantic) principles, plus fairly abstract principles about the prerequisites of action, *e.g.*, that one does not deliberate – or, perhaps, that there would be no point in deliberating – about what is necessary. They do not operate at the level of psychological determinism, nor do they talk about the freedom to do otherwise, *etc.* Likewise, it seems to me, Aristotle's and Epicurus' responses to these sorts of arguments remain at a similar logical/semantic level, and once the prerequisites of action have been saved from the threat posed by such arguments, both Aristotle and Epicurus feel free then to develop their theories of character development and action, without working truth-value gaps or causal indeterminacies directly into the resulting theories.

Now, once somebody has asserted that truth-value gaps and causal indeterminacies are needed to secure freedom of action, the natural questions to ask next – especially for opponents of the philosophers making these assertions – is how these gaps and indeterminacies relate, if at all, to the production of action, and whether these gaps and indeterminacies really are necessary once we have spelled out our action-theory. Both Chrysippus and Carneades *did* raise these sorts of questions, and in doing so, they helped advance the discussion past where it stood before. But I do not see any evidence that Aristotle and Epicurus considered these questions. In fact, insofar as we *do* have textual evidence concerning the development of character and the production of action, this evidence points *against* sticking in swerves either in the formation of character or the production of action (see chapters 2 and 3), whereas the passages we have are all consistent with my thesis that Epicurus is primarily concerned with guaranteeing that we are able to use our reason to control our actions and shape our character.

Finally, apart from textual considerations, we have no good grounds given the principle of charity to attribute to Epicurus the position that swerves are directly involved in any of the places where people have supposed they are, since the resulting positions are not philosophically strong, and in many cases actually would serve to undermine the sort of freedom Epicurus wishes to secure (see sections 2.3, 3.2, 3.3, and 4.4). I admit that Epicurus' arguments for positing the swerve are based upon a number of mistakes, but these are mistakes that we have good textual support for, at least. Furthermore, they are mistakes that are understandable and have precedent given the intellectual background Epicurus is operating against, and are ones I think we need to attribute to Epicurus in any case, on any interpretation. I see no reason to attribute to Epicurus additional, gratuitous confusions that have no precedent in past philosophers. I think that the other interpretations do attribute to Epicurus such additional, gratuitous confusions, and thus, on grounds of charity, the bivalence interpretation should be preferred.

Epilogue: Epicurus and the invention of libertarian free will

Most of what Epicurus and Lucretius say about our freedom is compatible with causal determinism. This should not surprise us. Epicurus is not concerned with the freedom required for genuine moral responsibility, but with securing a sort of freedom of action – a rational self-rule that allows us to control our actions and shape our character, so that we can attain a tranquil life. This type of freedom is compatible with causal determinism. However, Epicurus was led, by a series of philosophical mistakes – understandable mistakes, but mistakes nonetheless – to posit an indeterministic atomic motion to help defuse a threat to our freedom. The swerve plays only the subsidiary role of defusing the fatalist implications of the Master Argument and similar arguments based on the universal applicability of the Principle of Bivalence. Despite the swerve's relative unimportance in Epicurus' own theory of freedom, it is this element of his theory that in the end has had the greatest philosophical impact.[1]

If I am right that it would be anachronistic to saddle Epicurus with a libertarian response to the 'traditional' problem of the apparent incompatibility of determinism and the 'ability to do otherwise' necessary for genuine moral responsibility, this raises the following questions: how *did* the 'traditional' problem arise, who *was* the first person to put forward a libertarian response to this problem, and how was this transmitted into the western philosophical tradition? Also, what role did Epicurus' positing of the swerve play?

1 Despite its peripheral role in Epicurus' own thought, the disproportionate attention subsequently paid to the swerve is unsurprising. After all, ancient historians and doxographers are more likely to focus on what is distinctive and startling about Epicurus' theory, in order to have a counterpoint to contrast to the explicitly compatibilist theory of the Stoics, rather than noting their extensive common ground. Hostile critics, like Cicero, seized on what they took to be a ridiculous part of Epicurus' philosophy in order to have a stick to beat him with. And loyal Epicureans, knowing that Epicurus is the god-like savior of humanity, would feel bound to defend all of his divine pronouncements, such as that the sun is exactly the size that it appears, against misguided critics.

To answer these questions fully, and to justify those answers, would go well beyond the bounds of the present study. However, now that I have laid out how I think Epicurus' theory works, I would like to close this book by briefly telling the story, as I see it, of the way this theory helped lead to the creation by later philosophers of a libertarian solution to the problem of free will and determinism. I plan to fill out and defend in future work the claims sketched out here.

Epicurus helped shape the subsequent problem of free will and determinism through his influence on Carneades, and Carneades should be credited as the first person to come up with a libertarian position *vis-à-vis* the 'traditional' problem. This view requires arguing for three distinct theses: that the problem Carneades is confronting is fairly described as similar to the 'traditional' problem, that his solution to this problem is libertarian, and that Epicurus was the inspiration for Carneades' solution. It is often tricky to ascertain the exact influence of one philosopher on another, but this is not one of those cases. When Cicero describes Carneades' position, he says quite explicitly that Carneades developed it as a modification of the Epicurean position: Carneades' doctrine is that the Epicureans could maintain that there is a 'voluntary movement of the mind,' against the Stoic Chrysippus, without positing the swerve or any other sort of motion without a cause. (*De fato* xi 23)

To spell out what sort of problem Carneades is confronting, it will be helpful to refer back to the schema of different 'free will and determinism' problems, as involving a combination of three factors, detailed earlier (section 1.1):

Type of determinism *X* threatens (at least potentially) *Y*, and *Y* is a necessary condition for *Z*.

I have argued that Epicurus' primary concern is with fatalist arguments that hinge on *logical* determinism – the position that there is already a fact of the matter, and always has been, about what is going to occur in the future – but that he also opposed causal determinism because of the Interentailment Thesis. As described above (sections 6.3 and 6.4), Carneades uncouples logical and causal determinism. He maintains that logical determinism need not imply causal determinism, and that logical determinism has no unwelcome implications for our freedom: if it is simply my freely deciding to raise my arm at 12:15 EST on July 28, 2004 (as I just have) that makes it to have always been the case that I raise my arm at that time, and thus for the statement "Tim O'Keefe will raise his arm at 12:15 EST on July 28, 2004" to have been true for an eternity before

I raised my arm, the eternal truth of that statement does nothing to threaten my freedom.

However, Carneades does deny causal determinism – the thesis that the "laws of nature" along with past states of the universe determine exactly one unique future – because it is incompatible with there being a voluntary movement of the mind and with anything being in our power.[2] Carneades does not put the thesis of causal determinism in these terms, but he is clearly targeting this sort of doctrine. The Stoics, against whom Carneades is arguing, conceive of fate as an everlasting ordering and interconnection of causes, flowing from all eternity like the unwinding of a rope. And so, nature has contained in it already (and always has) the causes which will bring about what is going to occur. When Carneades attempts to pry apart logical and causal determinism, he gives examples of free action (like his going down to the Academy) and says that the statements describing these actions are true from eternity, but not in virtue of "an eternal stream of natural and necessary causation," or "foreordained causes" (*De fato* ix 19), or "immutable causes, eternally existing" (*De fato* xii 28), or a "nexus of eternal causes" (*De fato* xvi 38).

Carneades' denial of causal determinism, however, is most clear in his discussion of *epistemic* determinism. Carneades thinks that epistemic determinism entails causal determinism, and since causal determinism is false, so too is epistemic determinism. Carneades' argument proceeds from the assumption that to know what is going to occur in the future, one must know what presently obtaining causes will bring about that future event. For instance, in order for me to know that a major earthquake will occur in California a year hence, I would need to have information about the present disposition of California's various faults, the pressure they are exerting on one another, etc., along with the facts about how faults, rocks and dirt of various kinds, etc., behave, which all together will bring about the future quake. Carneades says that not even Apollo, however, can foretell events like Oedipus killing his father (although it has always been *true* that he would do so). That is because such actions, before they occurred, had no pre-existing causes that would bring them about, that Apollo could inspect in order to tell that they are going to occur (*De fato* xiv 32–33).

The parallel with a Laplacean omniscient demon is striking. Laplace claims that such a demon, knowing the present disposition of all of the matter in the universe, along with the laws of nature, would on this basis

2 *De fato* xi 23–5 and xiv 31–2.

be able to predict everything that was going to occur (as well as retrodict all that had occurred). Although Laplace affirms determinism and Carneades denies it, their epistemic examples serve similar functions: the demon's abilities illustrate Laplace's thesis of universal causal determinism, and the limitations facing even Apollo drive home what is involved in Carneades' denial of that thesis.

If causal determinism were true, according to Carneades, then nothing would be "in our power" (*De fato* xiv 31–32). What this amounts to can be seen more clearly by looking at how Carneades objects to the Stoic position. The Stoic Chrysippus replies to the 'Idle Argument' as follows: just because it is fated that you will recover from a snake-bite does not make your taking anti-venom in order to recover from the bite pointless. (See sections 6.3 and 6.4.) Chrysippus says that certain events are 'co-fated': for instance, it is fated (and causally determined) *both* that I will recover from the snake-bite *and* that I will take the anti-venom; it is through my fated action of taking the anti-venom that my fated recovery will occur (*De fato* xiii 30). The Stoics say that motions like my taking the anti-venom, which are brought about *by* fate *through* me, are "in my power," and they deny that we are free to choose *between* opposite actions (Alexander *On Fate* 181,13–182,20 L&S 62G).

Carneades, however, rejects the whole class of 'co-fated' events. He restates the 'Idle Argument' in terms of causes, instead of truth; Cicero believes that this restated argument is as tight as can be. Carneades argues that if everything is fated, everything occurs because of antecedent causes. This would make everything take place in a closely knit web of natural interconnection, which would make all things occur of necessity, and nothing would be in our power (*De fato* xiv 31). Given this context, and Carneades' repeated railings against causal determinism, for an action to be in our power most likely means that it is in our power either to perform it or not to perform it. And so, Carneades thinks that causal determinism threatens one's ability to do otherwise than one does, and for this reason he rejects causal determinism.

This may seem wrong, since Cicero derides Epicurus for positing 'motion without a cause,' whereas Carneades (via Cicero) affirms that every event, including human action, does have a cause. But even though every *event* has a cause, Carneades' position is still incompatibilist. We can best understand Carneades' position and the arguments he works through by comparing what he says to Roderick Chisholm's views on 'agent causation.' Like Carneades, Chisholm thinks that both causal determinism *and causal indeterminism* are incompatible with freedom.

Like Carneades, Chisholm thinks that merely uncaused events cannot be free, because freedom is not the same as randomness. So Chisholm proposes that every *event* has a cause, but not all events are caused *by other events* in accordance with exceptionless laws of nature. Instead, some events, such as voluntary human actions, are caused by the agent – by the person – yet how this 'agent causation' itself acts is not causally determined by previous events or states of affairs.[3]

This is quite similar to Carneades' description of the 'voluntary motion of the mind' that is in our power. All events, including human actions, have causes. However, voluntary actions do not have antecedent causes stretching back eternally to past events and states of affairs. Instead, these actions are simply the result of a 'voluntary motion of the mind,' a motion which has an intrinsic nature of being in our power and of obeying us (*De fato* xi 24–25).

Having this sort of ability to do otherwise than one does is a necessary condition both for the rationality of deliberation and action, and for moral responsibility. As noted above, Carneades' rejection of Chrysippus' 'co-fated' events occurs in his restatement of the Idle Argument, which concerns the question of whether determinism renders us helpless and makes action pointless. Cicero, who acts as Carneades' spokesman through the dialogue, also thinks that causal determinism would fetter the human mind in the chains of a fated necessity (*De fato* ix 20).

The case for attributing to Carneades a libertarian position on the incompatibility of determinism and the sort of free will necessary for moral responsibility is less direct, but still quite plausible. The key text is *De fato* xvii–xix 39–45, where Cicero takes up the question of whether fate is consistent with justified praise, blame, and punishment, and where he describes Chrysippus' attempt to make them compatible. Some people, according to Cicero, assert that not everything takes place by fate, because fate and freedom are incompatible. Their argument goes as follows: a necessary condition on justified praise, blame and punishment is that the assents, which produce our actions, be in our power. But if everything is fated, then everything takes place with an antecedent cause. Our assents are caused by our desires. But our desires would also then have antecedent causes, causes which are outside us and not in our power. (For instance, my vicious decision to eat a chicken patty made from factory farm-raised chickens is prompted by my hunger, along with a sense-impression of a chicken patty. But the cause of this sense-impression is an external object,

3 Chisholm (1964).

and that I had this sense-impression was not something in my power.) But if the causes of our assents are not in our power, then our assents themselves are not in our power.

However, Chrysippus wants everything to be fated and have antecedent causes, and also assent to be in our power. He tries to maintain both by distinguishing types of causes. He agrees that assents must be prompted by sense-impressions, *e.g.*, I would not reach for the chicken patty without the appropriate sense-impression. These sorts of auxiliary causes, however, which act as triggers to action, do not place assent out of our power. That is because they are not sufficient conditions on our actions, and what sort of action they prompt depends on the person, so that the cause of action is still internal to him, and the action in his power. The character of the person himself is the *principal* cause of his actions. So, for instance, the same sort of sense-impression which triggers my eating the chicken patty would not cause somebody to eat it who cares more about the suffering of de-beaked and overcrowded chickens than about his gustatory pleasure.[4]

So far, so good. Cicero presents Chrysippus' distinctions approvingly, and says that once they are accepted, the differences between the disputing parties over fate might seem merely verbal (*De fato* xix 44–45). But then he adds,

> This distinction [between antecedent and principal causes] is approved by both sides, but one of the two schools holds that although fate does govern those matters in which, when antecedent causes have occurred, it is not in our power to make the results turn out otherwise [*non sit in nostra potestate ut aliter illa eveniant*], yet fate is not present in the case of matters which are in our power. . .

Unfortunately, the text breaks off at this point. But it is not hard to see that the same Carneadean point is being made here, about in what sense actions must be 'in our power' in order for praise, blame, and punishments to be justified, as was being made earlier about in what sense actions must be in our power in order to escape the Idle Argument. Once an antecedent cause has occurred as a trigger to action, do I *then* have the ability to make results turn out otherwise, or not? Once the chicken-patty impression has struck me, do I have the ability either to eat the patty or not to? If I have this ability to do otherwise than I do, then my action is not fated. But if how I respond is 'up to me' merely in the Chrysippean sense that it causally depends on my present character, which is itself

4 My description of Chrysippus' position is perforce *very* brief and skips over various complications. Hankinson (1998) VII.1.d–e and VII.2.b, and Bobzien (1998*a*) chapters 5 and 6 give more detailed treatments and pointers to further literature.

'co-fated' and the way in which fate works its will through me, then my action is both fated and not truly in my power, so that praise, blame, and punishment would not be justified.

Ironically, the first person to put forward a libertarian theory of the freedom of the will may not himself have been a libertarian. As head of the skeptical academy, Carneades was in the business of refuting the arguments of others in order to show that they did not have the knowledge they thought they did. He did not confine himself to criticizing others' arguments, however. He also retailed arguments of his own in support of positive theses – not in order to show that they are true, but because doing so would help counterbalance the arguments for contradictory theses and bring his audience to realize that none of the opposing arguments establish their conclusions.[5]

Beyond Cicero, tracing the paths of historical influence becomes even murkier.[6] But one line by which this 'traditional' problem of free will, along with the libertarian solution to it, is likely then transmitted into the Western philosophical tradition is via St. Augustine, particularly in the position he lays out in *On free choice of the will* (*De libero arbitrio*). In addition to his deep familiarity with Cicero's *corpus* overall, Augustine is in particular familiar with what Cicero has to say about the incompatibility of free choice and epistemic determinism (*i.e.*, foreknowledge), as contained in works like *De fato* and *De divinatione*.[7] Part of his purpose in writing *On free choice of the will* is to reconcile divine foreknowledge and freedom. And so, even though he does not explicitly credit Cicero, the many points of overlap between Augustine's conception of freedom and the libertarian position reported by Cicero are likely not just coincidental. However, Augustine's purposes are in many ways importantly different

5 Cicero himself, in describing Carneades' position, certainly seems to endorse it. Such a provisional endorsement of a position as the most likely among those thus far examined is consistent with Cicero's own brand of skepticism (although we should be hesitant to immediately identify the position of the character 'Cicero' in his dialogues with that of the author Cicero). See Thorsrud (2002) for a description of Cicero's 'skepticism' as really being a form of moderate fallibilism, along with a defense of the more controversial claim that Cicero shares this fallibilism with Arcesilaus and Carneades.

6 One disclaimer: in sketching out the way in which Epicurus helped form the 'problem of free will,' from Carneades, through Cicero, to Augustine, I do not mean to deny that other streams of philosophical influence also contributed, *e.g.*, the work of the middle Platonists and the Aristotelian commentators. For more on the latter, see Bobzien (1998*b*). But I will not go into these other thinkers here.

7 Augustine reports Cicero's argument in *City of God* 5.9; the reply he gives to it there is basically the same as the one contained in *De lib. arb.* 3.2–4.

from Carneades'; let me note briefly the content of Augustine's doctrine and its goals.

Like Carneades, Augustine asserts that *voluntas* has a cause: it is a movement of the soul which is under our control (*De lib. arb.* 2.20). Also like Carneades (as reported in *De fato* xi 24–25), he makes this point by likening this movement of the soul to the movement of a body: just as it is the nature of a stone to move downwards, so to it is the nature of the soul to be able to move itself by the will, the difference being that *how* the soul exercises this power is up to it (*De lib. arb.* 3.1). He accepts the doctrine that sense-impressions function as triggering causes to action but are not sufficient to determine one's will. Augustine says that only something that is seen (in a sufficiently wide sense of 'seen') can incite the will to act. He adds that we control whether we accept or reject what we see, but we do not control what we see (*De lib. arb.* 3.25). This is supposed to help make all acts of will at least somewhat explicable: they have a motive, which is an object that the agent perceives as desirable.

Augustine emphasizes even more strongly than Cicero that will is a self-movement of the mind that has no cause beyond itself. He notes at many places that what we will is, in a very strong sense, within our power (*e.g.*, *De lib. arb.* 3.3). And so, the will, as a higher part of soul, cannot strictly speaking be overcome by passion – instead, a mind that sins of its own volition turns away from virtue and chooses to be a slave of desire (*De lib. arb.* 1.10–11). But Augustine also notes, as Cicero does not, that if this is so, the will also can ignore the verdict of right reason. Augustine maintains that the will is the cause of sin, and that there is no cause for the will beyond itself, because if there were a cause of the will beyond itself, there would be no sin (*De lib. arb.* 3.17). And so, the will can simply turn from a greater perceived good to a lesser one – a movement which is sin – for no reason whatsoever beyond its own decision. As Mann notes, "[One] aspect of the power of the human will is to reject the verdict of reason."[8] This autonomy of the will from both desire and from reason would not be welcomed by Epicurus; we will briefly explore below why Augustine insists on it.

In his discussion of the freedom of the will, Augustine does not bring up the 'Idle Argument' at all. Instead, just like the foes of fate that Cicero describes in *De fato* 39–45, Augustine insists that our actions being in our power, in the sense of our being able to choose one way or the other, is necessary for them to be justifiably subject to moral appraisal. When

8 Mann (2001) 46.

asked why God would allow people to have a free will, since free will is what allows evil into the world, one of Augustine's replies is that we cannot do right without having free will, and no action would be either a sin or a good deed if it were not performed by the will (*De lib. arb.* 2.1). Part of the nature of free will, however, is that it can be misused. Without this built-in liability, which allows us to sin, we would not be able to choose to live rightly.[9] But Augustine, in particular, wants to vindicate the justification of punishment, especially God's eternal punishment of sinners: because sinners turn away from virtue of their own volition, and this turning away from higher goods to lower ones is caused by the sinner's own will and *not* by God, God is just when He punishes sinners for it (*e.g.*, *De lib. arb.* 1.10–11, 2.19).

Augustine's other reason for insisting on this libertarian free will is in order to defuse the problem of evil. *On free choice of the will* opens with Augustine's interlocutor Evodius asking whether God is the cause of evil, and the main task of the book is to show that He is not. Since God is wholly good, He cannot create anything that is evil. In sin, the will turns from eternal higher goods (such as justice, conceived of by Augustine as akin to Platonic ideas in the mind of God) to changeable, lower ones (such as bodily pleasure). The will itself is good, the higher goods are good, the lower goods are good, and all of these are from God. The turning from higher to lower goods is evil, but this movement is *not* caused by God, but simply by the will itself and nothing else (*De lib. arb.* 2.19; see also 1.15).

Augustine's concern to construct a theodicy also helps to explain why he insists on the autonomy of will from both desire and from reason. As MacDonald notes, if free choice is supposed to explain the origin of evil in a world that is created entirely good, with no defect or corruption, Augustine realizes that this "requires him to maintain that the first sinners

9 *De lib. arb.* 2.18–19. See also *De lib. arb.* 3.18: in order for an action to be sinful, *i.e.*, culpable, one must be able to guard against it; i.e., one must have the ability not to perform it, and *De lib. arb.* 3.19 and 3.22: people are not liable to punishment because of the difficulty and ignorance that afflict them as a result of the Fall, which make it hard for them to do what is right, but because they had the ability to ask for help (from God) to overcome these obstacles and yet failed to do so, of their own free will. However, see Stump (2001) for considerations that Augustine may not be committed to PAP, but to the weaker principle that an agent is morally responsible for an act only if the act is not causally determined by anything outside the agent (so that he thinks causal determinism is incompatible with 'ultimate origination,' and such ultimate origination is a necessary condition on moral responsibility, to use the terminology from section 1.1). But Stump admits that the evidence is ambiguous, and for my purposes here the exact variety of Augustine's incompatibilism is not crucial.

are not created defective in any morally relevant way – that is, that the moral defects constituted by their primal sin are not preceded by any other morally relevant flaw in creation."[10] Choices like Satan's defection from the ranks of the angels and Adam and Eve's decision to eat the forbidden fruit illustrate the "sheer willfulness of sin."[11]

Near the end of *On free choice of the will*, Augustine brings together his concerns to provide a theodicy and to justify divine punishment, saying that God deserves no blame when somebody fails to do what he ought but deserves praise when somebody suffers what he ought (*De lib. arb.* 3.16), and that people repay their debt to God, their creator from whom all good things come, either by doing what they ought or by suffering what they ought (*De lib. arb.* 3.15).

By this point, we have traveled quite far from Epicurus' concerns. Carneades' modifications of Epicurus' position, in order to strengthen it as a counterweight to Stoic compatibilism, are quite understandable. So too are the ways in which Augustine appropriates for his own theological purposes what he found in Cicero of Carneades' theory. But if Epicurus had foreknown what the intellectual descendant of his theory was going to be like – a notion of a will, whereby we can perversely reject the verdicts of right reason, a notion which is used to defend the existence of a providential creator-god against the problem of evil and to justify eternal afterlife punishments at the hands of that god – he would have turned away in horror and dismay.

10 MacDonald (1999) 116. MacDonald's concern is with "primal sins" such as those of Adam, Eve, and Satan in particular, but his article is worth looking at for insight into Augustine's concept of the will in general. MacDonald tries to explain how Augustine's "claim that primal sin can have no cause should not be read as the claim that primal sin is wholly unmotivated by or discontinuous with the primal sinner's practical reasoning" (113). According to MacDonald, this sinning is a kind of negligence on the agent's part. I think that MacDonald's account of Augustine on sin is persuasive, although I am more sympathetic to it as an account of Augustine's thought rather than as an independently viable account of free choice, unlike MacDonald himself.

11 Mann (2001) 46. There are serious tensions in Augustine's thought. He wishes to claim that *we* (along with rebellious angels) are wholly responsible for evil but that *God* is responsible for all things that are good. Furthermore, he insists that because of original sin, we cannot now refrain from sinning without the help of God's grace, and that God's grace is the cause even of the will of faith; *i.e.*, the will to accept God's grace. (Otherwise, we would be responsible, and would receive credit, for the good action of willing to accept God's grace.) Whether he can consistently maintain all of these things is open to serious doubt. See Stump (2001) for a good introduction to the problem and for an attempt to help make Augustine's commitments consistent, and Kirwan (1989) chapters 6 and 7 for a more pessimistic assessment.

Appendix: Some texts

LUCRETIUS, DE RERUM NATURA 2 251–293

denique si semper motus conectitur omnis
et vetere exoritur <motu> novus ordine certo
nec declinando faciunt primordia motus
principium quoddam quod fati foedera rumpat,
ex infinito ne causam causa sequatur,
libera per terras unde haec animantibus exstat,
unde est haec, inquam, fatis avulsa voluntas
per quam progredimur quo ducit quemque voluptas,
declinamus item motus nec tempore certo
nec regione loci certa, sed ubi ipsa tulit mens?
nam dubio procul his rebus sua cuique voluntas
principium dat et hinc motus per membra rigantur.
nonne vides etiam patefactis tempore puncto
carceribus non posse tamen prorumpere equorum
vim cupidam tam de subito quam mens avet ipsa?
omnis enim totum per corpus materiai
copia conciri debet, concita per artus
omnis ut studium mentis conixa sequatur;
ut videas initum motus a corde creari
ex animique voluntate id procedere primum,
inde dari porro per totum corpus et artus.
nec similest ut cum impulsi procedimus ictu
viribus alterius magnis magnoque coactu.
nam tum materiem totius corporis omnem
persipicuumst nobis invitis ire rapique,
donec eam refrenavit per membra voluntas.
iamne vides igitur, quamquam vis extera multos
pellat et invitos cogat procedere saepe
praecipitesque rapi, tamen esse in pectore nostro
quiddam quod contra pugnare obstareque possit?
cuius ad arbitrium quoque copia materiai

cogitur interdum flecti per membra per artus
et proiecta refrenatur retroque residit.
quare in seminibus quoque idem fateare necessest,
esse aliam praeter plagas et pondera causam
motibus, unde haec est nobis innata potestas,
de nilo quoniam fieri nil posse videmus.
pondus enim prohibet ne plagis omnia fiant
externa quasi vi. sed ne mens ipsa necessum
intestinum habeat cunctis in rebus agendis
et devicta quasi cogatur ferre patique,
id facit exiguum clinamen principiorum
nec regione loci certa nec tempore certo.

Text is from L&S vol. 2 20F. See section 2.1 for the English translation.

LUCRETIUS, DE RERUM NATURA 4 877–896

nunc qui fiat uti passus proferre queamus,
cum volumus, quareque datum sit membra movere,
et quae res tantum hoc oneris protrudere nostri
corporis insuerit, dicam: tu percipe dicta.
dico animo nostro primum simulacra meandi
accidere atque animum pulsare, ut diximus ante.
inde voluntas fit; neque enim facere incipit ullam
rem quisquam, quam mens providit quid velit ante.
id quod providet, illius rei constat imago.
ergo animus cum sese ita commovet ut velit ire
inque gredi, ferit extemplo quae in corpore toto
per membra atque artus animai dissita vis est.
et facilest factu, quoniam coniuncta tenetur.
inde ea proporro corpus ferit, atque ita tota
paulatim moles protruditur atque movetur.
praeterea tum rarescit quoque corpus, et aer,
scilicet ut debet qui semper mobilis extat,
per patefacta venit penetratque foramina largus
et dispargitur ad partis ita quasque minutas
corporis.

The text is from L&S vol. 2 14E and Rouse (1937). See section 2.2 for the English translation.

EPICURUS, ON NATURE BOOK 25, PASSAGE [A]

(1) ἀπ[ό][1] τε [τῆς πρ]ώτης ἀρχῆς σπέρμ[ατα ἡμῖν ἀ]γωγὰ τὰ μὲν εἰς τάδ[ε] τὰ δ' εἰς τάδε τὰ δ' εἰς ἄμφω [ταῦ]τά [ἐ]στιν ἀεὶ [κα]ὶ πρά[ξ]εων [καὶ] διανοήσεων καὶ διαθέ[σε]ων καὶ πλεί[ω] καὶ ἐλάττωι. ὥστε παρ' ἡμᾶς π[οτε][2] ἁπλῶς τὸ ἀπογεγεννημένον ἤδη γείνεσθαι, [τ]οῖα ἢ τοῖα, καὶ τὰ ἐκ τοῦ περιέχοντος κ[α]τ' ἀνάγκην διὰ τοὺς πό[ρους] εἰσρέο[ν]τα παρ' ἡμᾶς π[ο]τε γε[ίνε]σθαι καὶ παρὰ τ[ὰς] ἡμε[τέρα]ς [ἐ]ξ ἡμῶν αὐτ[ῶν] δόξ[ας. ...] εἰ [π]αρὰ τὴν φ[ύ]σι[ν] α[. . .]ὑσ[....]υκ[..]θ[. . . . . .ει[...]ετησ[. . . . .] τα[. . . .]α [.]χε[....]ν[.]υ [. . .]ωσε[. . . . .]νεκε[...

(Lacuna of approx. 60 words, a few fragmentary lines I do not include here, and another lacuna of approx. 12 words)

(2)]εστήκει, ὧν οὐ[. . . ἀ]πολείπει τὰ πάθη τοῦ γίνε[σθαι, τὸ] νουθε[τ]εῖν τε ἀλλήλους καὶ μάχε[σ]θαι καὶ μεταρυθμίζειν ὡς ἔχοντας καὶ ἐν ἑαυτοῖς τὴν αἰτίαν καὶ οὐχὶ ἐν τῆι ἐξ ἀρχῆς μόνον συστάσει καὶ ἐν τῆι τοῦ περιέχοντος καὶ ἐπεισιόντος κατὰ τὸ αὐτόματον ἀνάγκηι. (3) εἰ γάρ τις καὶ τῶι νουθετεῖν καὶ τῶι νουθετεῖσθαι τὴν κατὰ τὸ αὐ[τό]μα[τ]ον ἀνάγκην προστι[θείη] ἀεὶ τοῦ [τό]θ' ἑαυτῶ[ι] ὑπάρχο[ντος], μὴ οὐχί πο[τε] δύν[ηται ταύτ]η [συ]νιέναι [. . . . .]αλλ[.................] ἡμεῖ[ν.................]πονε [*(lacuna of a few words)* (4) μεμ]φόμενος ἢ ἐπαινῶν· ἀλλ' ε[ἰ] μὲν τοῦτο πράττοι, τὸ [αὐτὸ] ἔργ[ο]ν ἂν εἴη [κ]ατα[λεί]πων ὃ ἐφ' ἡμῶν αὐτῶν [ποιεῖ] τὴν τῆς αἰτίας πρό[λη]ψιν, ἐννοοῦμεν[3] τὸ δό[γμα ...] μετατεθε[ι]μένο[ς

(a few fragmentary letters, and another lacuna of approx. 45 words)

(5) τοι[αύτ]ης πλάνης. περικά[τω] γὰρ ὁ τοιοῦτος λόγος τρέπεται, καὶ οὐδέποτε δύναται βεβαιῶσαι ὡς ἐστὶν τοιαῦτα πάντα οἷα τὰ κατ' ἀνάγκην καλούμενα· ἀλλὰ μάχεταί τινι περὶ αὐτοῦ τούτου ὡς δι' ἑαυτοῦ ἀβελτερευομένωι. (6) κἂν εἰς ἄπειρον φῆι πάλιν κατ' ἀνάγκην τοῦτο πράττειν ἀπὸ λόγων ἀεί, οὐκ ἐπιλογίζεται ἐν τῶι εἰς ἑαυτὸν τὴν αἰτίαν ἀνά[π]τειν τοῦ κα[τὰ τ]ρόπον λελογίσθαι εἰς δὲ τὸν ἀμφισβητοῦντα τοῦ μὴ κατὰ τρόπον. (7) εἰ δὲ μὴ ἃ πο[ιεῖ] ἀπολήγοι [ε]ἰς ἑαυτὸ[ν], ἀλλ' εἰς τὴν [ἀ]νάγ[κην] τ[ι]θείη, [ο]ὐδ' ἂν ε[..]κα[. . . . .]επ[*(lacuna approx. 30 words)* (8) εἰ τὸ δι' ἡμῶν] αὐτῶν καλούμενον τῶι τῆς ἀνάγκης ὀνόματι προσαγ[ο]ρεύειν[4] [ὄ]νομα μό[ν]ον μετατίθετα[ι] μη δ' ἐπιδίξει ὅτι τοιοῦτό τι ᾧ μοχθηρο[ί εἰσι τύ]ποι προειλ[η]φότες τὸ δι' ἡμῶ[ν αὐ]τῶν αἴτιον καλ[οῦμεν], οὔτ' ἰδ[ι. . . . . . *(lacuna approx. 25 words)* (9) γενέσθαι, ἀλ[λὰ κε]νὸν [καὶ] τὸ δι' ἀνάγκην καλ[εῖ]ν πρ[ὸ]ς ὧν φάτε. ἂν δὲ μ[ή] τις τοῦτο ἀποδείξει, μηδ' ἔχει ἡμῶν [τ]ι συνεργὸν μηδ' ὅρμημα ἀπο[τ]ρέπειν ὧν καλοῦντες δι' ἡμῶν αὐτῶν τὴν αἰτίαν συντελοῦμεν, ἀλλὰ πάντα ὅσ[α] νῦν δι' ἡμῶν αὐ[τῶ]ν ὀνομάζοντες τὴν αἰτίαν [εἶναι διαβ]ε[βα]ιούμεθα πράττε[ιν] κατὰ μώραν[5] ἀνάγκην προσαγορεύων,

1 Changed from ἐκ in L&S 20C.

2 Changed from π[ρῶτον] in L&S 20C.

3 Changed from ἐν ὧι οὗ μὲν in L&S 20C.

4 Changed from προσαγ[ο]ρεύων in L&S 20C.

5 Here I follow the text in L&S vol. 2 20B rather than Laursen (1988), who emends the text from μώραν to χώραν. Following Laursen's emendation would involve changing the translation from "foolish necessity" to "spatial necessity." Laursen (1988) 18 suggests that Epicurus is contrasting 'physical' and 'logical' determinism, while finally saying that there no important difference between them, but the sense on this reading would be quite unclear, so I follow Long and Sedley. Sedley notes that the μ is uncertain; if Laursen's further examination of the badly-damaged ms. makes the χ incontrovertible – which I doubt – then perhaps it was introduced as a scribal error for an original μ. Or Epicurus might here simply be quite unclear; it would not be the only place that occurs in this passage.

ὄνομα μόνον ἀμεί[ψ]ει· (10) ἔργον δ' οὐθὲν ἡμῶν μετακοσμήσει, ὥσπερ ἐπ' ἐνίων ὁ συνορῶν τὰ ποῖα κατ' ἀνάγκην ἐστὶν ἀποτρέπειν εἴωθε τοὺς προθυμουμένους παρὰ βίαν τι π[ρ]άττειν. (11) ζητήσει δ' ἡ διάνοια εὑρεῖν τὸ ποῖον [ο]ὖν τι δεῖ νομί[ζ]ειν τὸ ἐξ ἡ[μ]ῶν αὐτῶ[ν π]ως [πρ]αττόμενον [μ]ὴ προθυμ[ούμενον πράτ]τειν. οὐ γὰρ ἔχει ἄλ[λο τι οὐθὲν] εἰ μὴ φά[ναι τὸ] ποῖον [κατ' ἀνάγκην] ἐσ[τὶ καὶ] (*lacuna approx. 12 words*) ξ[................ το]ῦ ὀνό[ματος ... (*lacuna approx. 25 words*) (12) μάλιστα ἀδιανοήτων. ἂν δέ τις τοῦτο μὴ παραβιάζηται μηδ' αὖ ὃ ἐξελέγχει τε ἢ εἰσφέρει πρᾶγμα ἐκτιθεῖ, φωνὴ μόνον ἀμείβεται, καθάπερ πάλαι θρυλῶ. (13) οἱ δ' αἰτιολογήσαντες ἐξ ἀρχῆς ἱκανῶς, καὶ οὐ μό[ν]ον [τ]ῶν πρὸ αὐτῶν πολὺ διενέγκαντες ἀλλὰ καὶ τῶν ὕστερον πολλαπλ[α]σίως, ἔλαθον ἑαυτούς, καίπερ ἐν πολλοῖς μεγάλα κουφίσαντες, ε[ἰ]ς το τ[ὴ]ν ἀνάκγην καὶ ταὐτόματ[ο]ν πάντα α[ἰτι]ᾶσθαι. (14) ὁ δὴ λόγος αὐτὸς ὁ τοῦτο διδάσκων κατεάγνυτο καὶ ἐλάνθανεν τὸν ἄνδρα τοῖς ἔργοις πρὸς τὴν δόξαν συνκρού[ο]ντα· καὶ εἰ μὴ λήθη τις ἐπὶ τῶν ἔργων τῆς δόξης ἐνεγείνετο, συνεχῶς ἂν ἑαυτὸν ταράττοντα· ἧι δ' ἐκράτει τὸ τῆς δόξης κἂν τοῖς ἐσχάτοις π[ε]ριπεί[π]τοντα· ἧ[ι δὲ] μὴ ἐκράτει στάσεως ἐμπιμπλάμενον διὰ τὴν ὑπεναντιότητα τῶν ἔργων καὶ τῆς δόξης. (15) τούτων οὖν οὕτως ἐχόντων δεῖ κα[ὶ] περὶ οὗ λέγων ἐξ ἀρχῆς εἰς τὸ ταῦτα παρεκκαθαίρειν ἀφικόμην ἀποδιδόναι, μ[ὴ] κακ[όν τι] τοιοῦτ[ο. . . .

For the English translation, see section 4.2. Text is from L&S vol. 2 20C, with emendations from Laursen (1988) incorporated.

EPICURUS, ON NATURE BOOK 25, PASSAGE [B]

ἂν δὲ κ[αὶ] βαδίζη[ι] διὰ τὴν ἐξ ἑαυτοῦ ἤδη α[ἰ]τίαν εἰς τὸ ὅμοιον τῆι ἐ[ξ] ἀρχῆς συστάσει φαύληι οὔσ[η]ι, ἔτι μᾶλλον ἐνίοτε κακίζομεν, ἐν νουθετητικῶι μέντοι μᾶλλον τρόπω[ι] καὶ οὐχ ὥσπερ τὰ ἄγρια τῶν ζώιων [κ]α[θ]αίρομεν μὲν ὁμοίως αὐτὰ τὰ ἀπογεγε[ν]νημένα [κ]αὶ τὴ[ν] σύστασιν εἰς ἕν τι συμπλέκοντες, οὐ μὴν ο[ὔ]τε τῶι νουθε[τ]ητικῶι τρόπωι καὶ ἐπανορθωτ[ι]κῶι οὔτε τῶι ἁπλῶς ἀ[ντι]ποι[η]τικῶι χρώμεθα[. . . . . .]μ[. . . . .]καθ[α]ίρομεν

For the English translation, see section 4.2.1. Text is from Laursen (1988).

EPICURUS, ON NATURE BOOK 25, PASSAGE [C]

(0) [ἀ]ποβαινόντων κατὰ [τ]ὰς συνωσθείσας, ἀλ[λ]ὰ καὶ αἱ συνωσθεῖσαι δηλόνως ὁμοίως. φύ[σ]ιν [γ]ὰρ εἶχον συνωσ[θ]εῖσαι τοιαῦτα ἀπογ[ενν]ᾶν καὶ τοιουτο[.] .[. . .]. εσθαι αἱ αὐ[ταὶ] κα[τὰ] τὸν [ἀ]π[ὸ] τοῦ αὐτο[ῦ δ]ιαστήματος τρόπον. [κ]αὶ τ[ὸ] ἀπ[ο]γενν[. . . .]ν τα[.]ε δ[. . . . .]ωσ φ[. . . . .]ς[. . . . .].τ.ο

Lacuna of a few words

ῳ]ην [ῳ] ι [ῳ γ[γ]νεσθαι κατὰ τὸν π[ρ]οειρημένον τρόπον καὶ τῶν αὐ[τ]ῶν ἀπεργαστικὰ εἶναι. (1) πολλὰ δὲ καὶ τῶνδε καὶ τῶνδε φύσιν ἔχοντα ἀπεργαστικὰ γίγνεσθαι δι' ἑαυτὰ οὐ γίγνεται ἀ[πε]ργαστικά, οὐ διὰ τὴν αὐτὴν αἰτίαν τῶν τε ἀτόμων καὶ ἑαυτῶν. (2) οἷς δὴ καὶ μάλιστα μαχόμεθα καὶ ἐπιτιμῶμεν [. .]σοῦντες κατὰ τὴν ἐξ ἀρχῆς [τα]ραχώδη φύσιν ἔχοντα κα[θά]περ ἐπὶ τῶν πάντων ζώιων. (3) οὐδὲν γὰρ αὐτοῖς συνήργηκεν εἰς ἔνια ἔργα τε καὶ μεγέθη ἔργων καὶ διαθέσεων ἡ τῶν ἀτόμων φύσις, ἀλλ' αὐτὰ τὰ ἀπογεγεννημένα τὴν πᾶσα[ν ἢ] τὴν πλε[ί]στην κέκ[τ]ητ[αι] αἰτίαν τῶνδέ τ[ι]νων, (4) ἐκ δ' ἐκείνης [ἔ]νιαι τῶ[ν ἀ]τόμων κινήσεις ταραχώδε[ι]ς κ[ινο]ῦνται, οὐχὶ δ[ι]ὰ τὰς ἀτόμου[ς] πάντω[ς ἀλλὰ διὰ] τ[ὰ ἐμ]π[ί]πτον[τα. . . . . . . ἐκ τοῦ] περιέχοντος [εἰς] τὴν φυσικὴ[ν . . . .]η[. .]τω[. . . . .]τεστ[. . . .]υπασησκει[. . . . . .] . . [αἰτί]ας [ο]ὔσης κα[ὶ . . . .τῆς τῶν] ἀτόμ[ων ἐξ ἀρ]χῆς συ[στάσε]ως καὶ [. . . .]ωμ[. . . . . ἀθ]ροί[σ]εως [. . . . . ἐ]ξ αὐτου τοῦ ἀ[πογενν]ηθέντος εἴπερ [. . . . . . .]μ . . ἀπάντων [

Lacuna of about 20 words

σεσθαι μαχόμεν[οι πο]λλοῖς ἅμα τῶν ἀν[θρώ]πων καὶ νουθε[τοῦν]τες, ὃ τῆι τοῦ αὐτοῦ τρ]όπου κατ' ἀνάγκην α[ἰ]τία[ι] ὑπεναντίον ἐστίν. (5) οὕτως, ἐπειδὰν ἀπογεννηθῆ[ι] τι λαμβάνον τινὰ ἑτερότητ[α τῶ]ν ἀτόμων κατά τ[ινα] τρόπον διαληπτικόν, οὐ τὸν ὡς ἀφ' ἑτέρου διαστήματος, ἰσχάνε[ι] τὴν ἐξ [ἑ]αυτοῦ αἰτίαν· (6) εἶτα αναδίδωσιν εὐθὺς μέχρι τῶν πρώτων φύσεων καὶ μίαν πως ἅπασαν αὐτὴ[ν] ποιεῖ. (7) ὅθεν δὴ καὶ οἱ μὴ δυνάμενοι κατὰ τρόπον τὰ τοιαῦτα διαιρεῖν χειμ[ά]ζουσιν ἑαυτοὺς περ[ὶ] τὴν τῶν αἰτιῶν ἀπόφασιν, καὶ το[ύτων ἐπ' αὐ]τῶν [. .] τοῖς μὲν μᾶλλο[ν, τοῖς δ' ἧ]ττον μαχ[όμε]θα καὶ ἐ[π]ι[τιμ]ῶμεν κα[ὶ . . . .]μεν ν.[. . . . . .].[.].λα[. . . . .].[.]ε[. . . . .]. . .[.]. . . .[. . .]γαρ ε[.]α[. . . . . .]ατ[. . . . .]συσ . . [. . . . .]μ. .[. . . . .].λτ[. . . . .]ιση[

For the English translation, see section 4.3. Text is from Laursen (1988).

EPICURUS, LETTER TO HERODOTUS 43–44

Κινοῦνταί τε συνεχῶς αἱ ἄτομοι [...] τὸν αἰῶνα, καὶ αἱ μὲν εἰς μακρὰν ἀπ' ἀλλήλων διιστάμεναι, αἱ δὲ αὐτοῦ τὸν παλμὸν ἴσχουσιν, ὅταν τύχωσι τῇ περιπλοκῇ κεκλειμέναι ἢ στεγαζόμεναι παρὰ τῶν πλεκτικῶν.

44. Ἥ τε γὰρ τοῦ κενοῦ φύσις ἡ διορίζουσα ἑκάστην αὐτὴν τοῦτο παρασκευάζει, τὴν ὑπέρεισιν οὐχ οἵα τε οὖσα ποιεῖσθαι· ἥ τε στερεότης ἡ ὑπάρχουσα αὐταῖς κατὰ τὴν σύγκρουσιν τὸν ἀποπαλμὸν ποιεῖ, ἐφ' ὁπόσον ἂν ἡ περιπλοκὴ τὴν ἀποκατάστασιν ἐκ τῆς συγκρούσεως διδῷ. ἀρχὴ δὲ τούτων οὐκ ἔστιν, ἀιδίων τῶν ἀτόμων οὐσῶν καὶ τοῦ κενοῦ.

For the English translation, see section 5.2. Text is from L&S vol. 2 IIA.

References

Algra, K., Barnes, J., Mansfeld, J., and Schofeld, M., eds. 1999. *The Cambridge History of Hellenistic Philosophy*. Cambridge: Cambridge University Press.

Annas, J. 1992. *Hellenistic Philosophy of Mind*. Berkeley: University of California Press.

1993. "Epicurus on Agency," in *Passions and Perceptions: Studies in Hellenistic Philosophy of Mind, Proceedings of the 5th Symposium Hellenisticum*, J. Brunschwig and M. Nussbaum, eds. Cambridge: Cambridge University Press.

Armstrong, D. 1980. *The Nature of Mind*. St. Lucia, Queensland: University of Queensland Press.

Arrighetti, G., ed. 1973. *Epicuro, Opere*. Second edition. Turin: Giulio Einaudi editore.

Asmis, E. 1970. *Epicurus' Theory of Free Will and Its Origins in Aristotle* (diss. Yale University).

1984. *Epicurus' Scientific Method*. Ithaca: Cornell University Press.

1990. "Free Action and the Swerve." *Oxford Studies in Ancient Philosophy* 8, 275–290.

Ayer, A. J. 1954. *Philosophical Essays*. London: Macmillan and Co.

Bailey, C. 1928. *The Greek Atomists and Epicurus*. Oxford (reprinted 1964, New York: Russell and Russell).

1947. *Titi Lvcreti Cari. De Rervm Natvra: Libri Sex*. Oxford: Clarendon Press.

Baker, L. 1987. *Saving Belief*. Princeton: Princeton University Press.

Barnes, J. 1982. "The Beliefs of a Pyrrhonist." *Proceedings of the Cambridge Philological Society* 28, 1–29.

1984. *The Complete Works of Aristotle. The Revised Oxford Translation*. Princeton: Princeton University Press.

1988. "Bits and Pieces," in Barnes and Mignucci (1988) 225–294.

Barnes, J., Bobzien, S., and Mignucci, M. 1999. "Logic," in Algra *et al.* (1999) 77–176.

Barnes, J., Burnyeat, M. and Schofield, M., eds. 1980. *Doubt and Dogmatism*. Oxford: Oxford University Press.

Barnes, J., and Mignucci, M., eds. 1988. *Matter and Metaphysics: Fourth Symposium Hellenisticum*. Naples: Bibliopolis.

Bernstein, M. 2002. "Fatalism," in Kane (2002) 65–81.
Berofsky, B. 2002. "Ifs, Cans, and Free Will: The Issues," in Kane (2002) 181–201.
Berryman, S. 1997. "Horror Vacui in the Third Century BCE: When is a Theory not a Theory?" in R. Sorabji, ed., *Aristotle and After*, BICS suppl. vol. II (1997), 147–157.
2002. "Aristotle on *Pneuma* and Animal Self-Motion." *Oxford Studies in Ancient Philosophy* 23, 85–97.
2003. "Ancient Automata and Mechanical Explanation." *Phronesis* 48, 344–369.
Bobzien, S. 1998*a*. *Determinism and Freedom in Stoic Philosophy*. Oxford: Clarendon Press.
1998*b*. "The Inadvertent Conception and Late Birth of the Free-Will Problem." *Phronesis* 43, 133–175.
2000. "Did Epicurus Discover the Free Will Problem?" *Oxford Studies in Ancient Philosophy* 19, 287–337.
Burnyeat, M. 1978. "The Upside-Down Back-to-Front Sceptic of Lucretius IV 472." *Philologus* 122, 197–206.
1980. "Can the Sceptic live his Scepticism?" in Barnes *et al.* (1980), 20–53.
1997. "The Sceptic in His Place and Time," in M. Burnyeat and M. Frede, eds. *The Original Sceptics: A Controversy*. Indianapolis: Hackett, 92–126.
Chisholm, R. 1964. "Human Freedom and the Self," in G. Watson, ed. *Free Will.* Oxford: Oxford University Press (1982), 7–29.
Churchland, P. 1988. *Matter and Consciousness. A Contemporary Introduction to the Philosophy of Mind.* Revised edition. Cambridge, MA: The MIT Press.
Cooper, J. 1999. "Pleasure and Desire in Epicurus," in *Reason and Emotion. Essays on Ancient Moral Psychology and Ethical Theory*. Princeton: Princeton University Press, 485–514.
Couissin, P. 1983. "The Stoicism of the New Academy," in *The Skeptical Tradition*, M. Burnyeat, ed. Berkeley: University of California Press, 31–64.
Curd, P. "Why Democritus Was Not a Skeptic," in *Essays in Ancient Greek Philosophy, Vol. 6: Before Plato*, A. Preus, ed. Binghamton: State University of New York Press, 149–169.
Dennett, D. 1984. *Elbow Room. The Varieties of Free Will Worth Wanting.* Cambridge, MA: The MIT Press.
DeWitt, N. 1954. *Epicurus and His Philosophy*. Minneapolis: University of Minnesota Press.
Diels, H. and Kranz, W. 1985. *Die Fragmente der Vorsokratiker*. Zurich: Weidmann.
Dorandi, T. 1999. "Chronology," in Algra *et al.* (1999) 31–54.
Englert, W. 1987. *Epicurus on the Swerve and Voluntary Action*. American Classical Studies, 16. Atlanta: Scholar's Press.
Everson, S. 1999. "Epicurean Psychology," in Algra *et al.* (1999) 542–559.
Fischer, J. 2002. "Frankfurt-type Examples and Semi-Compatibilism," in Kane (2002) 281–308.

Fischer, J., and Ravizza, M. 1998. *Responsibility and Control. A Theory of Moral Responsibility.* Cambridge: Cambridge University Press.
Frankfurt, H. 1969. "Alternate Possibilities and Moral Responsibility." *Journal of Philosophy* 66, 829–839.
Fowler, D. 2002. *Lucretius on Atomic Motion: A Commentary on* De rerum natura *2.1–332*. Oxford: Oxford University Press.
Frede, M. 1980. "The Original Notion of Cause," in Barnes *et al.* (1980) 217–249.
Furley, D. 1967. *Two Studies in the Greek Atomists.* Princeton: Princeton University Press.
1989*a*. "Aristotle and the Atomists on Motion in a Void," in *Cosmic Problems.* Cambridge: Cambridge University Press, 77–90.
1989*b*. "Weight and Motion in Democritus' Theory," in *Cosmic Problems.* Cambridge: Cambridge University Press, 91–102.
1994. "Self-Movers," in Gill and Lennox (1994) 3–14.
Ganson, T. 1999. "Democritus against Reducing Sensible Qualities." *Ancient Philosophy* 19, 201–215.
Gaskin, R. 1995. *The Sea Battle and the Master Argument: Aristotle and Diodorus Cronus on the Metaphysics of the Future.* Berlin and New York: Walter de Gruyter.
Gill, L., and Lennox, J. eds. 1994. *Self-Motion: From Aristotle to Newton.* Princeton: Princeton University Press.
Haji, I. 2002. "Compatibilist Views of Freedom and Responsibility," in Kane (2002) 202–28.
Hankinson, R. J. 1995. *The Sceptics.* London and New York: Routledge.
1996. "Cicero's Rope," in K. Algra, P. van der Horst, and D. Runia, eds., *Polyhistor: Studies in the History and Historiography of Ancient Philosophy.* Leiden: E. J. Brill, 185–205.
1998. *Cause and Explanation in Ancient Greek Thought.* Oxford: Clarendon Press.
Heil, J. 1992. *The Nature of True Minds.* Cambridge: Cambridge University Press.
Hicks, R. D. 1962. *Stoic and Epicurean.* New York: Russell and Russell Inc.
Hintikka, J. 1973. *Time and Necessity. Studies in Aristotle's Theory of Modality.* Oxford: Oxford University Press.
Hocutt, M. 1974. "Aristotle's Four Becauses." *Philosophy* 49, 385–399.
Huby, P. 1967. "The First Discovery of the Freewill Problem." *Philosophy* 42, 353–362.
Inwood, B., and Gerson, L. P. 1997. *Hellenistic Philosophy: Introductory Readings.* Second edition. Indianapolis: Hackett.
James, W. 1890. *The Principles of Psychology, Volume One.* Authorized Edition, 1950. New York: Dover Publications.
Kane, R. 1996. *The Significance of Free Will.* New York: Oxford University Press.
ed. 2002. *The Oxford Handbook of Free Will.* Oxford: Oxford University Press.
Kapitan, T. 2002. "A Master Argument for Incompatibilism?" in Kane (2002) 127–157.

Kim, J. 1989. "The Myth of Nonreductive Materialism." Presidential address, Central Division, *Proceedings and Addresses of the American Philosophical Association*, 43, 3: 31–48. (anthologized in R. Warner and T. Szubka, eds., 1994. *The Mind–Body Problem*, Oxford: Blackwell, 242–260.)

Kirk, G. S., Raven, J. E., and Schofield, M. 1983. *The Presocratic Philosophers.* Second Edition. Cambridge: Cambridge University Press.

Kirwen, C. 1989. *Augustine.* London: Routledge.

Laursen, S. 1987. "Epicurus *On Nature* Book xxv." *Cronache Ercolanesi* 17, 77–78.

1988. "Epicurus *On Nature* Book xxv: Long-Sedley 20 B, C, and J." *Cronarche Ercolanesi* 18, 7–18.

Llewelyn, J. E. 1966. "The Inconceivability of Pessimistic Determinism." *Analysis* 27, 39–44.

Long, A. A. 1986. *Hellenistic Philosophy: Stoics, Epicureans, Sceptics.* Berkeley and Los Angeles: University of California Press.

Long, A. A., and Sedley, D. 1987. *The Hellenistic Philosophers.* 2 vols. Cambridge: Cambridge University Press.

Macdonald, S. 1999. "Primal Sin," in *The Augustinian Tradition*, G. Matthews, ed. Berkeley: University of California Press, 110–139.

Mackie, J. L. 1982. *The Miracle of Theism.* Oxford: Clarendon Press.

Malcolm, N. 1968. "The Conceivability of Mechanism." *Philosophical Review* 77, 45–72.

Mann, W. 2001. "Augustine on Evil and Original Sin," in *The Cambridge Companion to Augustine.* Eleonose Stump and Norman Kretzmann, eds. Cambridge: Cambridge University Press, 40–48.

Mansfeld, J. 1999. "Sources," in Algra *et al.* (1999), 1–30.

McPherran, M. 1987. "Skeptical Homeopathy and Self-Refutation." *Phronesis* 32, 290–328.

Mitsis, P. 1988. *Epicurus' Ethical Theory: The Pleasures of Invulnerability.* Ithaca, NY: Cornell University Press.

O'Brien, D. 1981. *Theories of Weight in the Ancient World: Four Essays on Democritus, Plato and Aristotle. A Study in the Development of Ideas. Volume One: Democritus, Weight and Size: An Exercise in the Reconstruction of Early Greek Philosophy.* Paris: Les Belles Lettres.

O'Keefe, T. 1996. "Does Epicurus Need the Swerve as an *Archê* of Collisions?" *Phronesis* 41, 305–317.

1997. "The Ontological Status of Sensible Qualities for Democritus and Epicurus." *Ancient Philosophy* 17, 119–134.

2001*a*. "Would a Society of Wise Epicureans Be Just?" *Ancient Philosophy* 21, 133–146.

2001*b*. "Is Epicurean Friendship Altruistic?" *Apeiron* 34, 269–305.

2002. "The Reductionist and Compatibilist Argument of Epicurus' *On Nature* Book 25." *Phronesis* 47, 153–186.

2003*a*. Review of Fowler (2002). *Ancient Philosophy* 23, 461–468.

2003*b*. "Lucretius on the Cycle of Life and the Fear of Death." *Apeiron* 36, 43–65.

2003c. Review of Warren (2002). *Notre Dame Philosophical Reviews*, May 2003. <http://ndpr.icaap.org/content/archives/2003/5/okeefe/warren.html>

Pereboom, D. 2001. *Living Without Free Will.* Cambridge: Cambridge University Press.

Prior, A. 1967. *Past, Present and Future.* Oxford: Clarendon Press.

Purinton, J. 1996. "Epicurus on the degrees of responsibility of 'things begotten' for their actions: a new reading of *On Nature* xxv," in G. Giannantoni and M. Gigante, eds., *Epicureismo Greco e Romano: Atti del Congresso Internazionale Napoli, 19–26 maggio 1993*, vol. 1. Naples, 155–168.

1999. "Epicurus on 'Free Volition' and the Atomic Swerve." *Phronesis* 44, 253–299.

Rackham, H., trans. 1931. *Cicero: De Finibus Bonorum et Malorum.* Second edition. Cambridge, MA: Harvard University Press (Loeb Classical Library).

trans. 1942. *Cicero: De Oratore III, De Fato, Paradoxa Stoicorum, De Partitione Oratoria.* Cambridge, MA: Harvard University Press (Loeb Classical Library).

Rescher, N. 1963. "An Interpretation of Aristotle's Doctrine of Future Contingency and Excluded Middle," in N. Rescher, *Studies in the History of Arabic Logic.* Pittsburgh: University of Pittsburgh Press, 43–54.

Rist, J. M. 1972. *Epicurus: An Introduction.* Cambridge: Cambridge University Press.

Rouse, W. H. D., trans. 1937. *Lucretius. De Rerum Natura.* Cambridge, MA: Harvard University Press (Loeb Classical Library).

Ryle, G. 1960. *Dilemmas.* Cambridge: Cambridge University Press.

Sandbach, F. H. 1985. Aristotle and the Stoics (*Proceedings of the Cambridge Philological Society*, suppl. 10.)

Saunders, T. 1984. "Free Will and the Atomic Swerve in Lucretius." *Symbolae Osloenses* 59, 37–59.

Sedley, D. 1974. "The Structure of Epicurus' *On Nature.*" *Cronache Ercolanesi* 4, 89–92.

1977. "Diodorus Cronus and Hellenistic Philosophy." *Proceedings of the Cambridge Philological Society* 203, 74–120.

1983. "Epicurus' refutation of determinism," in G. Macchiaroli, ed., *ΣΥΖΗΤΗΣΙΣ. studi sull'epicureismo greco e romano offerti a Marcello Gigante.* Naples: Bibliopolis, 11–51.

1988a. "Epicurean anti-reductionism," in Barnes and Mignucci (1988) 297–327.

1988b. "Two conceptions of vacuum." *Phronesis* 27, 175–193.

1998. *Lucretius and the Transformation of Greek Wisdom.* Cambridge: Cambridge University Press.

Sorabji, R. 1980. *Necessity, Cause and Blame.* London: Duckworth.

Stump, E. 2001. "Augustine on Free Will," in *The Cambridge Companion to Augustine.* Eleonore Stump and Norman Kretzmann, eds. Cambridge: Cambridge University Press, 124–147.

Thorsrud, H. 2002. "Cicero on his Academic Predecessors: The Fallibilism of Arcesilaus and Carneades." *Journal of the History of Philosophy* 40, 1–18.

Tooley, M. 1997. *Time, Tense, and Causation.* Oxford: Clarendon Press.

van Inwagen, P. 1983. *An Essay on Free Will.* Oxford: Clarendon Press.

van Rijen, J. 1989. *Aspects of Aristotle's Logic of Modalities.* Dordrecht: Kluwer.

Vlastos, G. 1969. "Reasons and Causes in the *Phaedo.*" *Philosophical Review* 78, 291–325 (revised version reprinted in G. Vlastos (1973), *Platonic Studies,* Princeton: Princeton University Press; page references are to this reprinting).

Wardy, R. 1988. "Eleatic Pluralism." *Archiv für Geschichte der Philosophie* 70, 125–146.

Warren. J. 2002. *Epicurus and Democritean Ethics: An Archaeology of Ataraxia.* Cambridge: Cambridge University Press.

Zagzebski, L. 2002. "Recent Works on Divine Foreknowledge and Free Will," in Kane (2002) 45–64.

Zeller, E. 1962. *The Stoics, Epicureans and Sceptics.* New York: Russell and Russell Inc.

Index

Lightning Source UK Ltd.
Milton Keynes UK
UKHW01f0608210518
322891UK00001B/104/P

9 780521 114912